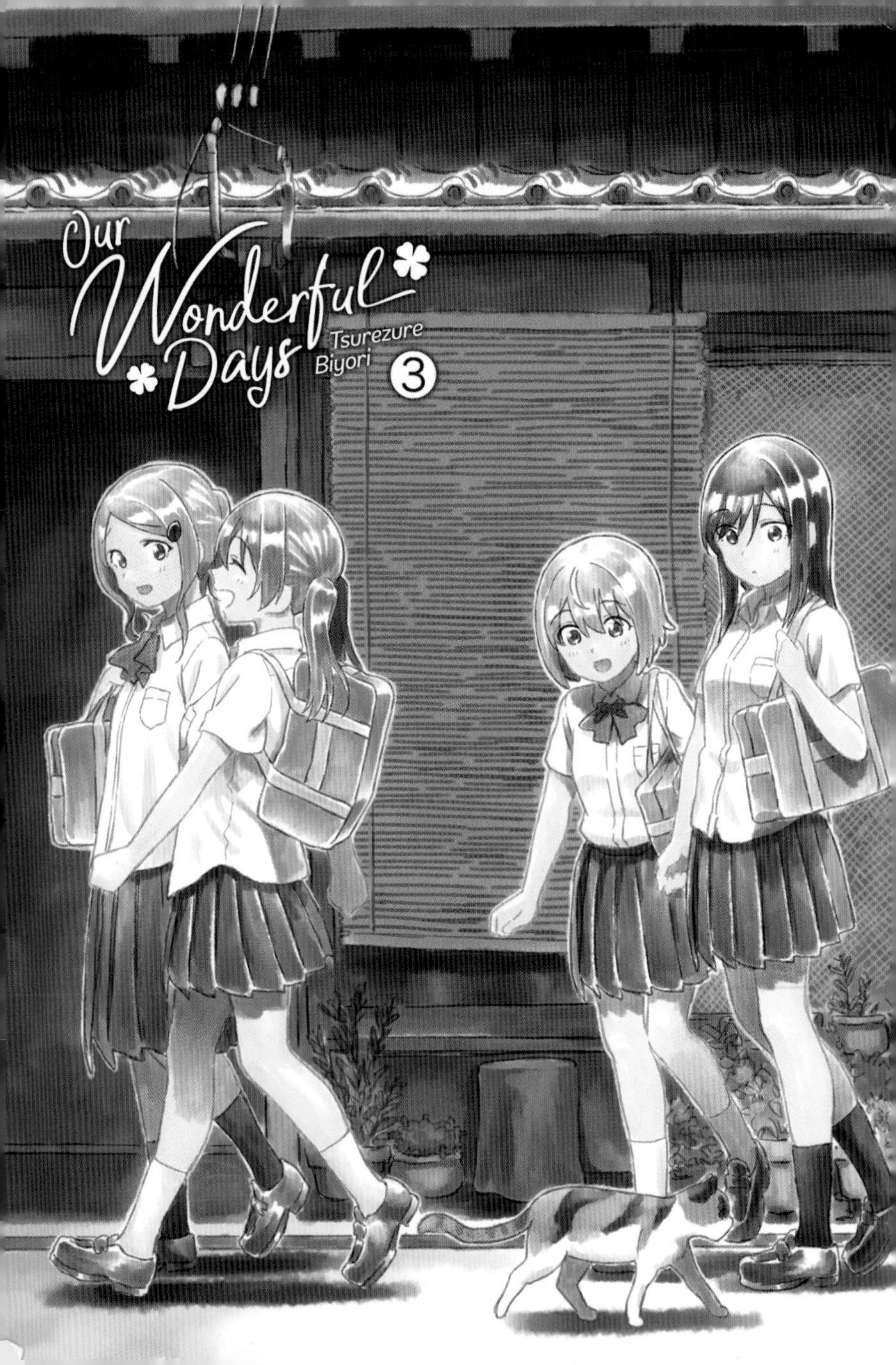
Our Wonderful Days
Tsurezure Biyori
3

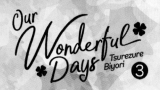

Our **Wonderful** *Tsurezure*
Days *Biyori* ❸

story & art by Kei Hamuro

CONTENTS

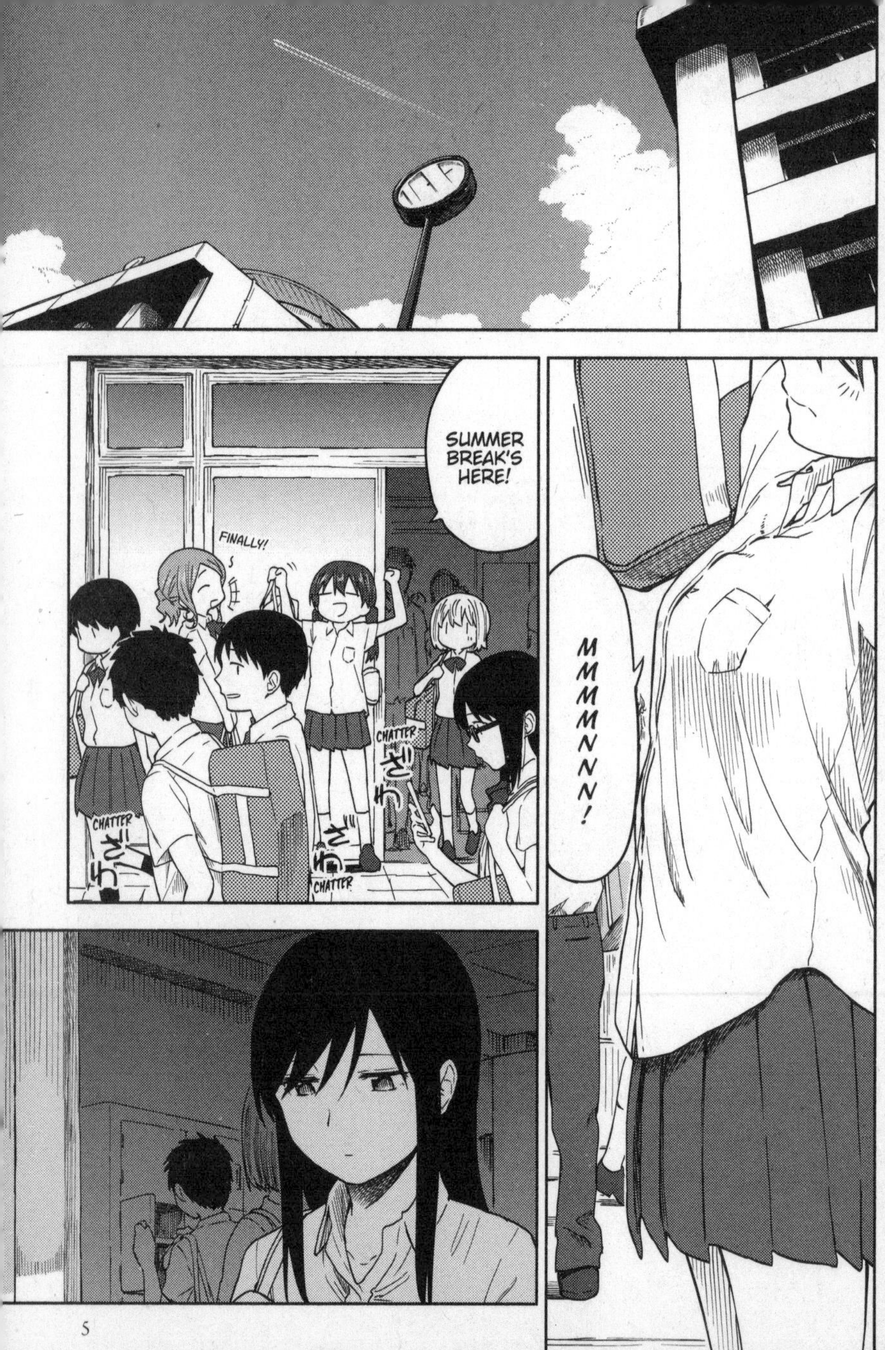
MMMMMNNNN!
SUMMER BREAK'S HERE!
FINALLY!
CHATTER
ざわ
CHATTER
ざわ
CHATTER
ざわ

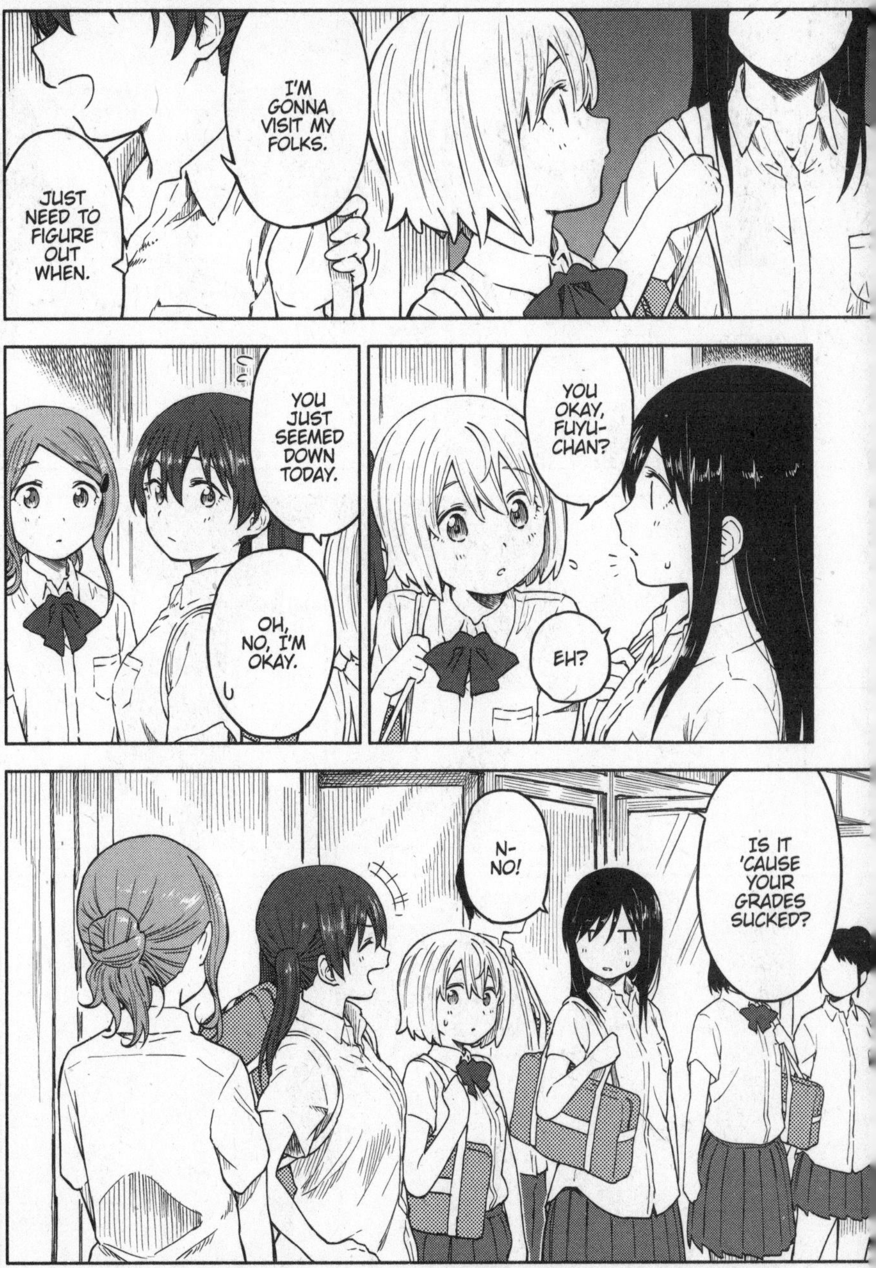
I'M GONNA VISIT MY FOLKS.
JUST NEED TO FIGURE OUT WHEN.
YOU OKAY, FUYU-CHAN?
EH?
YOU JUST SEEMED DOWN TODAY.
OH, NO, I'M OKAY.
IS IT 'CAUSE YOUR GRADES SUCKED?
N-NO!

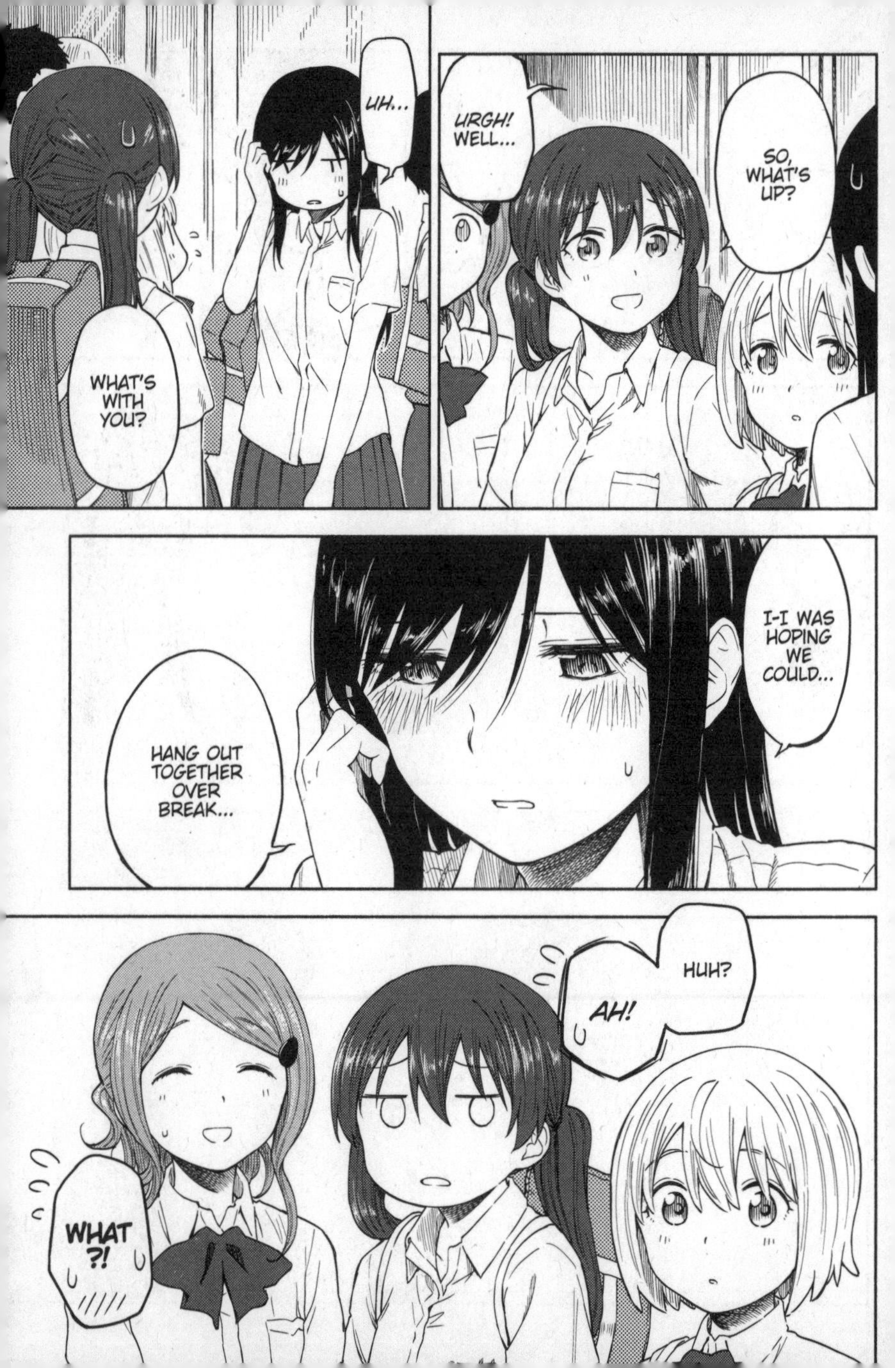
URGH! WELL...
SO, WHAT'S UP?
UH...
WHAT'S WITH YOU?
I-I WAS HOPING WE COULD...
HANG OUT TOGETHER OVER BREAK...
HUH? AH!
WHAT ?!

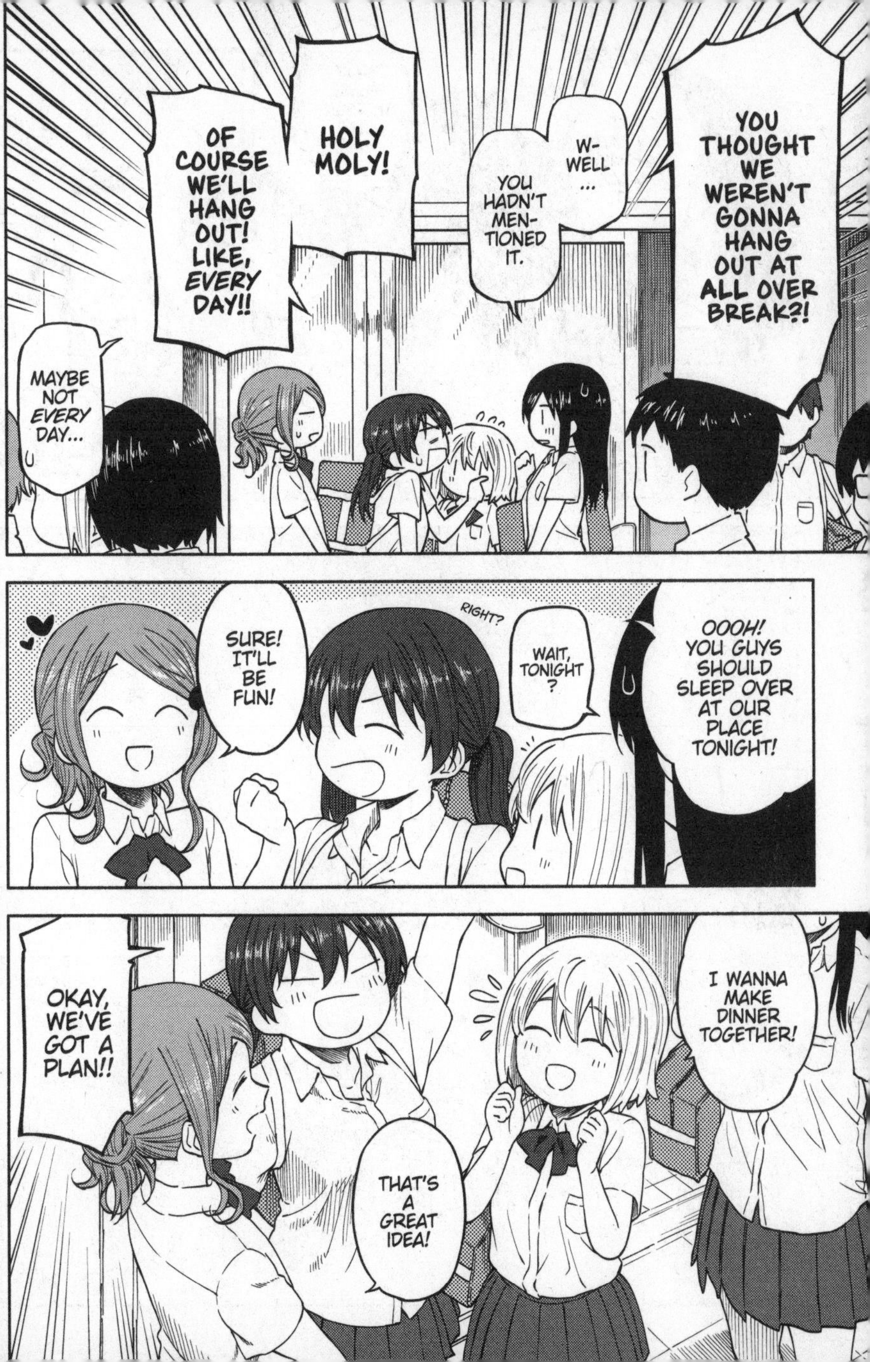
YOU THOUGHT WE WEREN'T GONNA HANG OUT AT ALL OVER BREAK?!
W-WELL ...
YOU HADN'T MEN-TIONED IT.
HOLY MOLY!
OF COURSE WE'LL HANG OUT! LIKE, EVERY DAY!!
MAYBE NOT EVERY DAY...
OOOH! YOU GUYS SHOULD SLEEP OVER AT OUR PLACE TONIGHT!
WAIT, TONIGHT?
RIGHT?
SURE! IT'LL BE FUN!
I WANNA MAKE DINNER TOGETHER!
OKAY, WE'VE GOT A PLAN!!
THAT'S A GREAT IDEA!

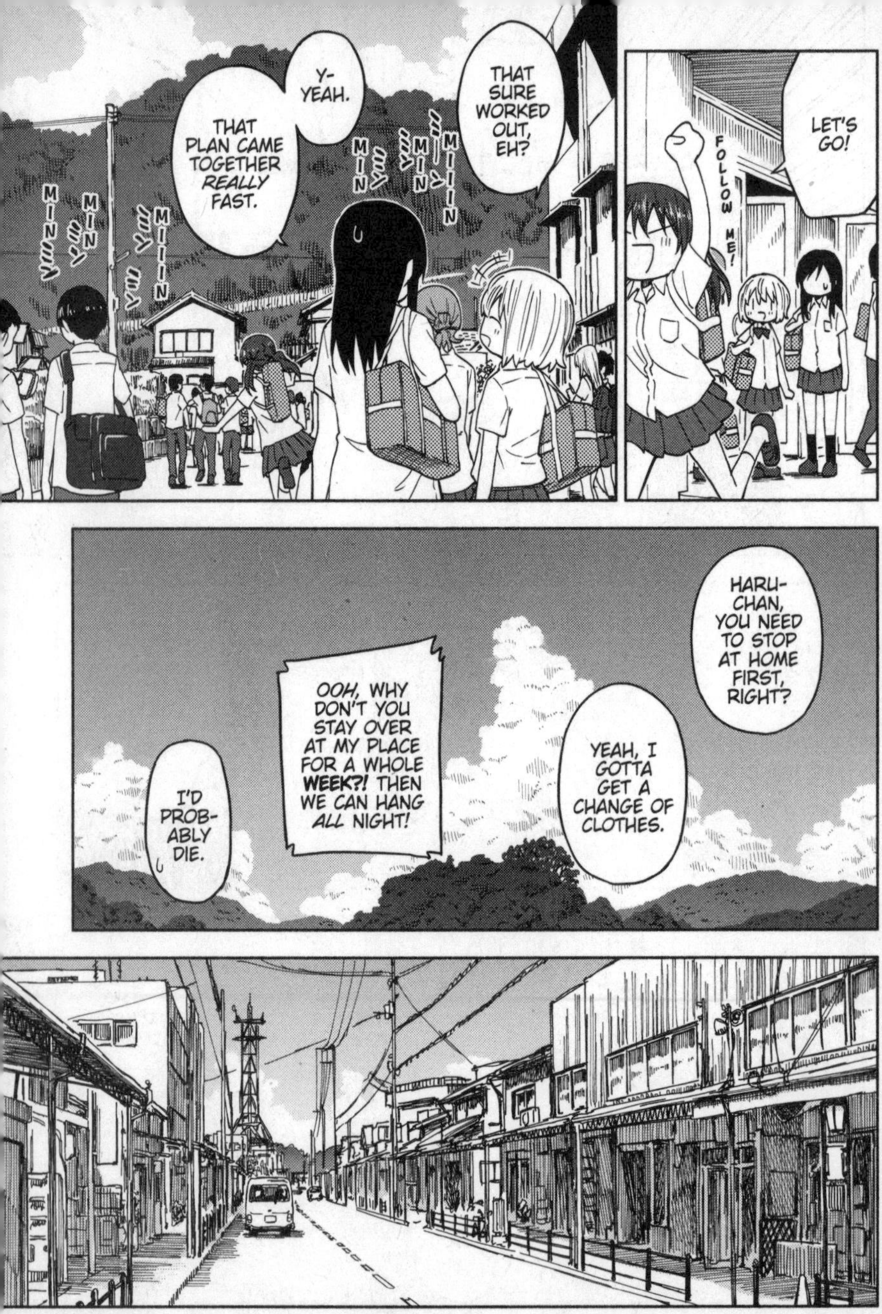
LET'S GO!
FOLLOW ME!
THAT SURE WORKED OUT, EH?
Y-YEAH.
THAT PLAN CAME TOGETHER REALLY FAST.
MIIIIN
MIN
MIN
MIIIN
MIN
MIN
HARU-CHAN, YOU NEED TO STOP AT HOME FIRST, RIGHT?
YEAH, I GOTTA GET A CHANGE OF CLOTHES.
OOH, WHY DON'T YOU STAY OVER AT MY PLACE FOR A WHOLE WEEK?! THEN WE CAN HANG ALL NIGHT!
I'D PROBABLY DIE.

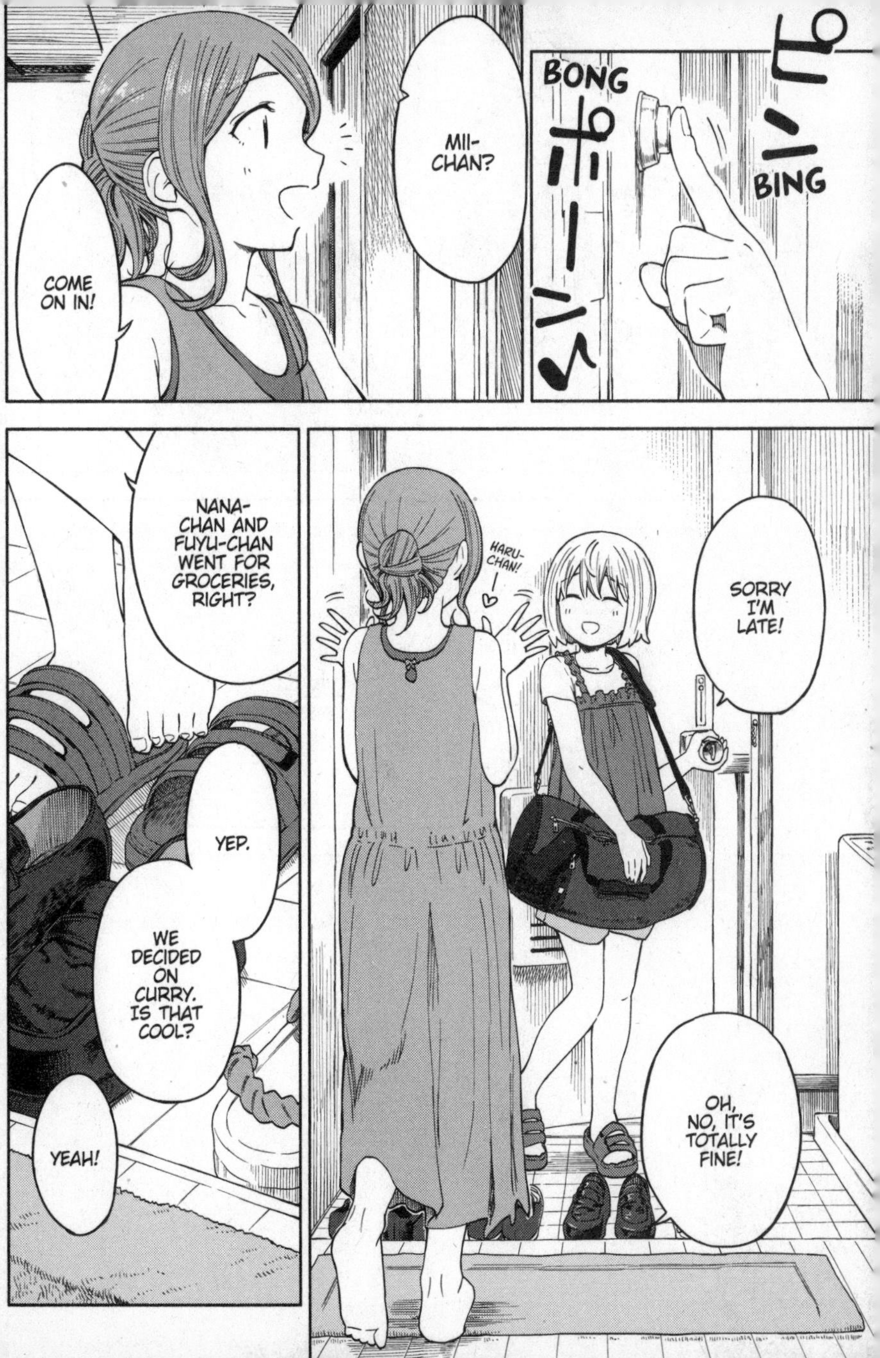
ピン
BING
ポーン♪
BONG
MII-CHAN?
COME ON IN!
SORRY I'M LATE!
HARU-CHAN!
OH, NO, IT'S TOTALLY FINE!
NANA-CHAN AND FUYU-CHAN WENT FOR GROCERIES, RIGHT?
YEP.
WE DECIDED ON CURRY. IS THAT COOL?
YEAH!

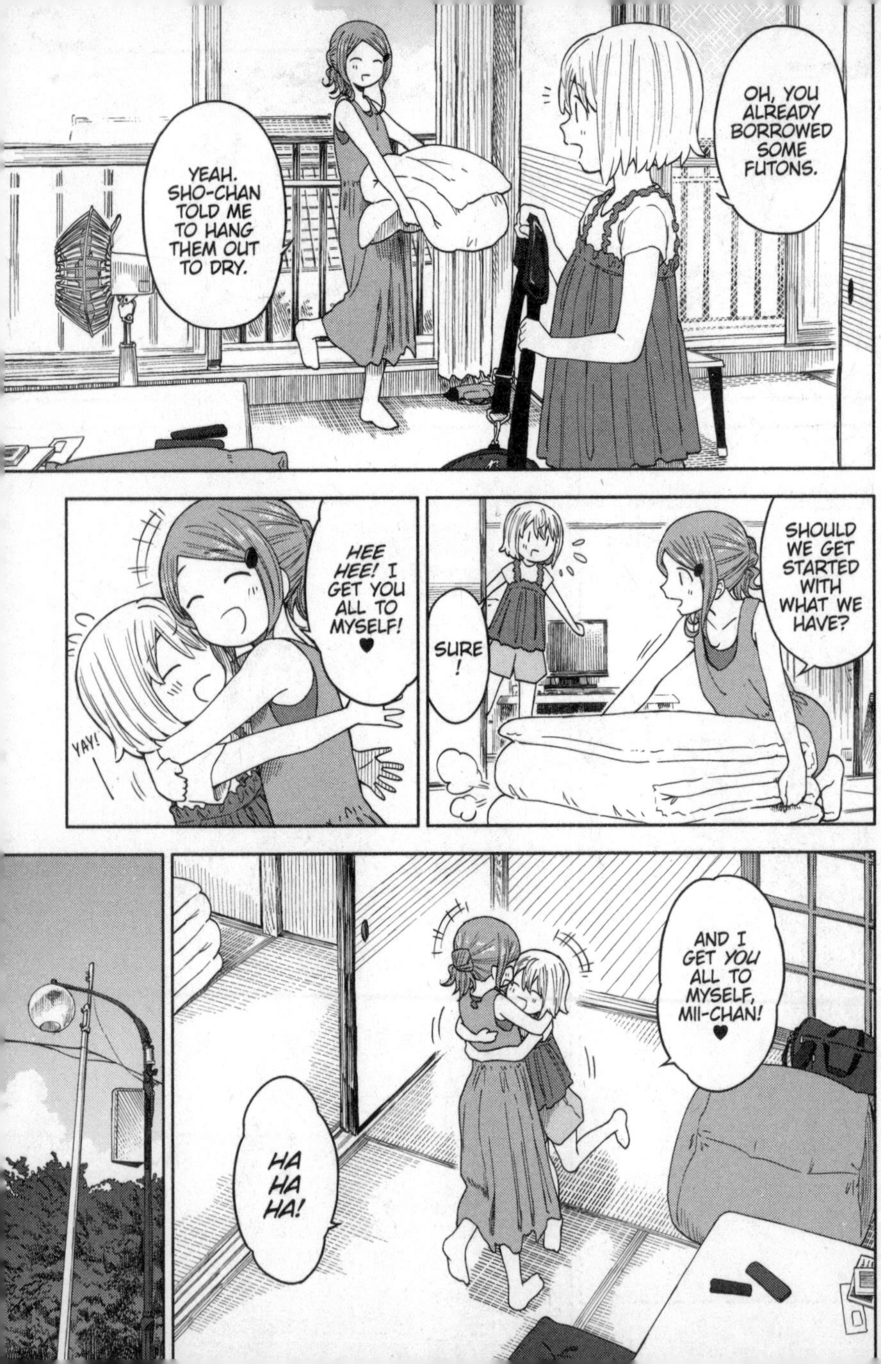
OH, YOU ALREADY BORROWED SOME FUTONS.
YEAH. SHO-CHAN TOLD ME TO HANG THEM OUT TO DRY.
SHOULD WE GET STARTED WITH WHAT WE HAVE?
SURE!
HEE HEE! I GET YOU ALL TO MYSELF! ♥
YAY!
AND I GET *YOU* ALL TO MYSELF, MII-CHAN! ♥
HA HA HA!

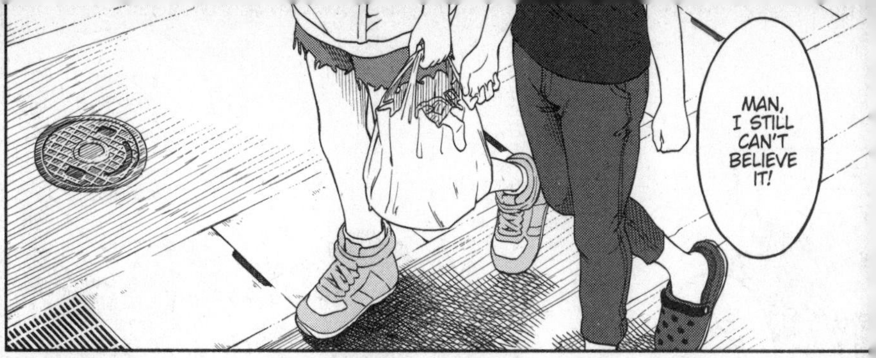
MAN, I STILL CAN'T BELIEVE IT!

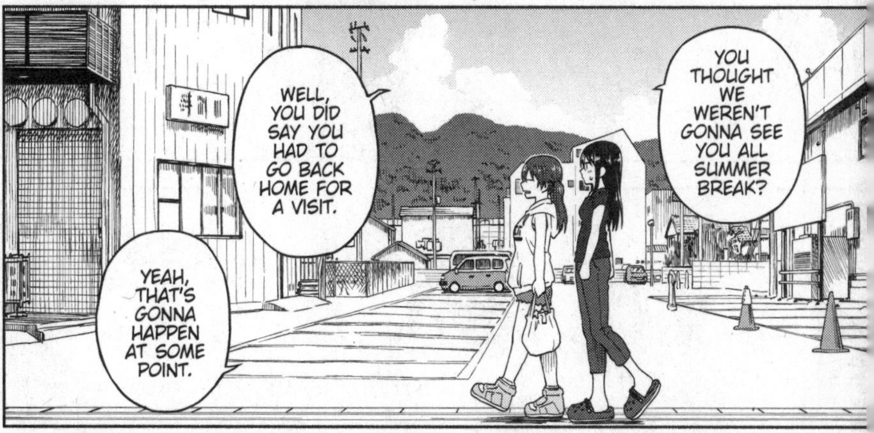
YOU THOUGHT WE WEREN'T GONNA SEE YOU ALL SUMMER BREAK?
WELL, YOU DID SAY YOU HAD TO GO BACK HOME FOR A VISIT.
YEAH, THAT'S GONNA HAPPEN AT SOME POINT.

Sign: Business Hotel

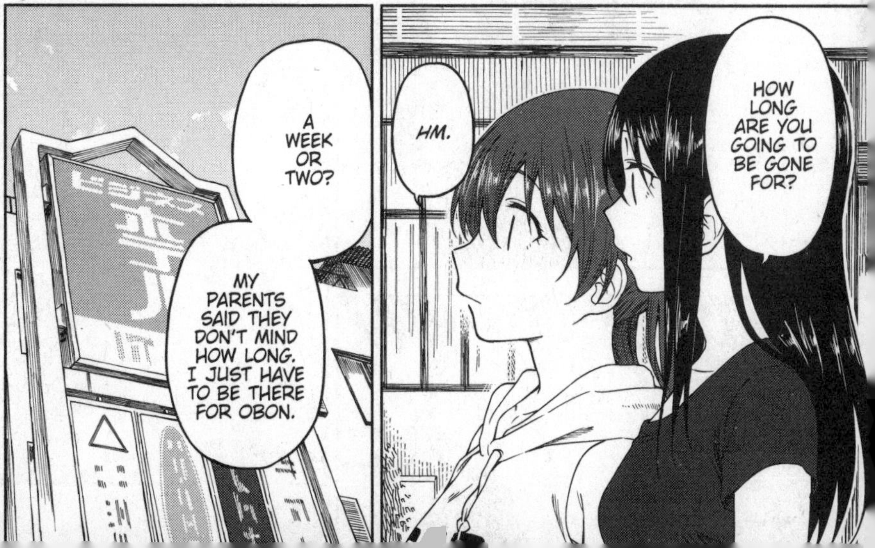
HOW LONG ARE YOU GOING TO BE GONE FOR?
HM.
A WEEK OR TWO?
MY PARENTS SAID THEY DON'T MIND HOW LONG. I JUST HAVE TO BE THERE FOR OBON.

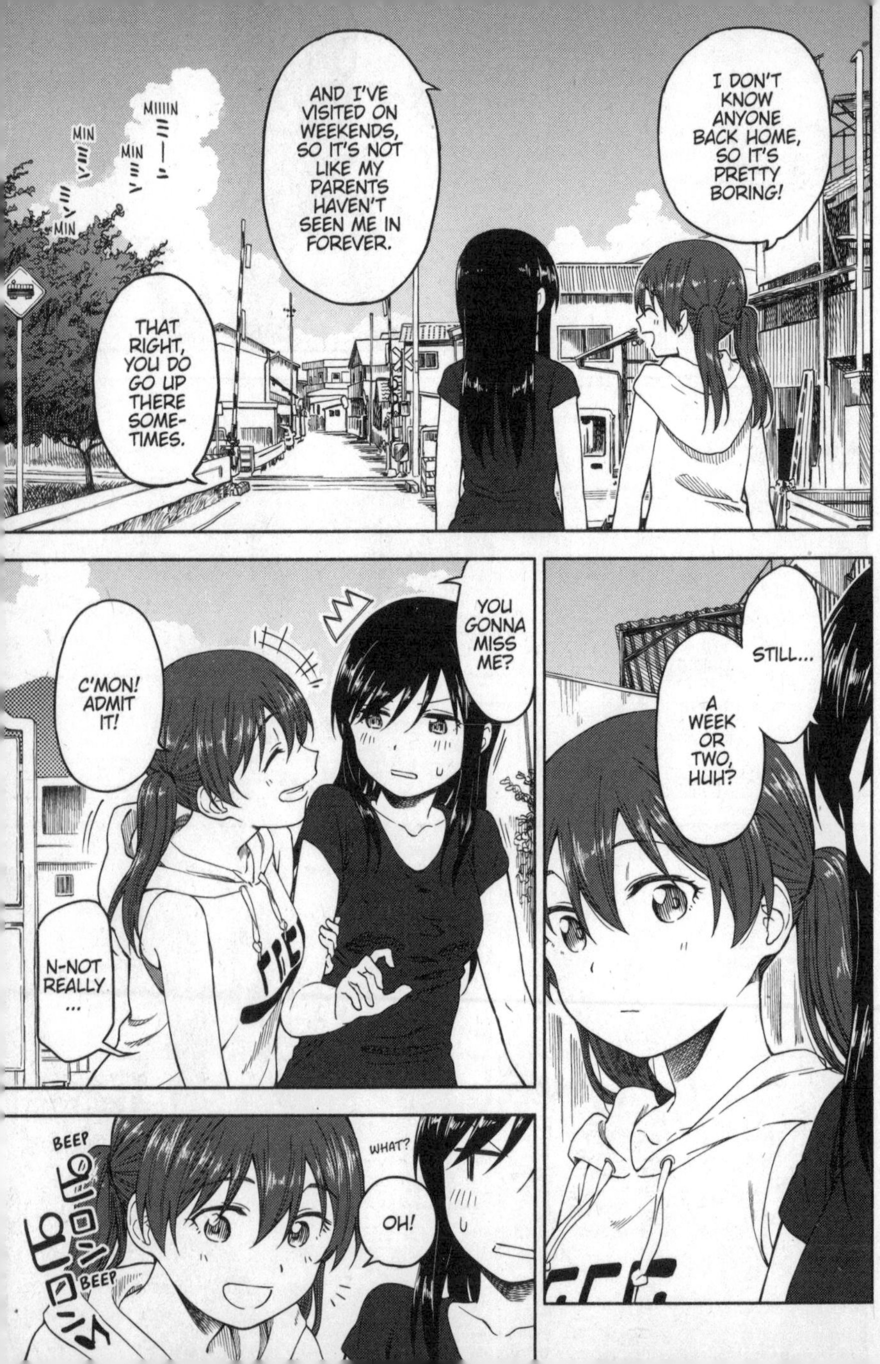
I DON'T KNOW ANYONE BACK HOME, SO IT'S PRETTY BORING!
AND I'VE VISITED ON WEEKENDS, SO IT'S NOT LIKE MY PARENTS HAVEN'T SEEN ME IN FOREVER.
MIIIIN
MIN
MIN
MIN
THAT RIGHT, YOU DO GO UP THERE SOME-TIMES.
STILL...
A WEEK OR TWO, HUH?
YOU GONNA MISS ME?
C'MON! ADMIT IT!
N-NOT REALLY ...
WHAT?
OH!
BEEP
BEEP

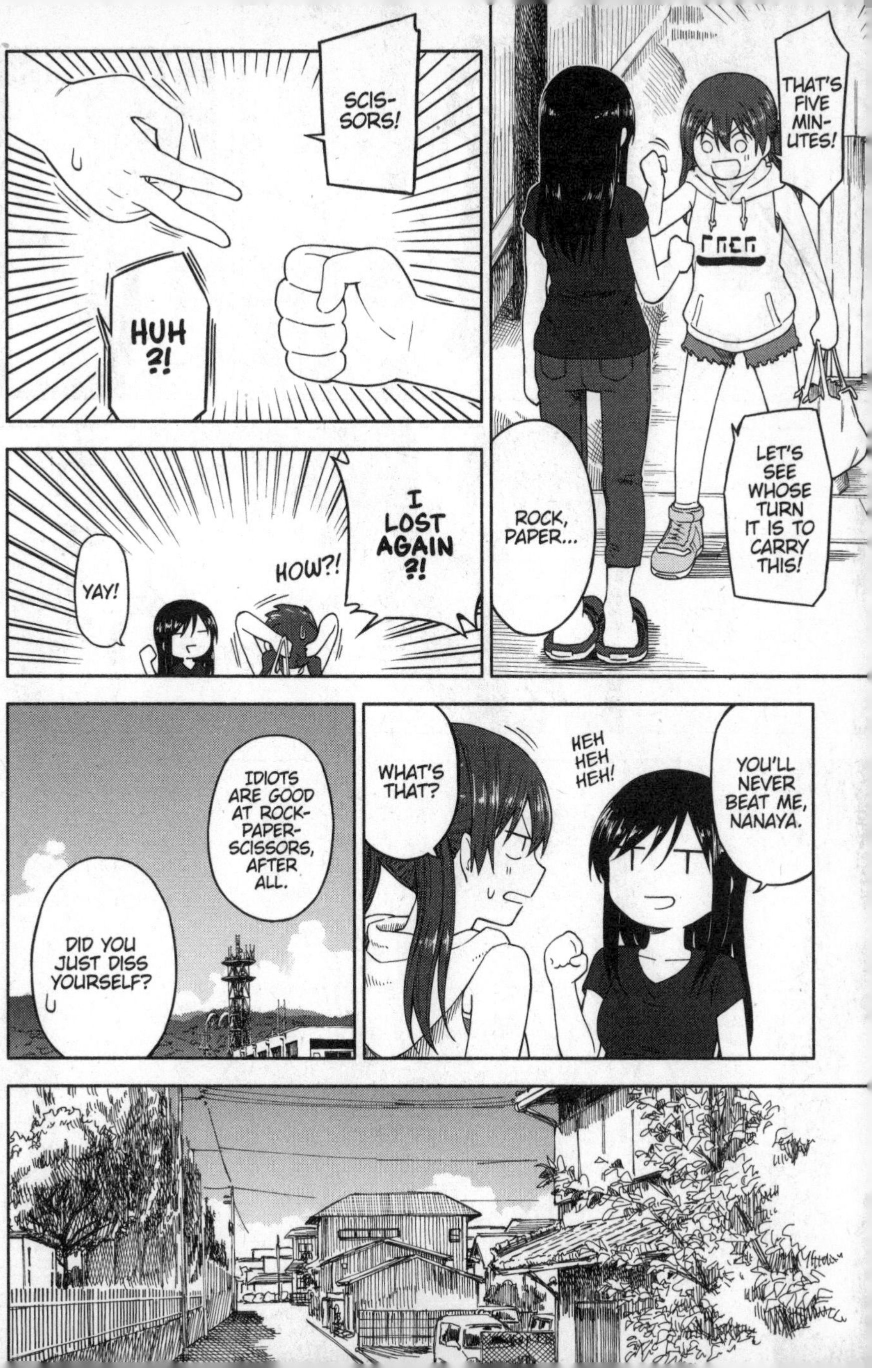
THAT'S FIVE MIN-UTES!
LET'S SEE WHOSE TURN IT IS TO CARRY THIS!
ROCK, PAPER...
SCIS-SORS!
HUH?!
I LOST AGAIN?!
HOW?!
YAY!
YOU'LL NEVER BEAT ME, NANAYA.
HEH HEH HEH!
WHAT'S THAT?
IDIOTS ARE GOOD AT ROCK-PAPER-SCISSORS, AFTER ALL.
DID YOU JUST DISS YOURSELF?

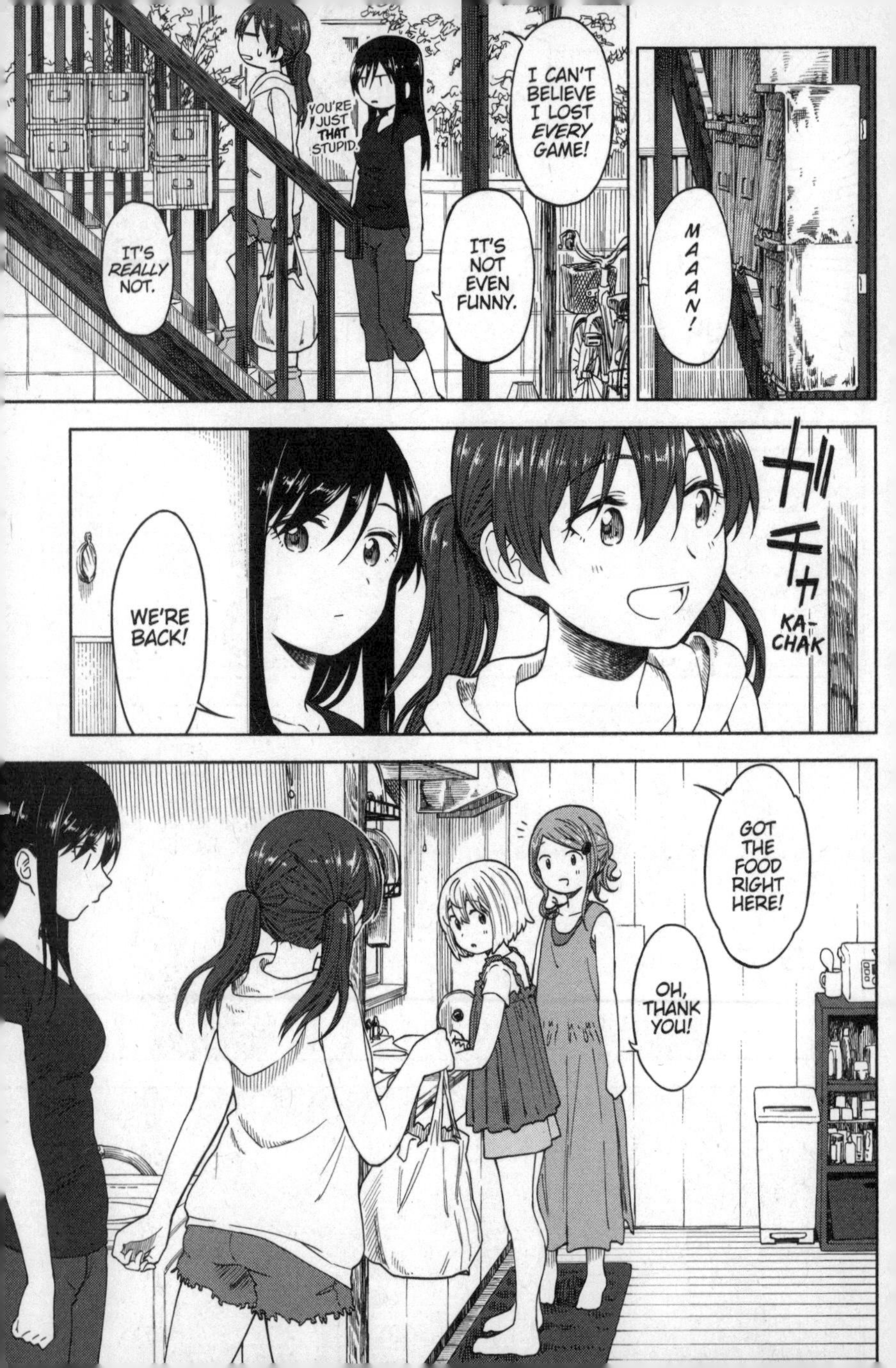
MAAAN!
I CAN'T BELIEVE I LOST EVERY GAME!
YOU'RE JUST THAT STUPID.
IT'S NOT EVEN FUNNY.
IT'S REALLY NOT.
ガチャ
KA-CHAK
WE'RE BACK!
GOT THE FOOD RIGHT HERE!
OH, THANK YOU!

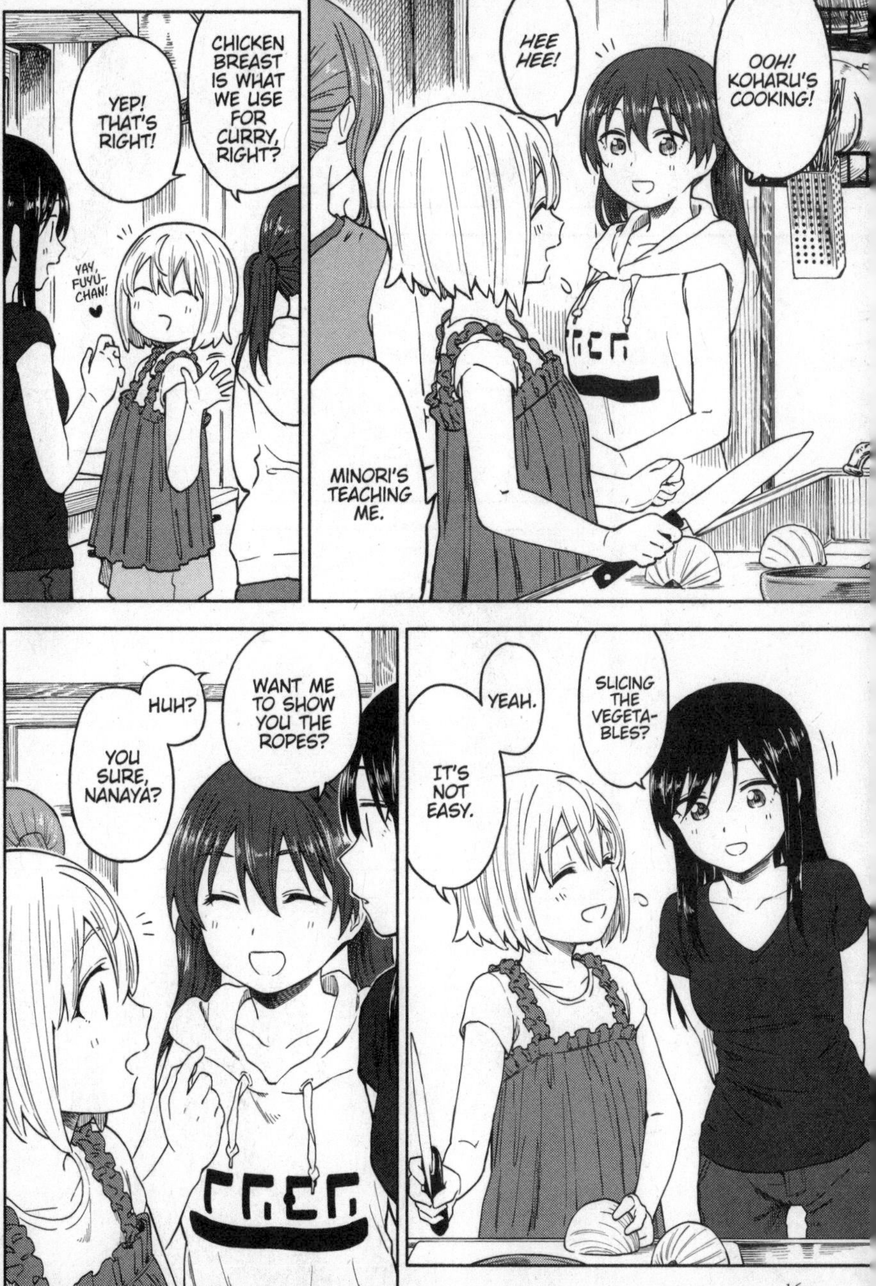
OOH! KOHARU'S COOKING!
HEE HEE!
MINORI'S TEACHING ME.
CHICKEN BREAST IS WHAT WE USE FOR CURRY, RIGHT?
YEP! THAT'S RIGHT!
YAY, FUYU-CHAN!
SLICING THE VEGETA-BLES?
YEAH.
IT'S NOT EASY.
WANT ME TO SHOW YOU THE ROPES?
HUH?
YOU SURE, NANAYA?

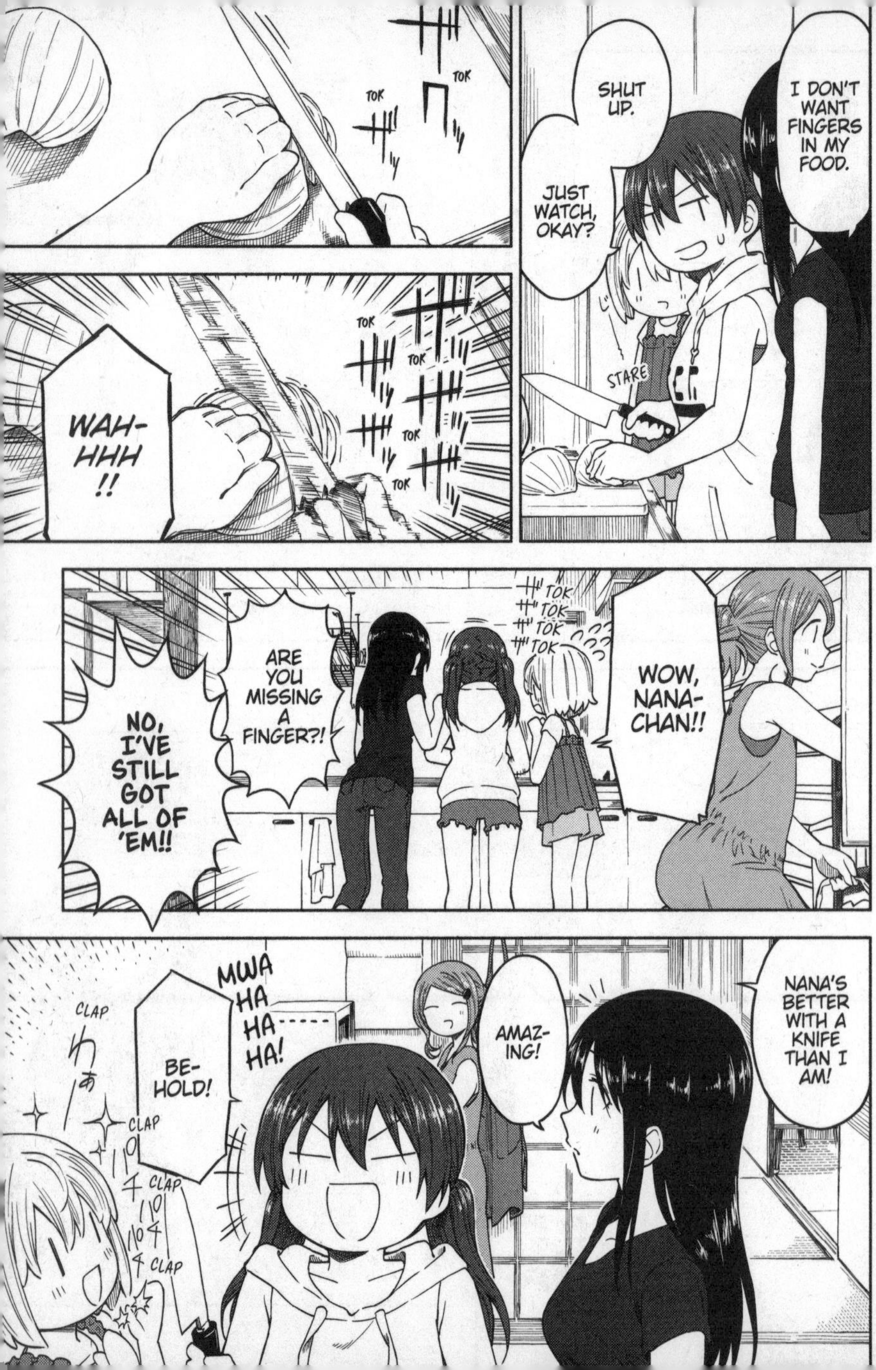

I DON'T WANT FINGERS IN MY FOOD.
SHUT UP.
JUST WATCH, OKAY?
STARE
TOK
TOK
TOK
TOK
TOK
TOK
WAH-HHH!!
WOW, NANA-CHAN!!
TOK
TOK
TOK
TOK
ARE YOU MISSING A FINGER?!
NO, I'VE STILL GOT ALL OF 'EM!!
NANA'S BETTER WITH A KNIFE THAN I AM!
AMAZ-ING!
MWA HA HA HA!
BE-HOLD!
CLAP
CLAP
CLAP
CLAP

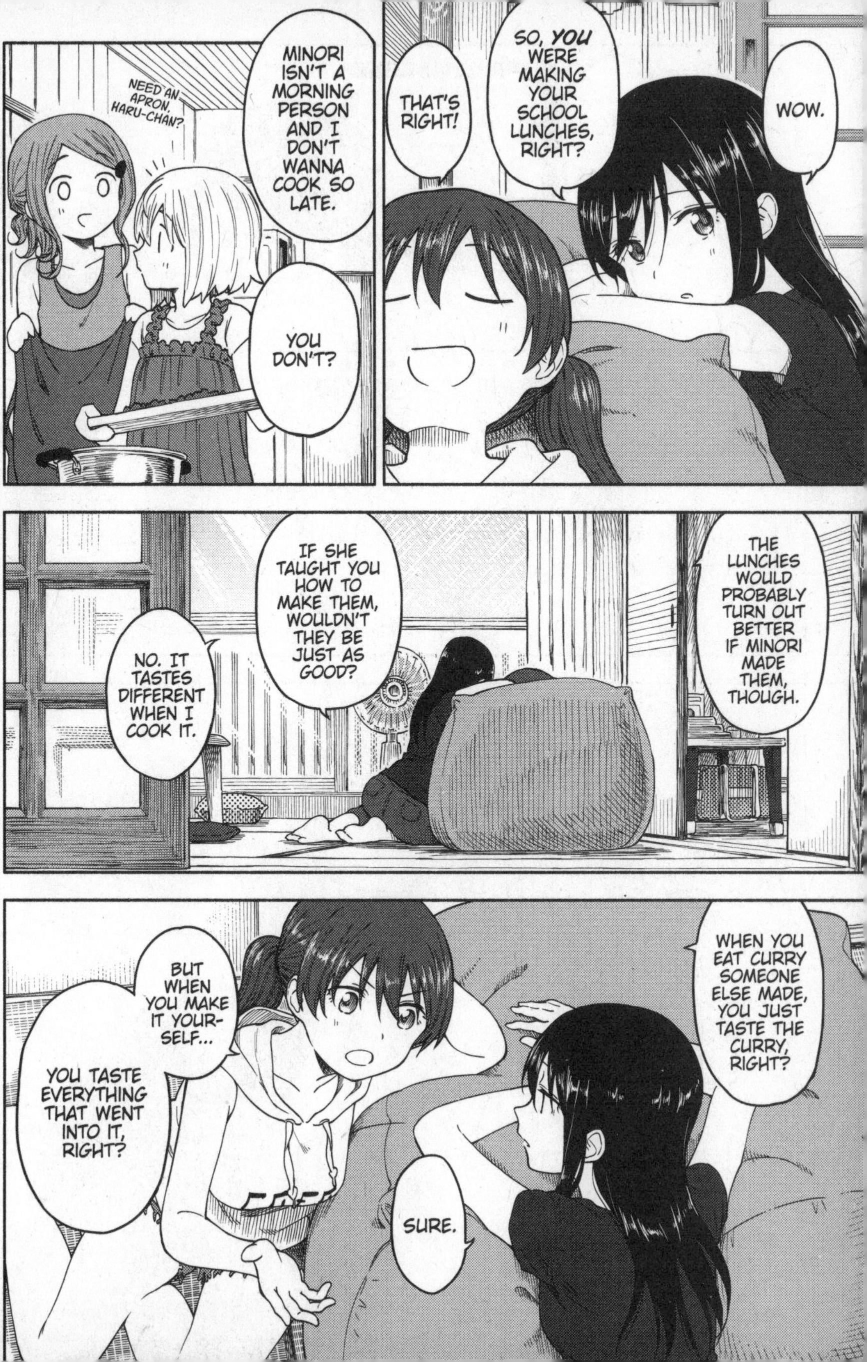
WOW.
SO, YOU WERE MAKING YOUR SCHOOL LUNCHES, RIGHT?
THAT'S RIGHT!
MINORI ISN'T A MORNING PERSON AND I DON'T WANNA COOK SO LATE.
NEED AN APRON, HARU-CHAN?
YOU DON'T?
THE LUNCHES WOULD PROBABLY TURN OUT BETTER IF MINORI MADE THEM, THOUGH.
IF SHE TAUGHT YOU HOW TO MAKE THEM, WOULDN'T THEY BE JUST AS GOOD?
NO. IT TASTES DIFFERENT WHEN I COOK IT.
WHEN YOU EAT CURRY SOMEONE ELSE MADE, YOU JUST TASTE THE CURRY, RIGHT?
SURE.
BUT WHEN YOU MAKE IT YOUR-SELF...
YOU TASTE EVERYTHING THAT WENT INTO IT, RIGHT?

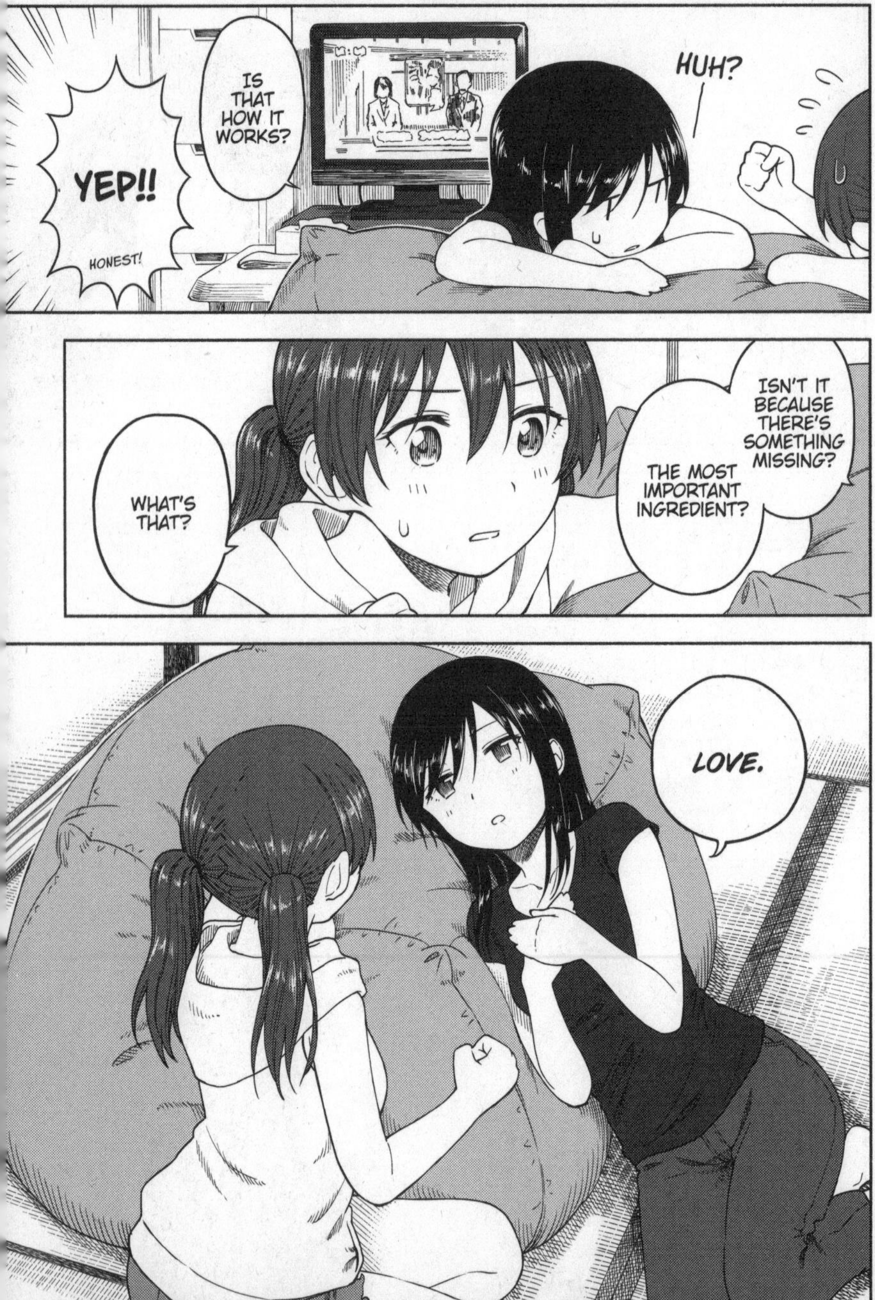
HUH?
IS THAT HOW IT WORKS?
YEP!!
HONEST!
ISN'T IT BECAUSE THERE'S SOMETHING MISSING?
THE MOST IMPORTANT INGREDIENT?
WHAT'S THAT?
LOVE.

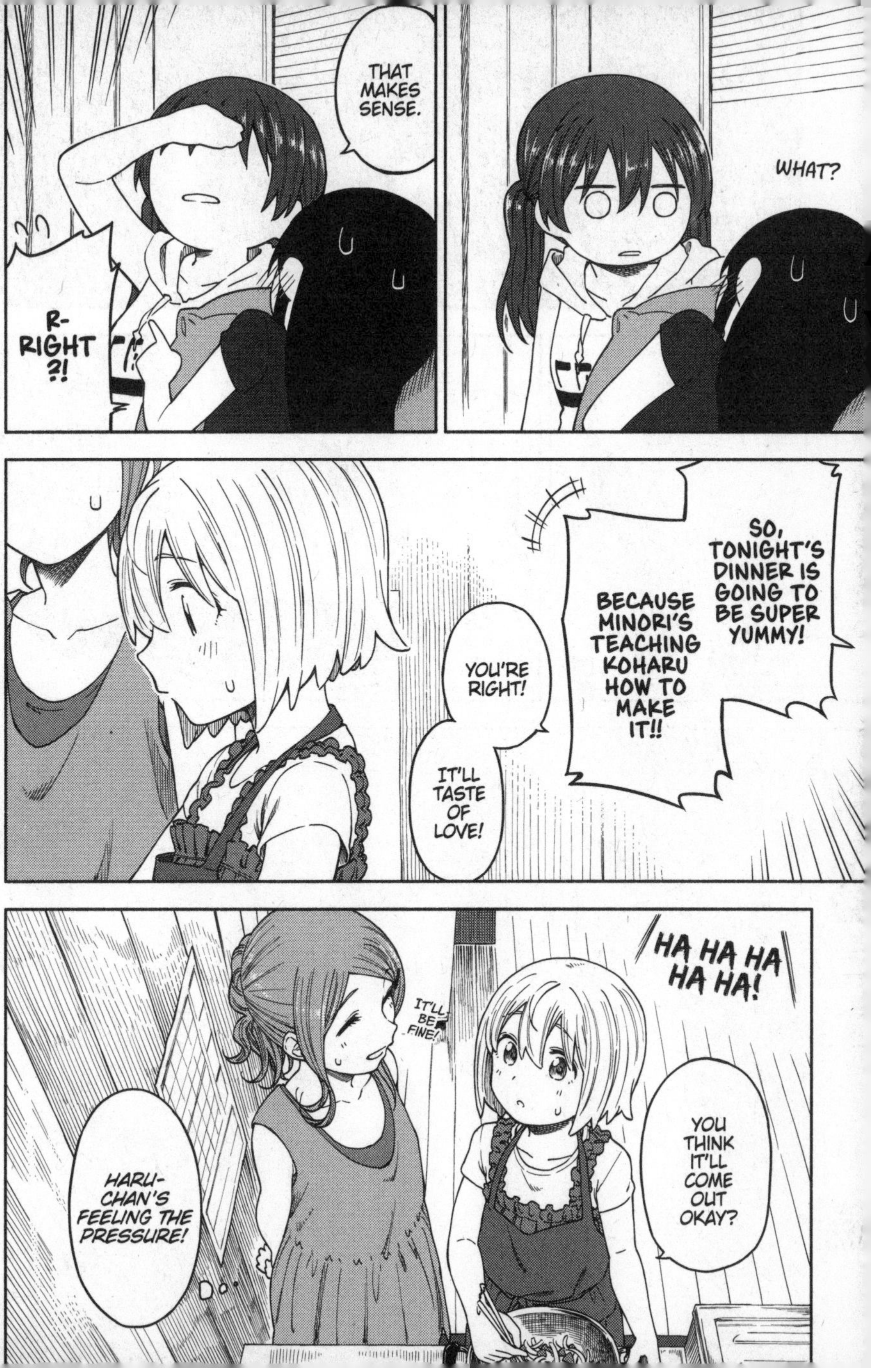
WHAT?
THAT MAKES SENSE.
R-RIGHT?!
SO, TONIGHT'S DINNER IS GOING TO BE SUPER YUMMY!
BECAUSE MINORI'S TEACHING KOHARU HOW TO MAKE IT!!
YOU'RE RIGHT!
IT'LL TASTE OF LOVE!
HA HA HA HA HA!
YOU THINK IT'LL COME OUT OKAY?
IT'LL BE FINE!
HARU-CHAN'S FEELING THE PRESSURE!

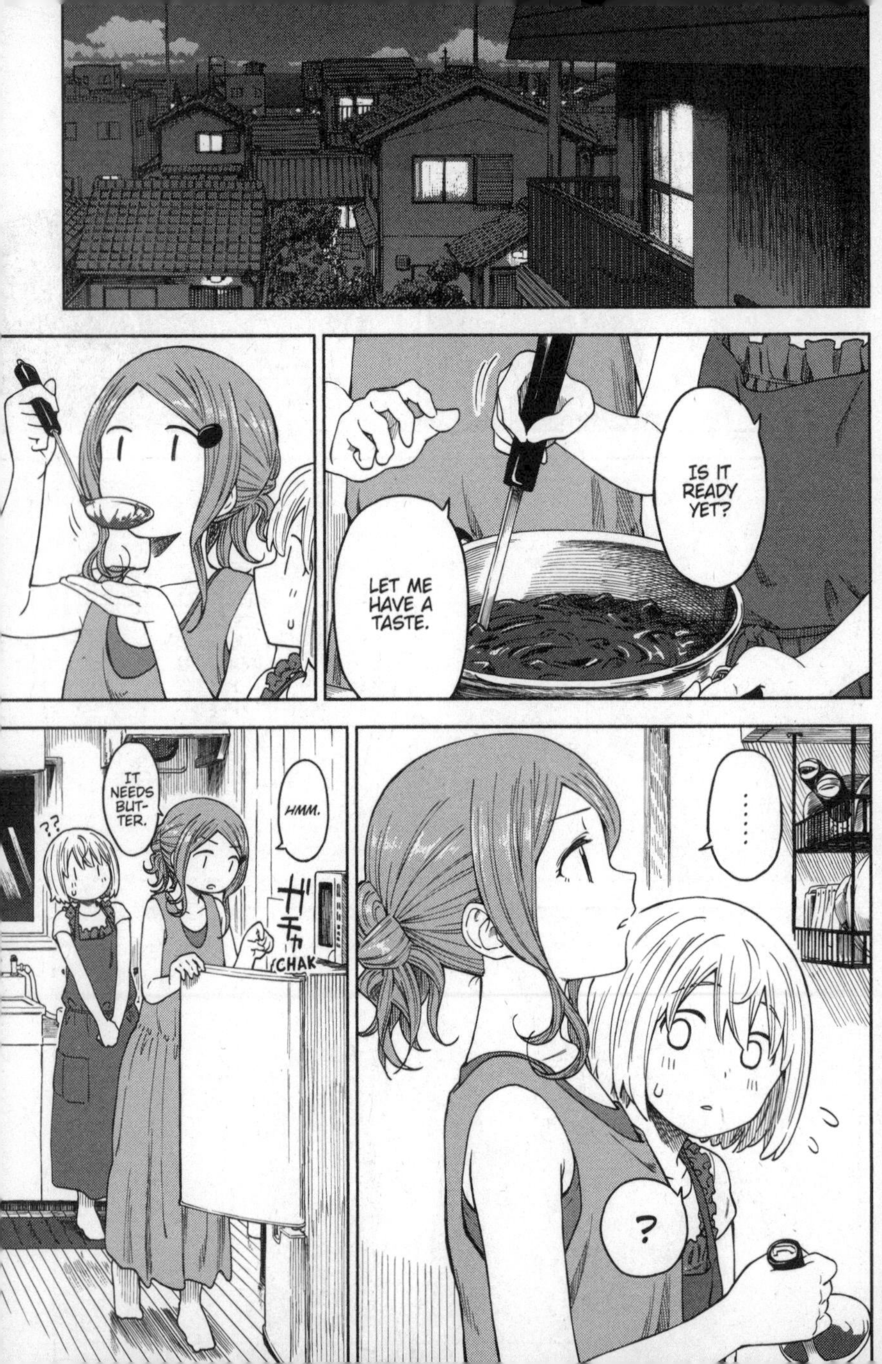
IS IT READY YET?
LET ME HAVE A TASTE.
......
?
HMM.
IT NEEDS BUT-TER.
??
ガチャ
CHAK

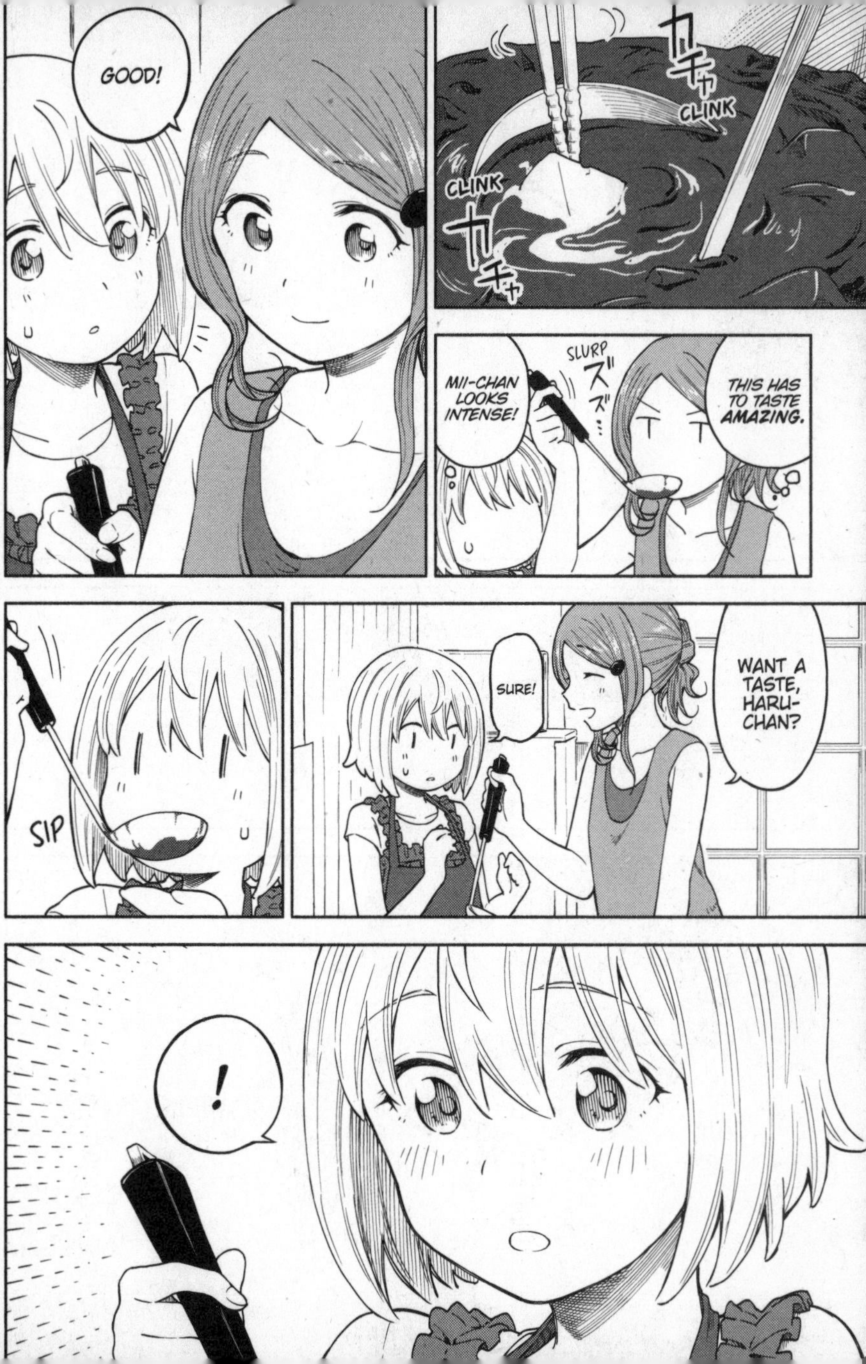
カチャ
CLINK
CLINK
カチャ
THIS HAS TO TASTE AMAZING.
SLURP
ズズ…
MII-CHAN LOOKS INTENSE!
GOOD!
WANT A TASTE, HARU-CHAN?
SURE!
SIP
!

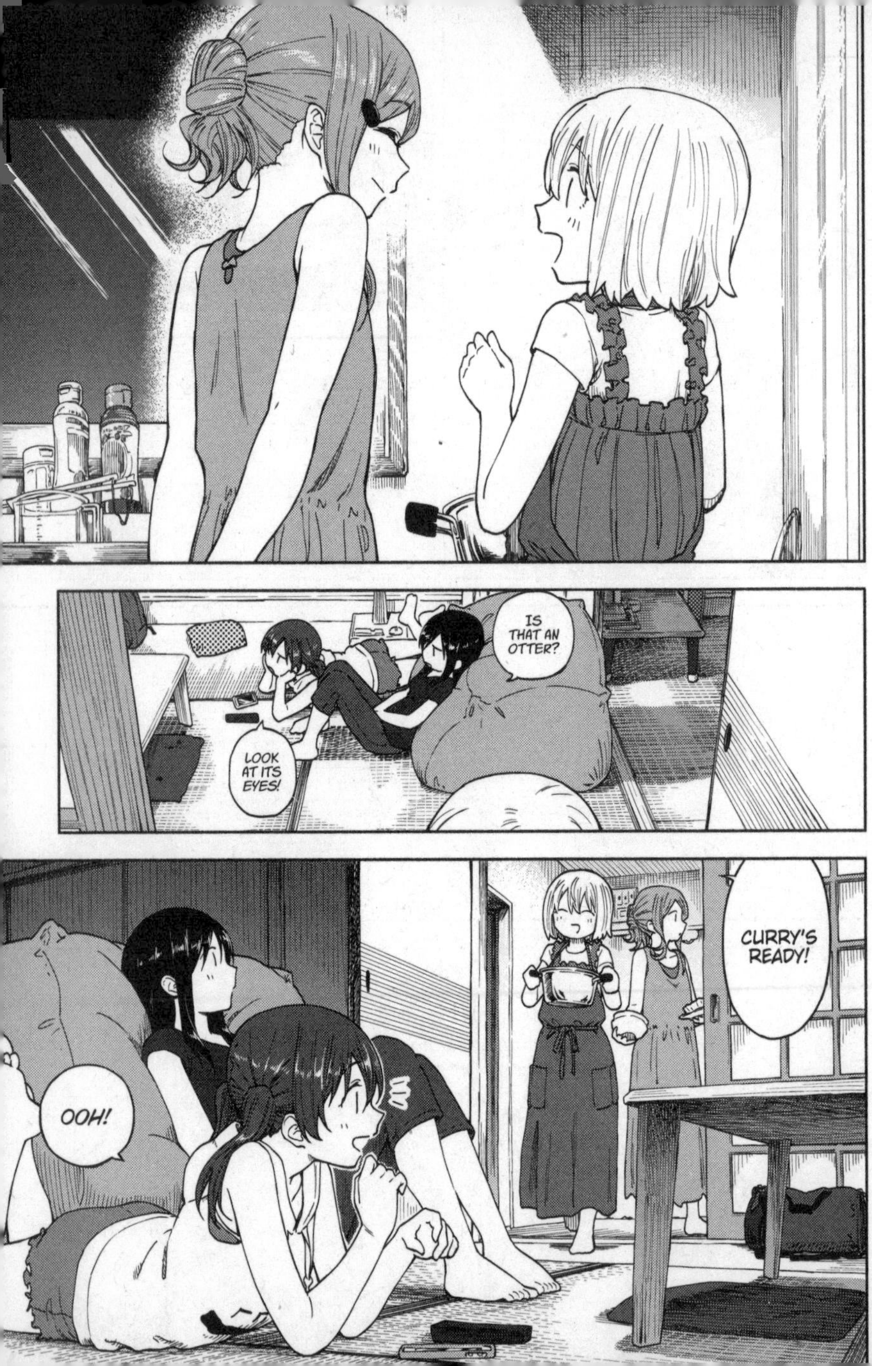
IS THAT AN OTTER?
LOOK AT ITS EYES!
CURRY'S READY!
OOH!

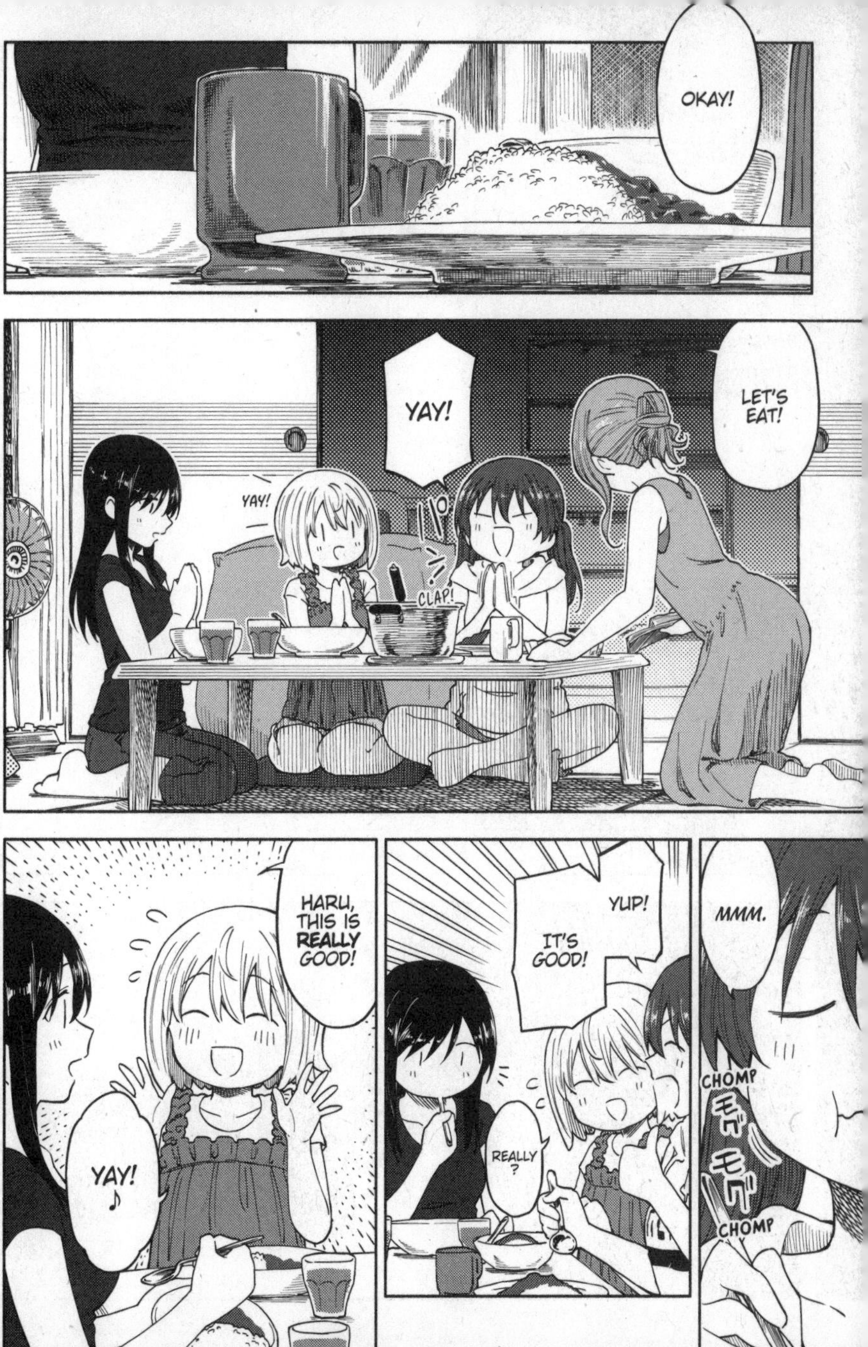
OKAY!
LET'S EAT!
YAY!
CLAP!
YAY!
MMM.
CHOMP
モグ
モグ
CHOMP
YUP!
IT'S GOOD!
REALLY?
HARU, THIS IS **REALLY** GOOD!
YAY! ♪

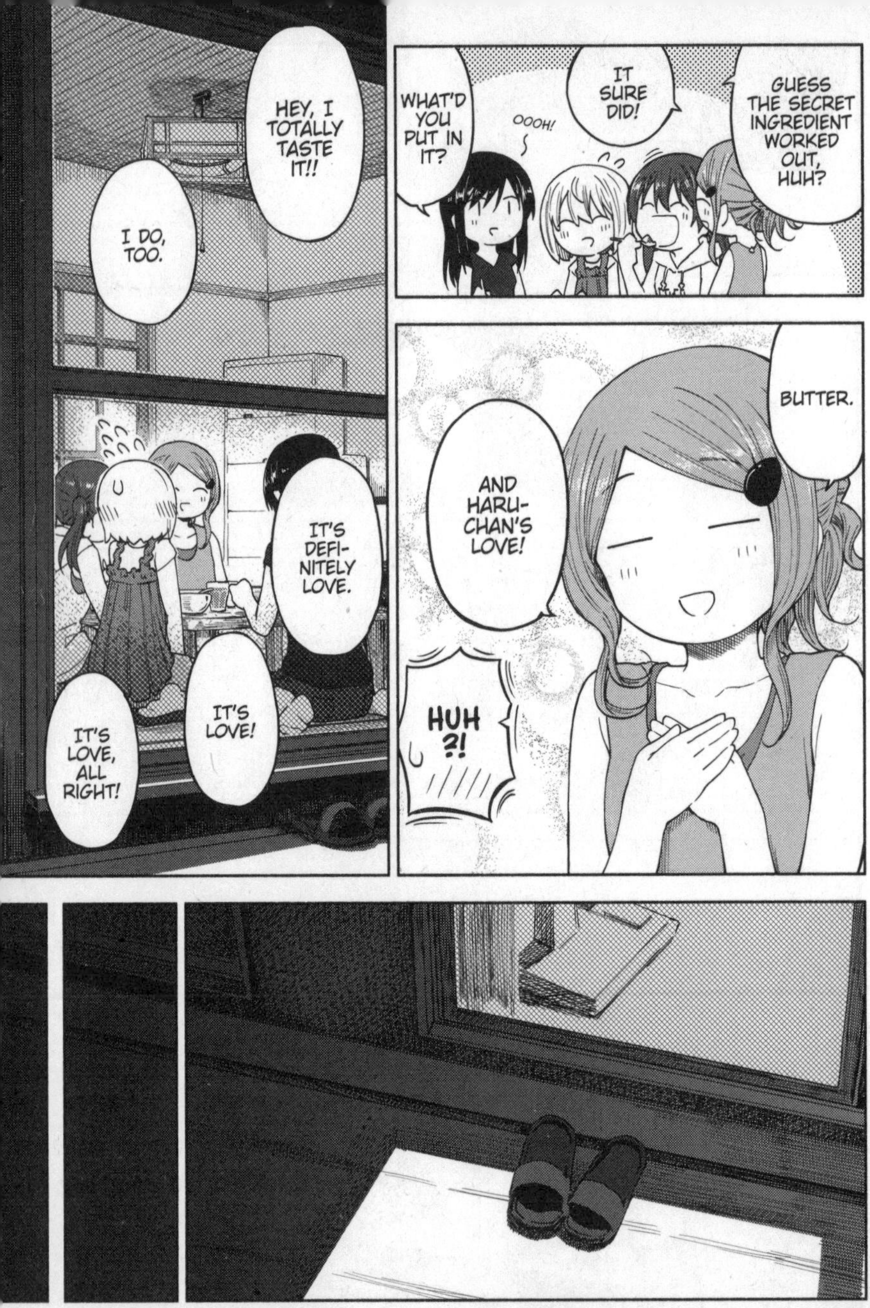
GUESS THE SECRET INGREDIENT WORKED OUT, HUH?
IT SURE DID!
OOOH!
WHAT'D YOU PUT IN IT?
BUTTER.
AND HARU-CHAN'S LOVE!
HUH ?!
HEY, I TOTALLY TASTE IT!!
I DO, TOO.
IT'S DEFINITELY LOVE.
IT'S LOVE!
IT'S LOVE, ALL RIGHT!

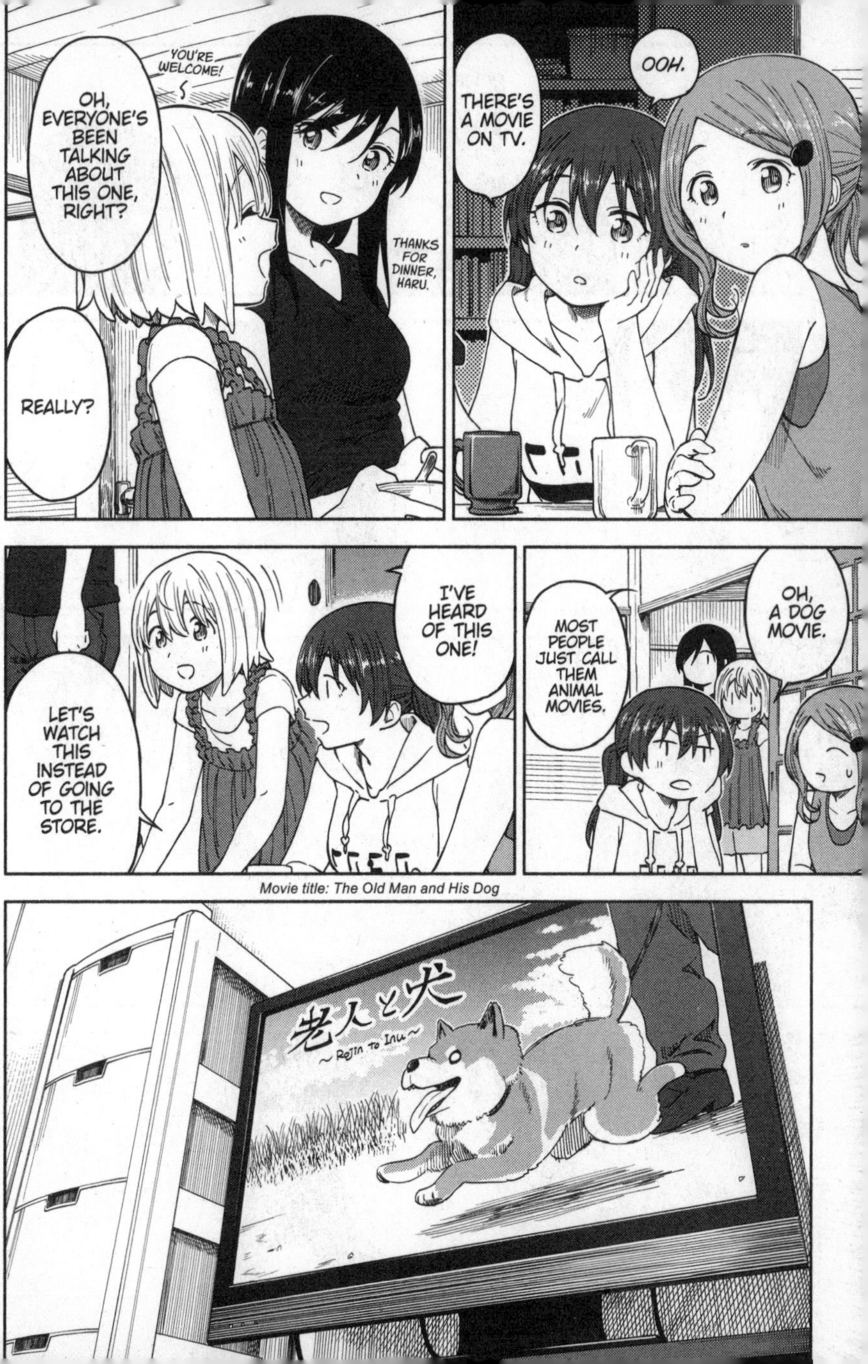
OOH.
THERE'S A MOVIE ON TV.
THANKS FOR DINNER, HARU.
YOU'RE WELCOME!
OH, EVERYONE'S BEEN TALKING ABOUT THIS ONE, RIGHT?
REALLY?
OH, A DOG MOVIE.
MOST PEOPLE JUST CALL THEM ANIMAL MOVIES.
I'VE HEARD OF THIS ONE!
LET'S WATCH THIS INSTEAD OF GOING TO THE STORE.
Movie title: The Old Man and His Dog
老人と犬
~Rojin to Inu~

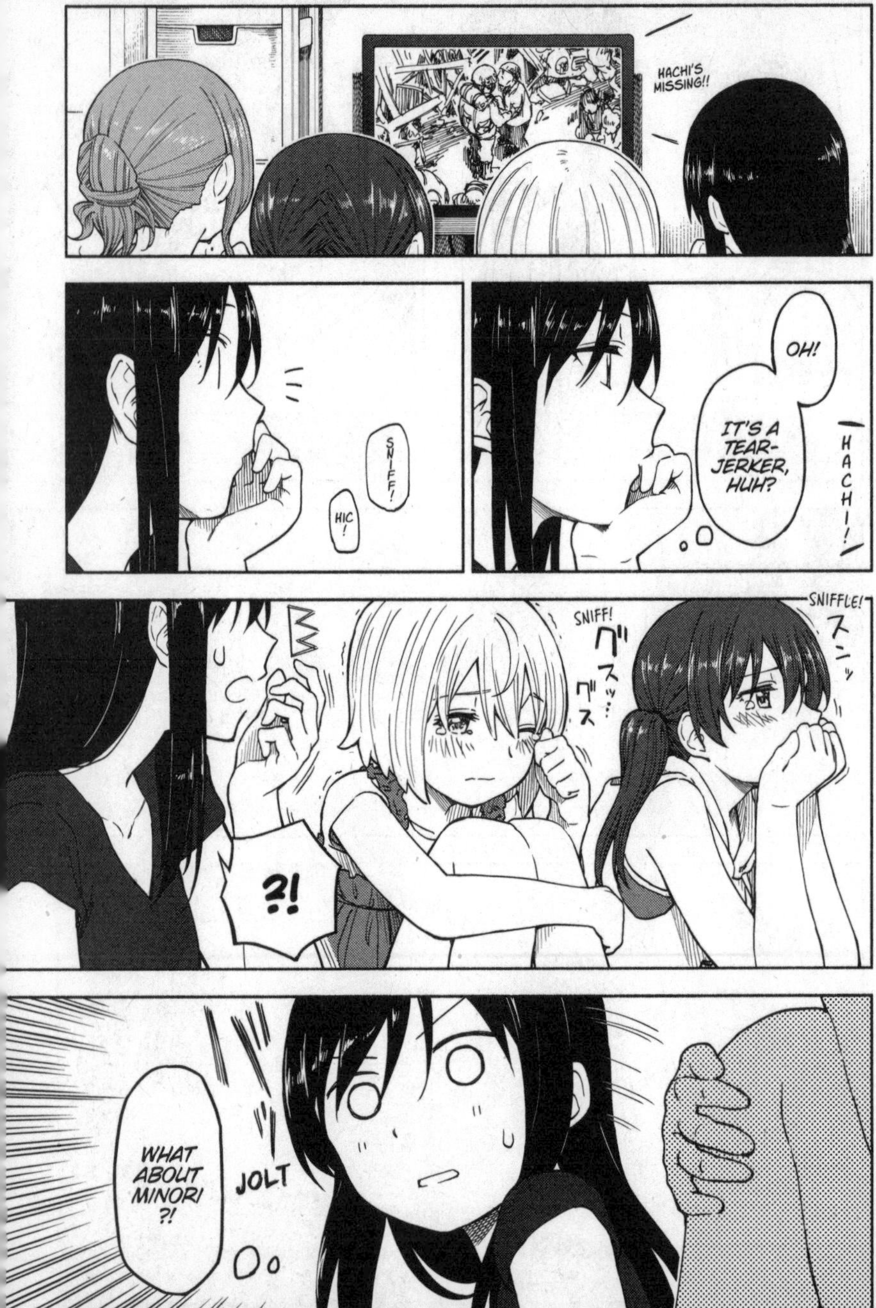

HACHI'S MISSING!!
OH!
IT'S A TEAR-JERKER, HUH?
HACHI!
SNIFF!
HIC!
SNIFFLE!
スンッ
SNIFF!
グスッ グス
?!
JOLT
WHAT ABOUT MINORI?!

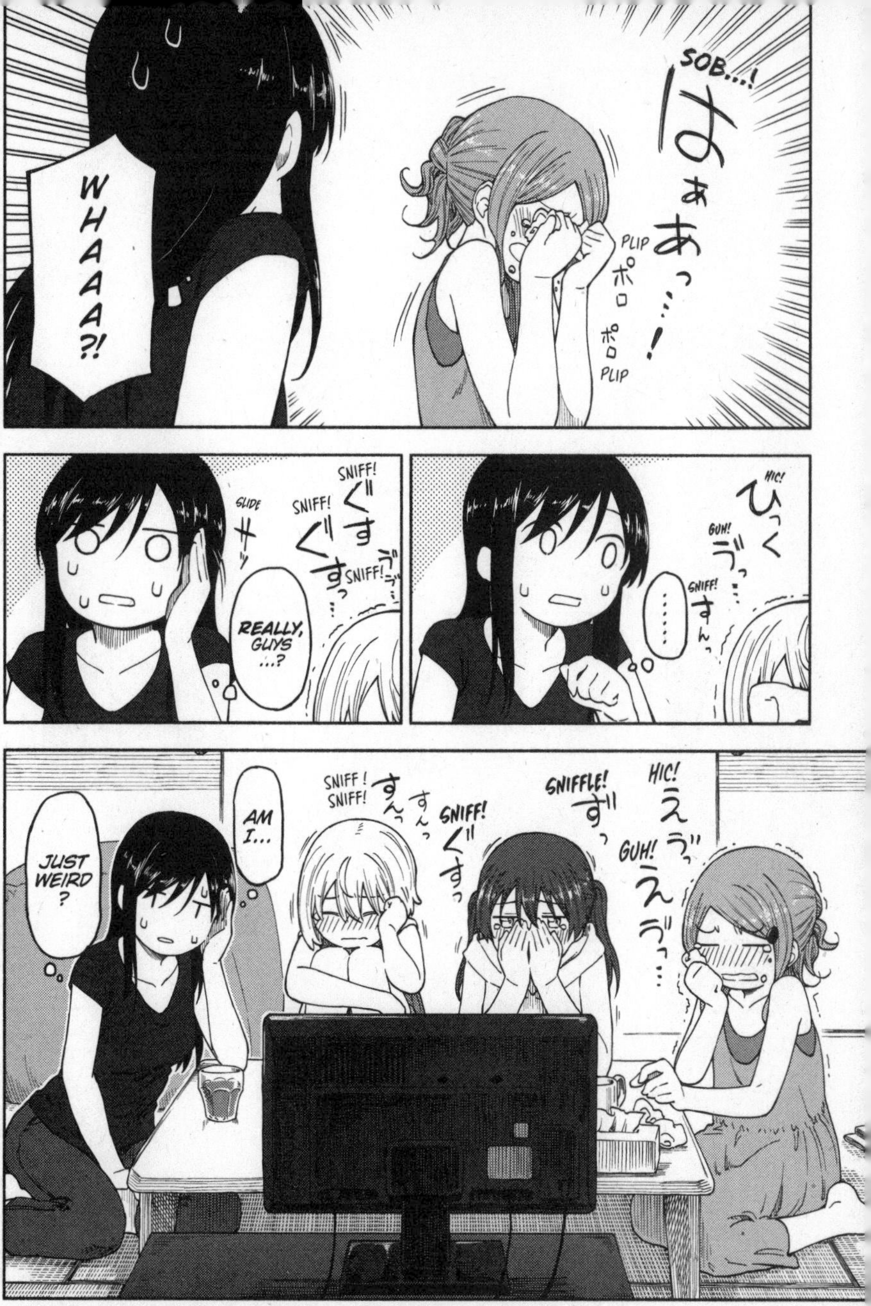
SOB....!
はぁあっ…!
PLIP ポロ
ポロ PLIP
WHAAAA?!
HIC! ひっく
GUH! ゔっ…
SNIFF! すんっ
……
SNIFF! ぐす
SNIFF! ぐすっ…
SNIFF! ゔっ…
SLIDE ザッ
REALLY, GUYS ...?
HIC! えゔっ
GUH! えゔっ…
SNIFFLE! ずっ
SNIFF! ぐすっ
SNIFF! SNIFF! すんっ すんっ
AM I...
JUST WEIRD?

Our Wonderful Days

story & art by Kei Hamuro

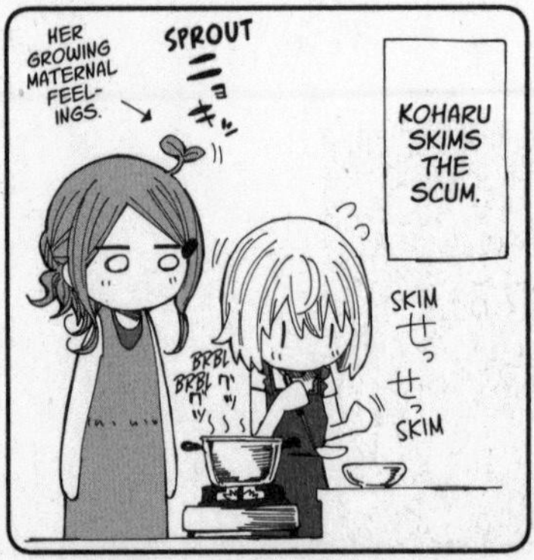
KOHARU SKIMS THE SCUM.
SPROUT
ニョキッ
HER GROWING MATERNAL FEEL- INGS.
SKIM
せっ
せっ
SKIM
BRBL
BRBL

Our *Wonderful* *Days* Tsurezure Biyori

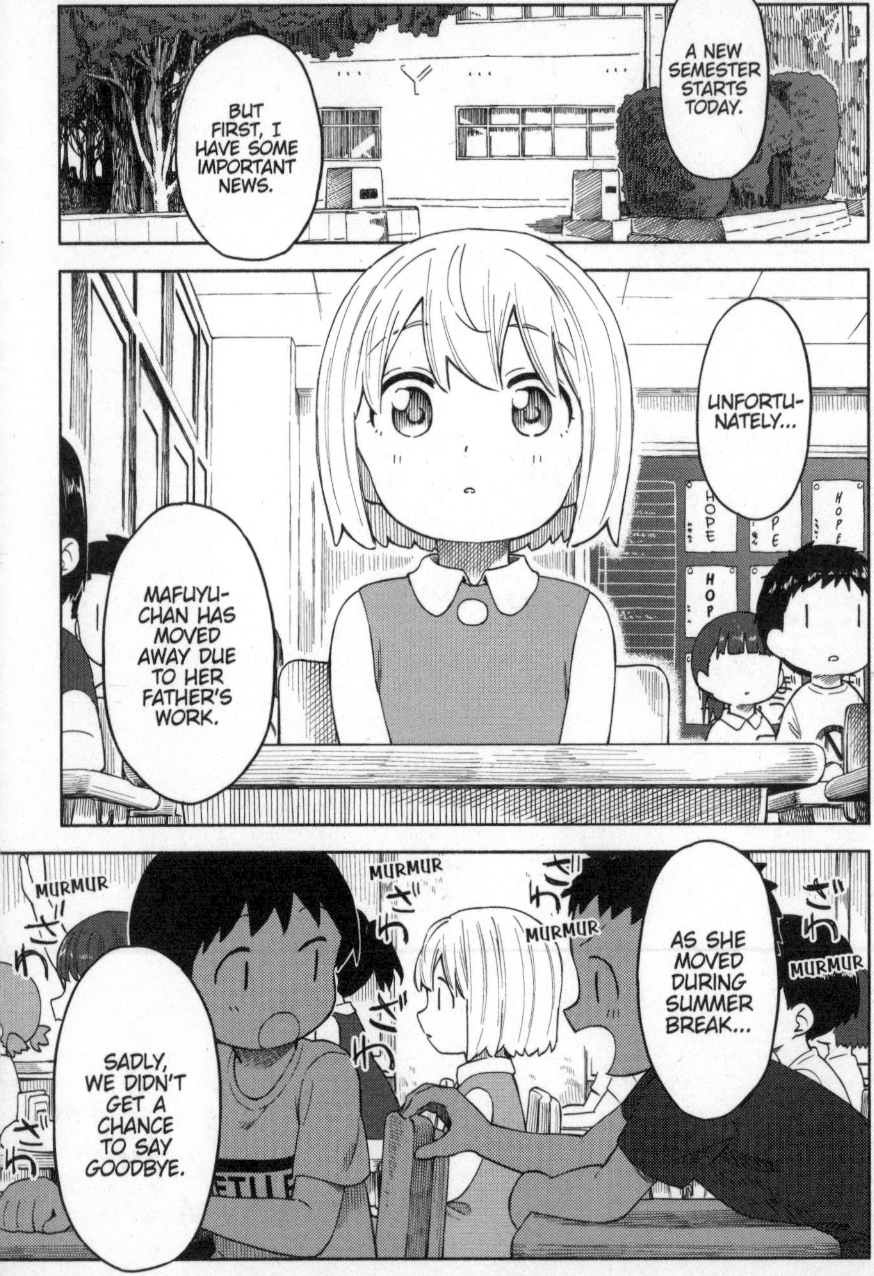
A NEW SEMESTER STARTS TODAY.
BUT FIRST, I HAVE SOME IMPORTANT NEWS.
UNFORTU-NATELY...
MAFUYU-CHAN HAS MOVED AWAY DUE TO HER FATHER'S WORK.
AS SHE MOVED DURING SUMMER BREAK...
MURMUR
MURMUR
MURMUR
MURMUR
SADLY, WE DIDN'T GET A CHANCE TO SAY GOODBYE.

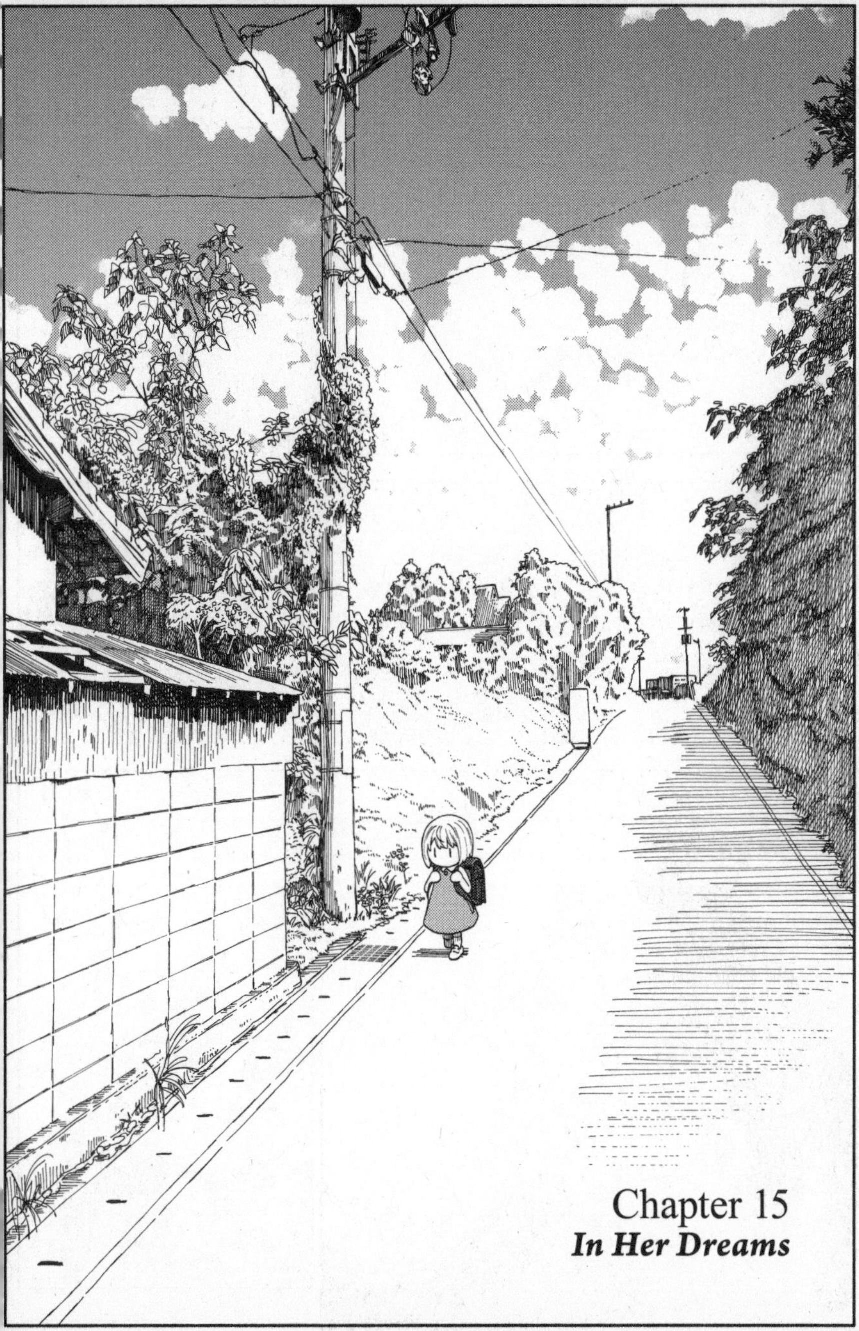

Chapter 15
In Her Dreams

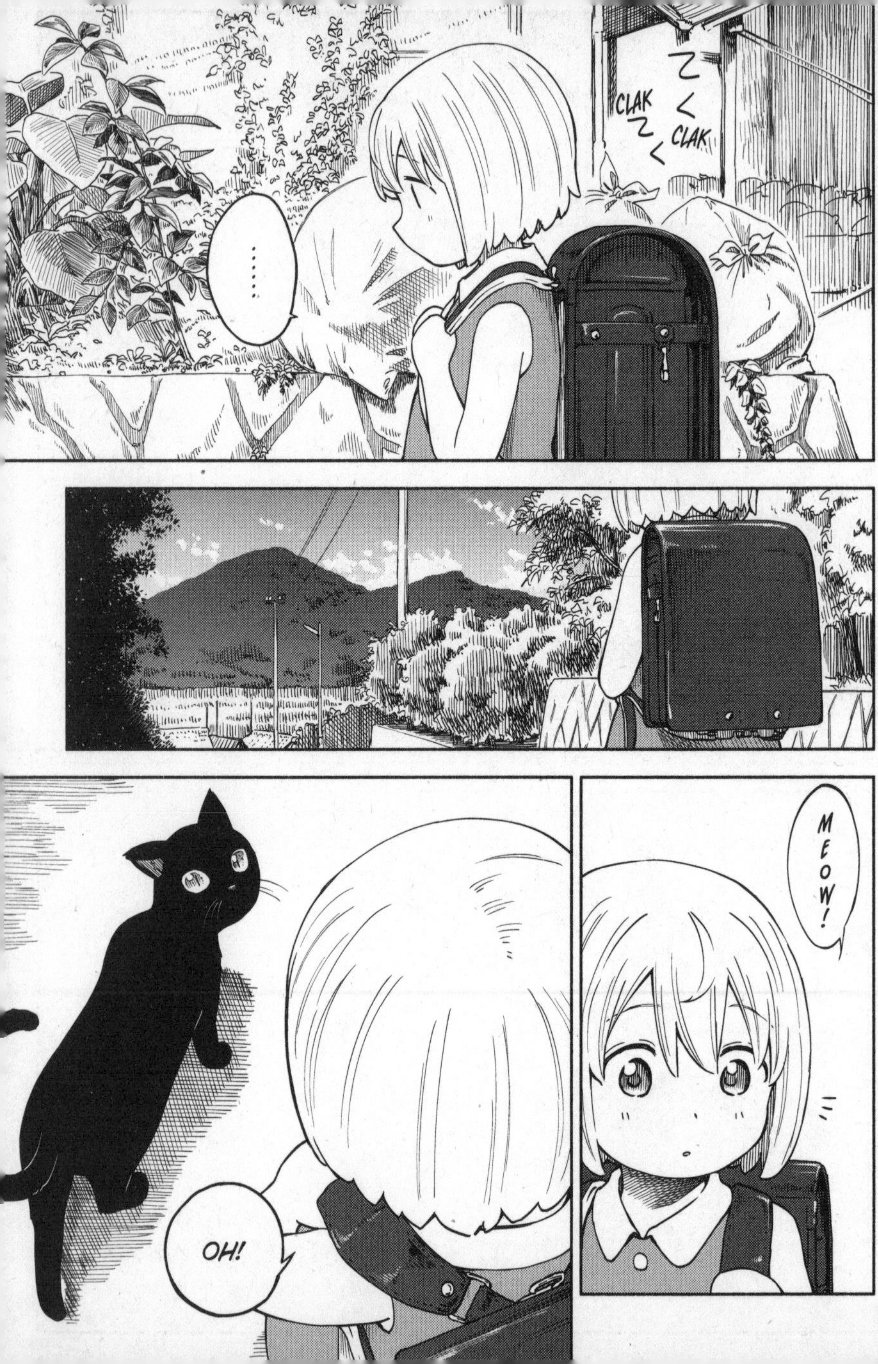
CLAK CLAK
……
MEOW!
OH!

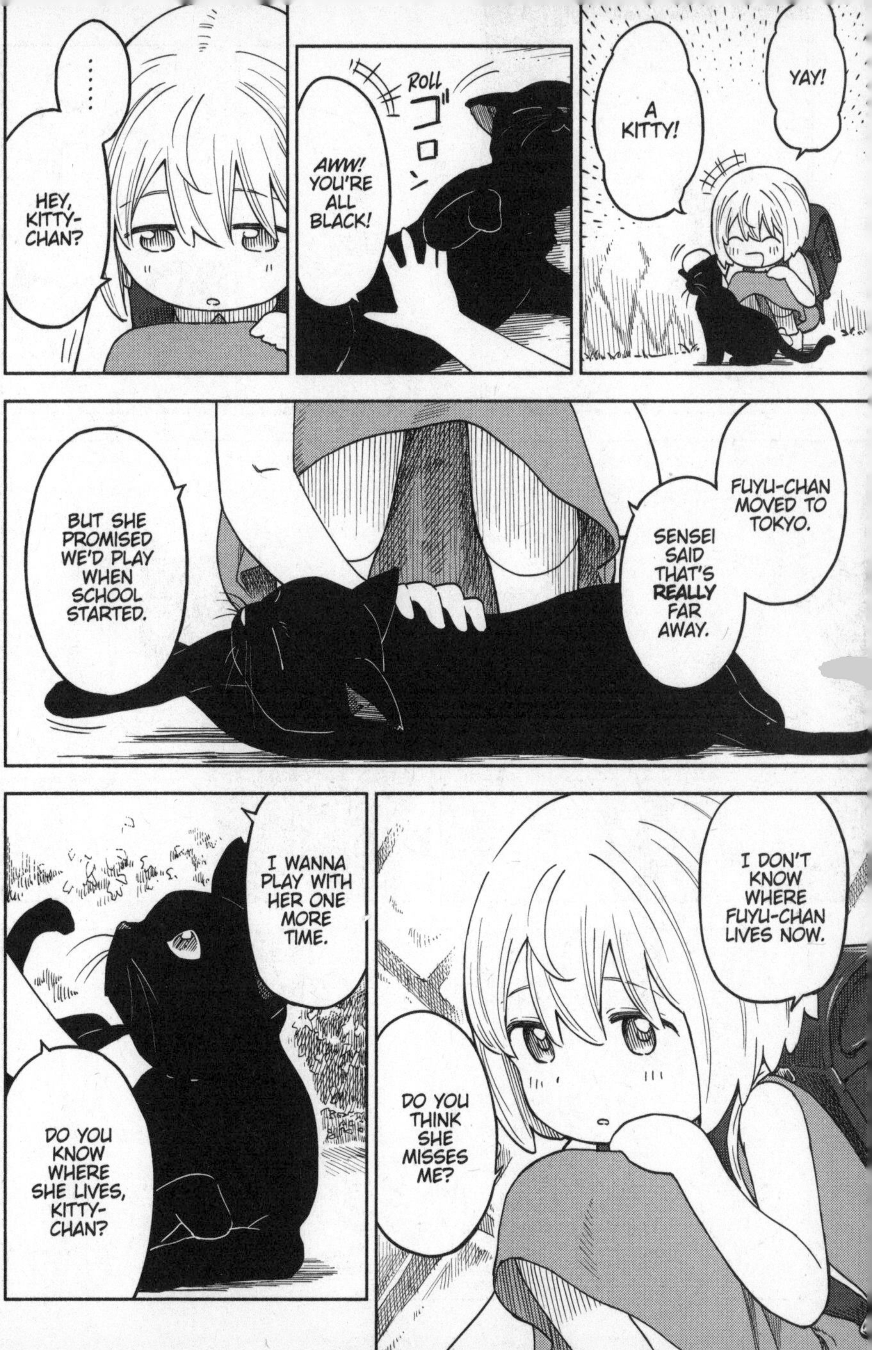
YAY!
A KITTY!
ROLL
ゴロ
AWW! YOU'RE ALL BLACK!
......
HEY, KITTY-CHAN?
FUYU-CHAN MOVED TO TOKYO.
SENSEI SAID THAT'S REALLY FAR AWAY.
BUT SHE PROMISED WE'D PLAY WHEN SCHOOL STARTED.
I DON'T KNOW WHERE FUYU-CHAN LIVES NOW.
DO YOU THINK SHE MISSES ME?
I WANNA PLAY WITH HER ONE MORE TIME.
DO YOU KNOW WHERE SHE LIVES, KITTY-CHAN?

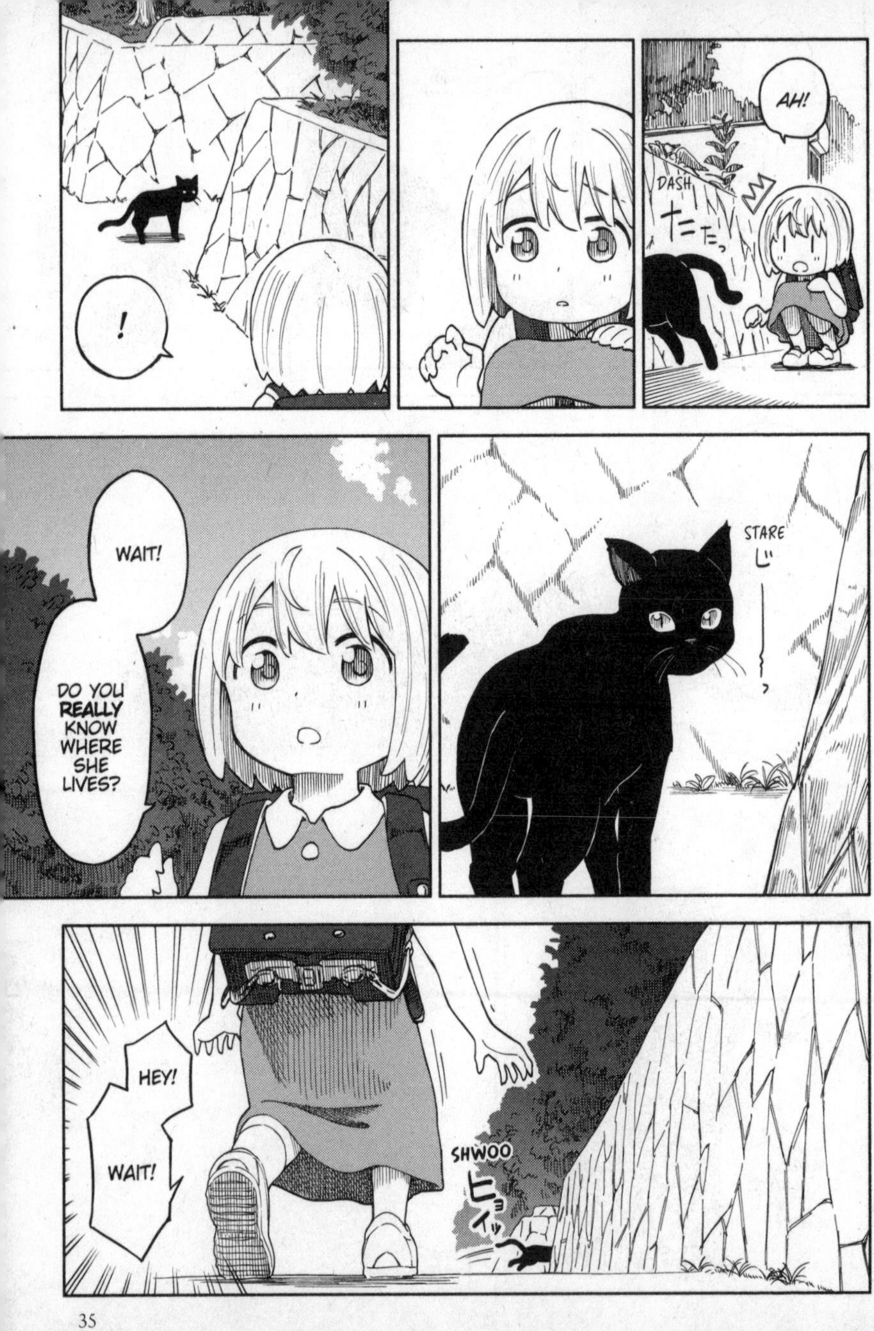
AH!
DASH
たたっ
!
STARE
じー
WAIT!
DO YOU REALLY KNOW WHERE SHE LIVES?
HEY!
WAIT!
SHWOO
ヒョイッ

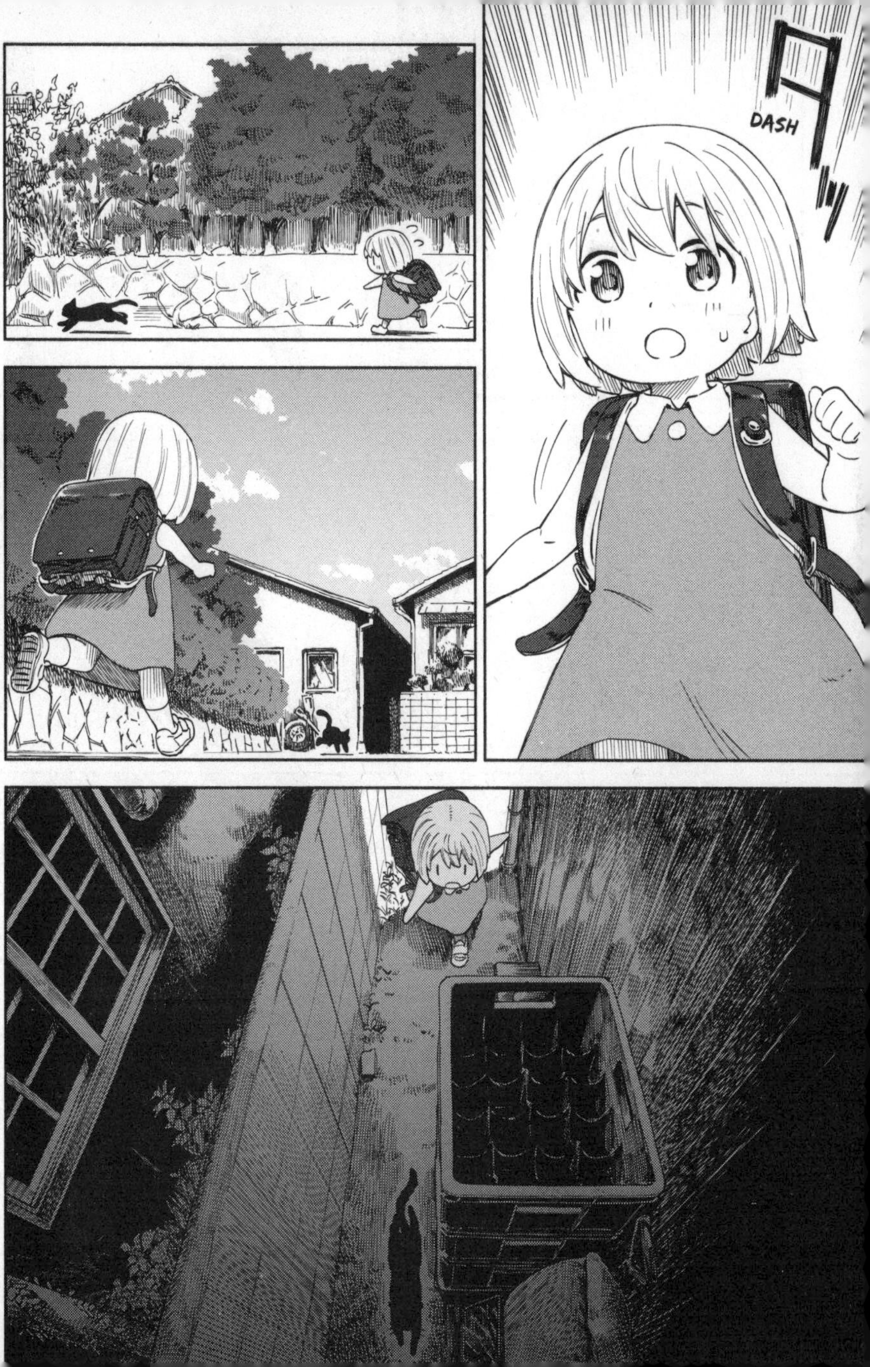
タッ
DASH

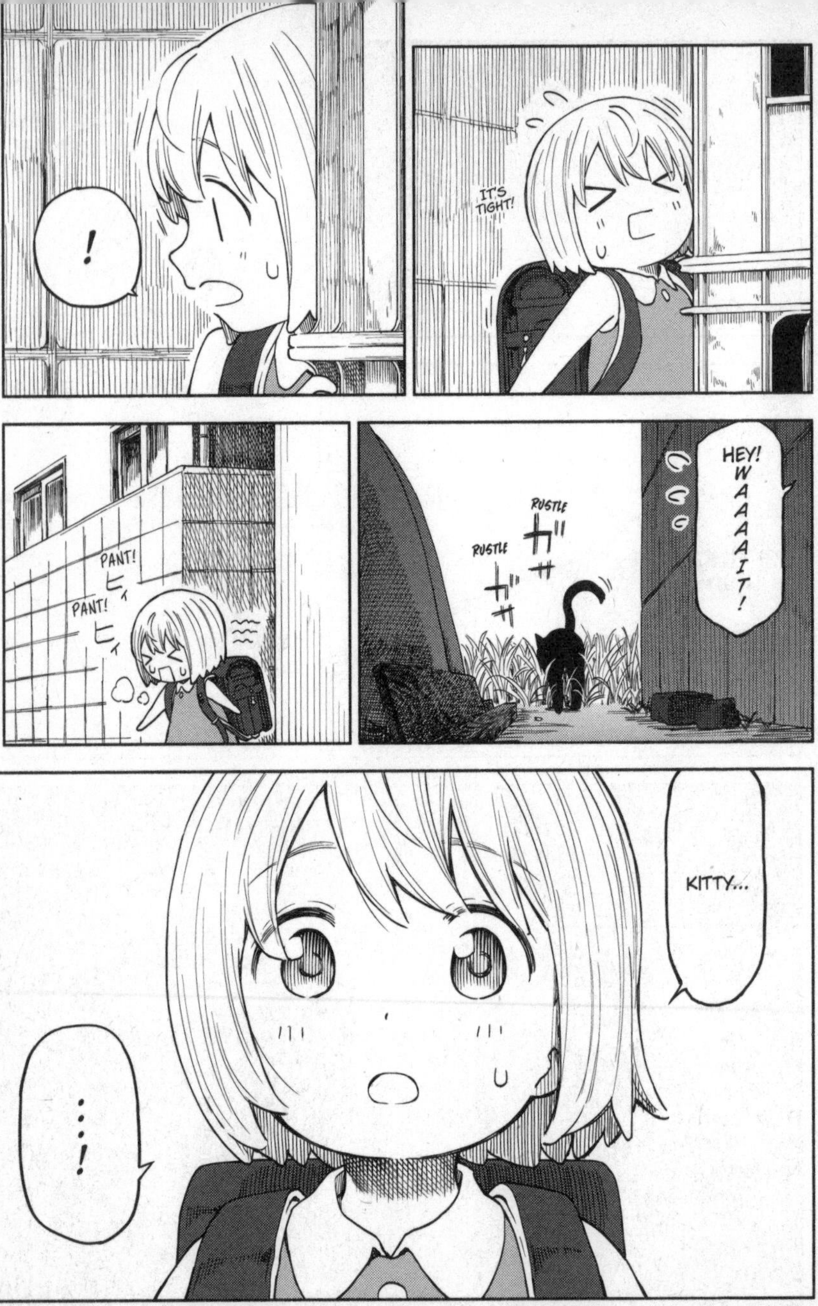
IT'S TIGHT!
!
HEY! WAAAAAIT!
RUSTLE
RUSTLE
PANT!
PANT!
KITTY...
...!

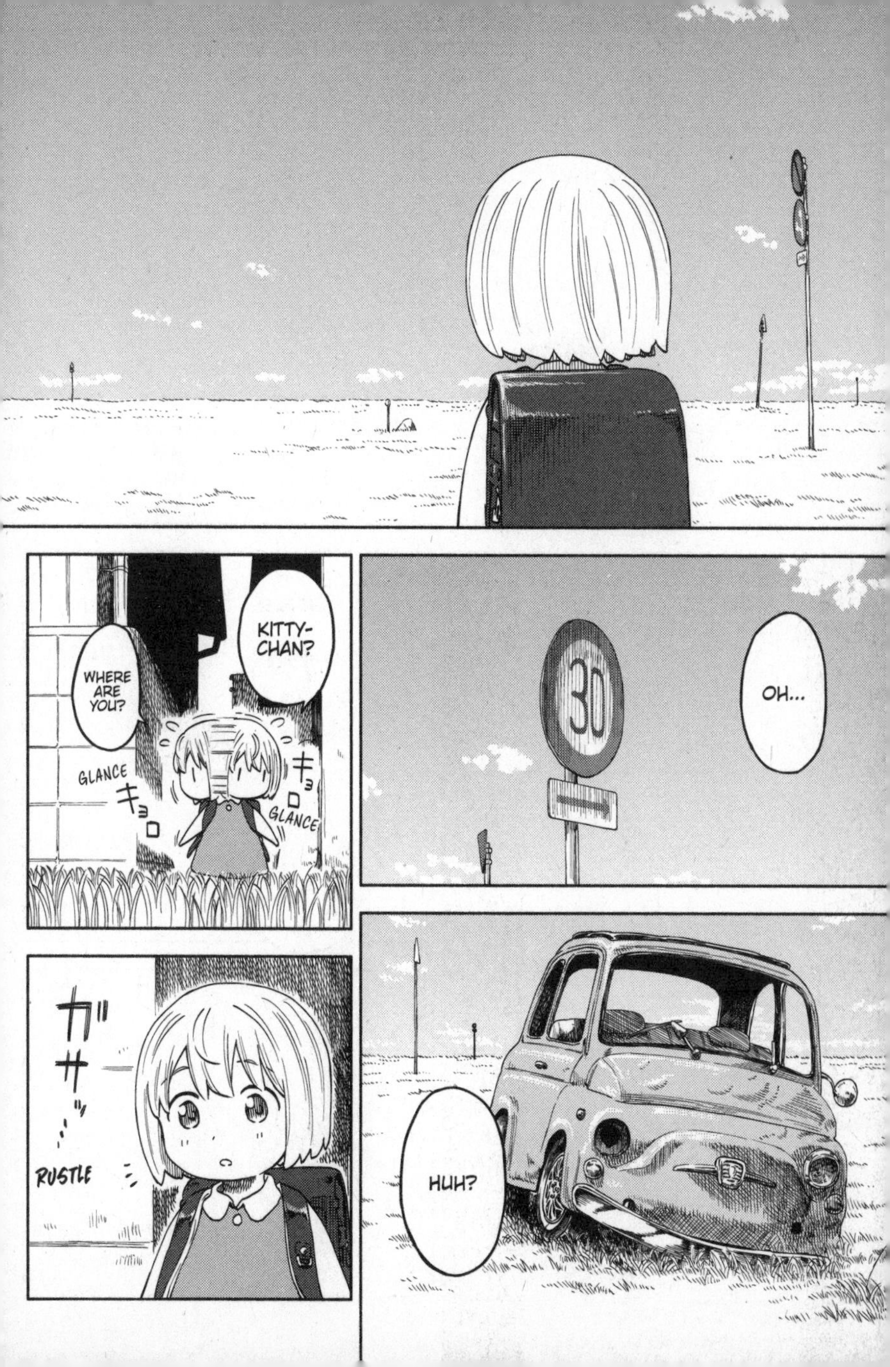
OH...
KITTY-CHAN?
WHERE ARE YOU?
キョロ
GLANCE
キョロ
GLANCE
HUH?
ガサッ
RUSTLE

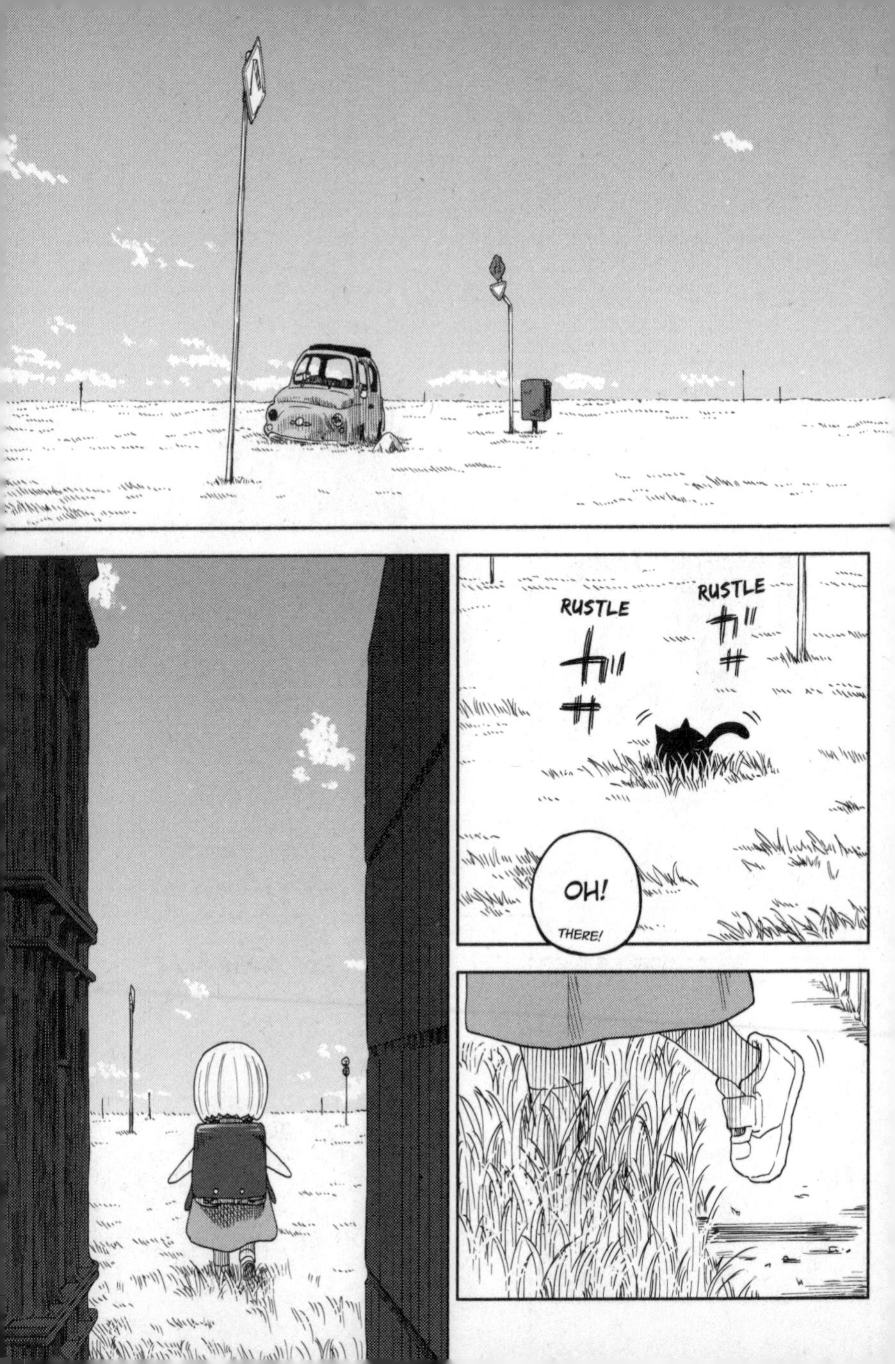
RUSTLE
RUSTLE
OH!
THERE!

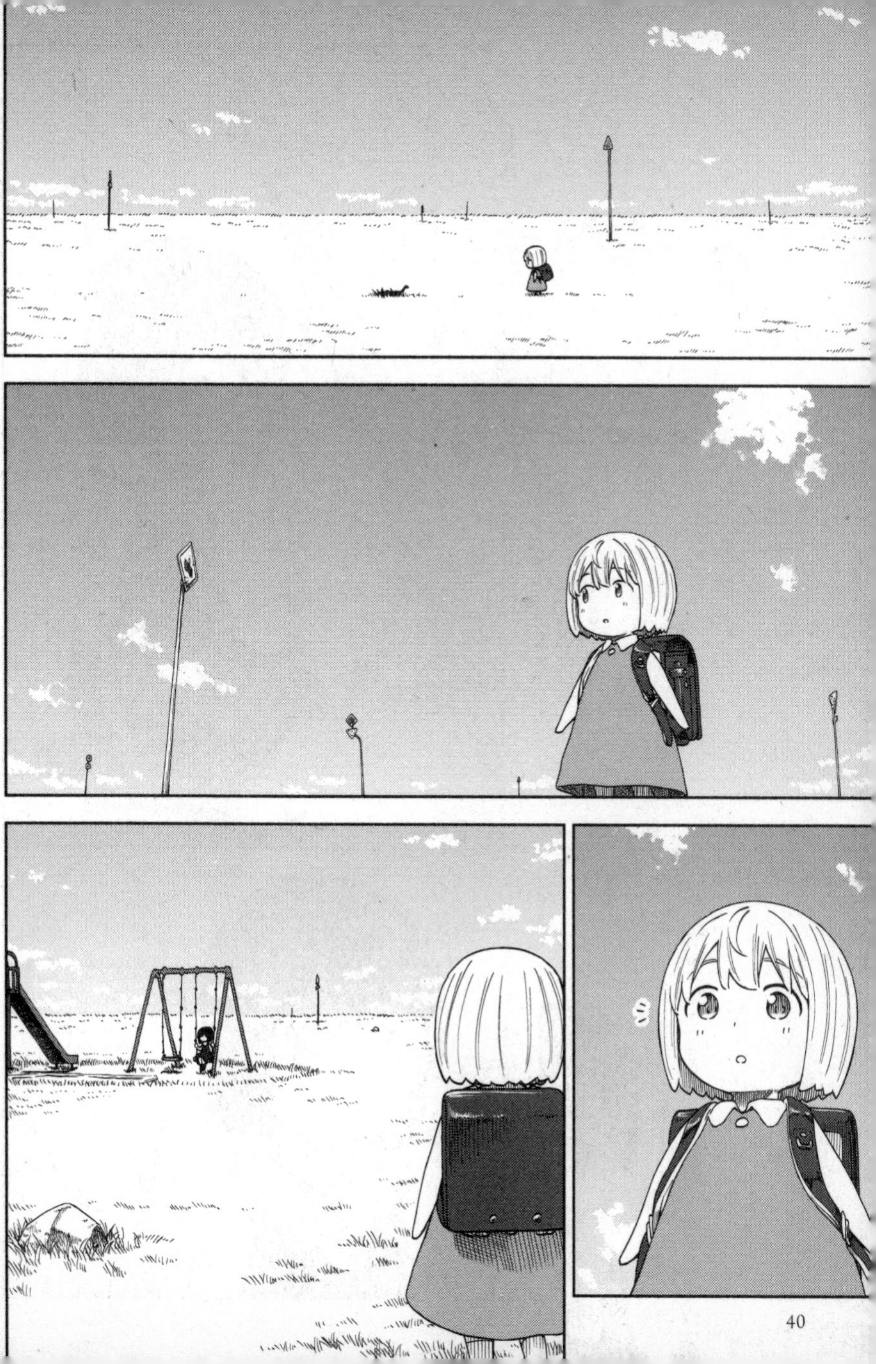

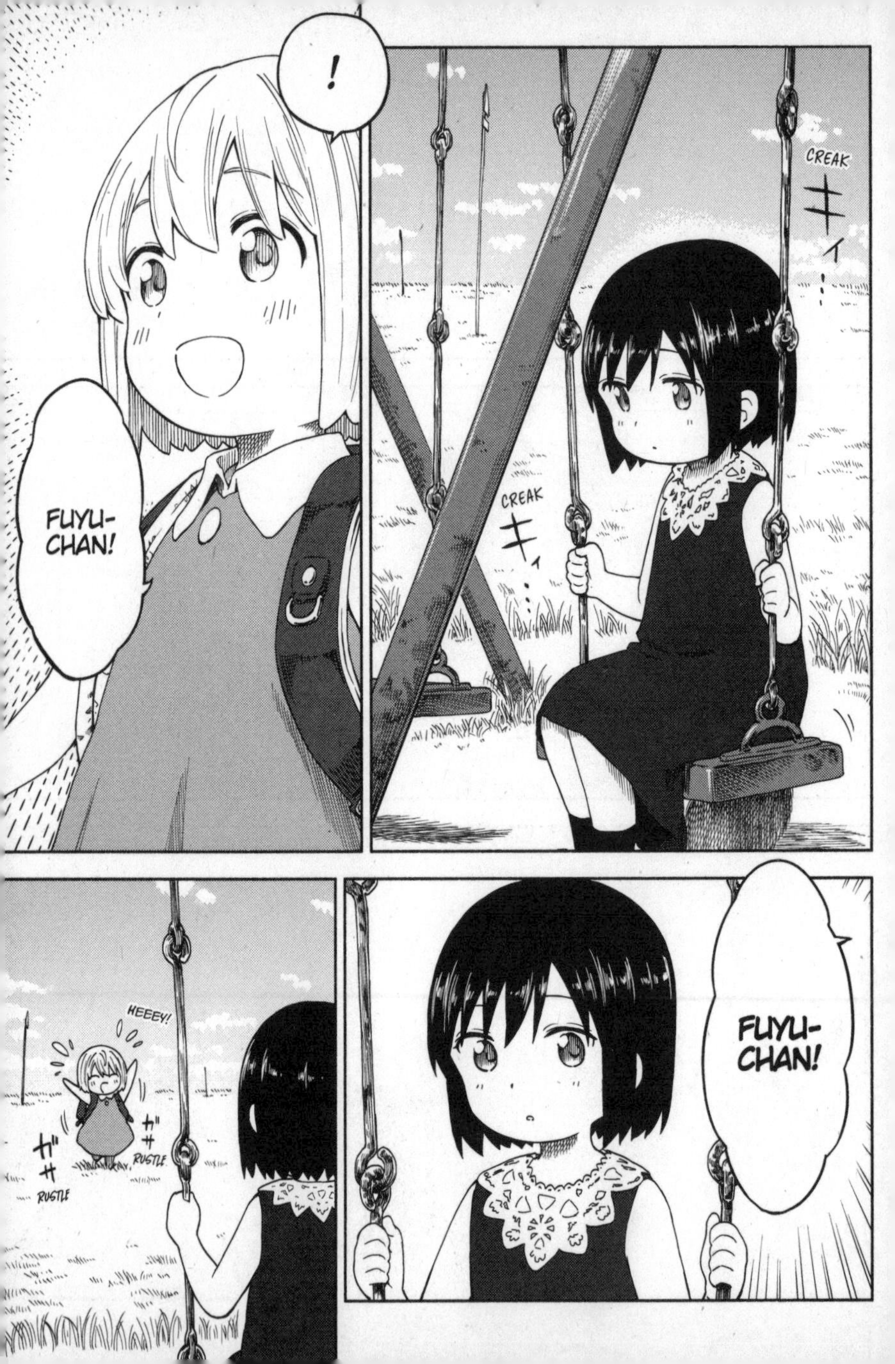
CREAK
キィ…
CREAK
キィ…
!
FUYU-CHAN!
FUYU-CHAN!
HEEEY!
ガサ
RUSTLE
ガサ
RUSTLE

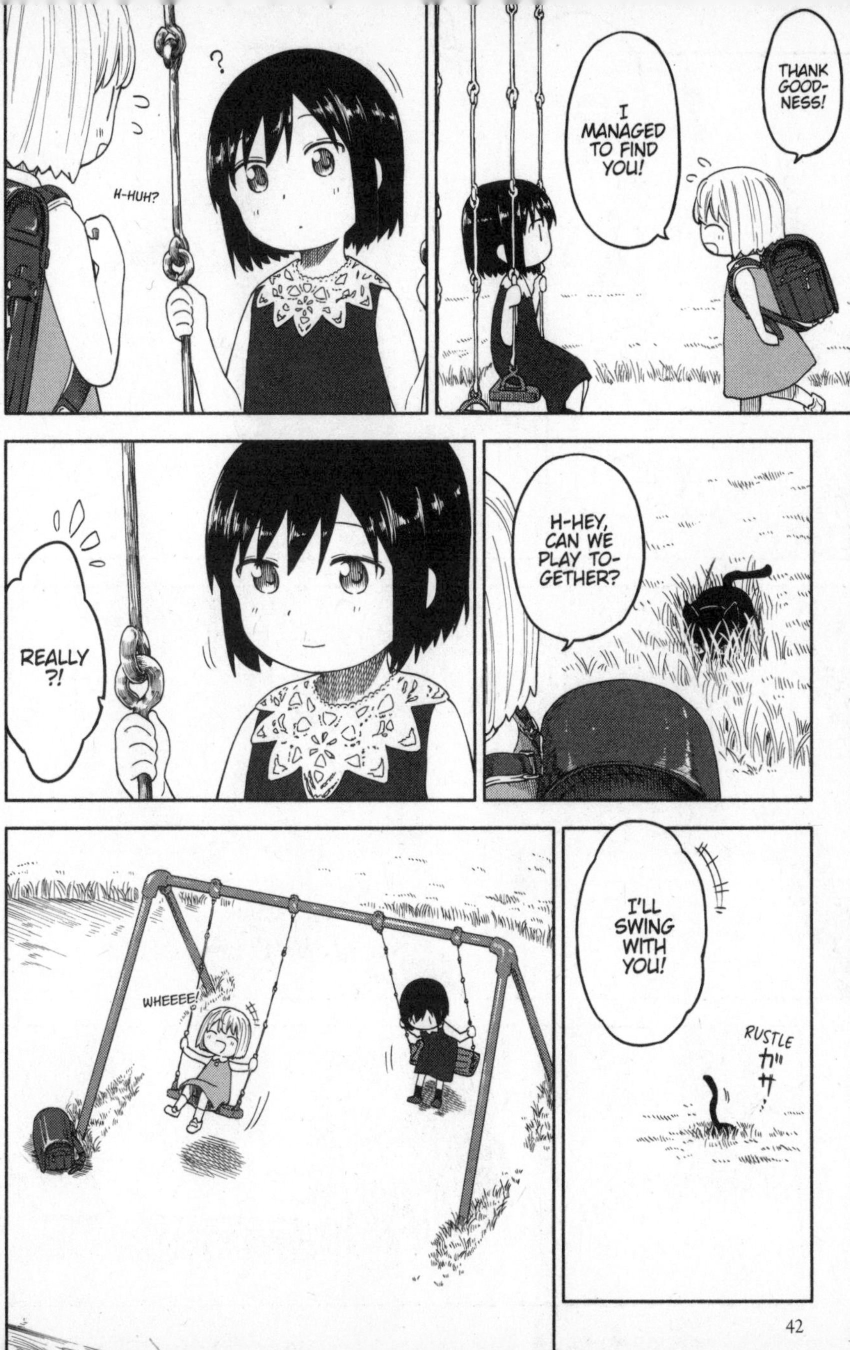
THANK GOOD-NESS!
I MANAGED TO FIND YOU!
H-HUH?
H-HEY, CAN WE PLAY TO-GETHER?
REALLY ?!
I'LL SWING WITH YOU!
RUSTLE
ガサ
WHEEEE!

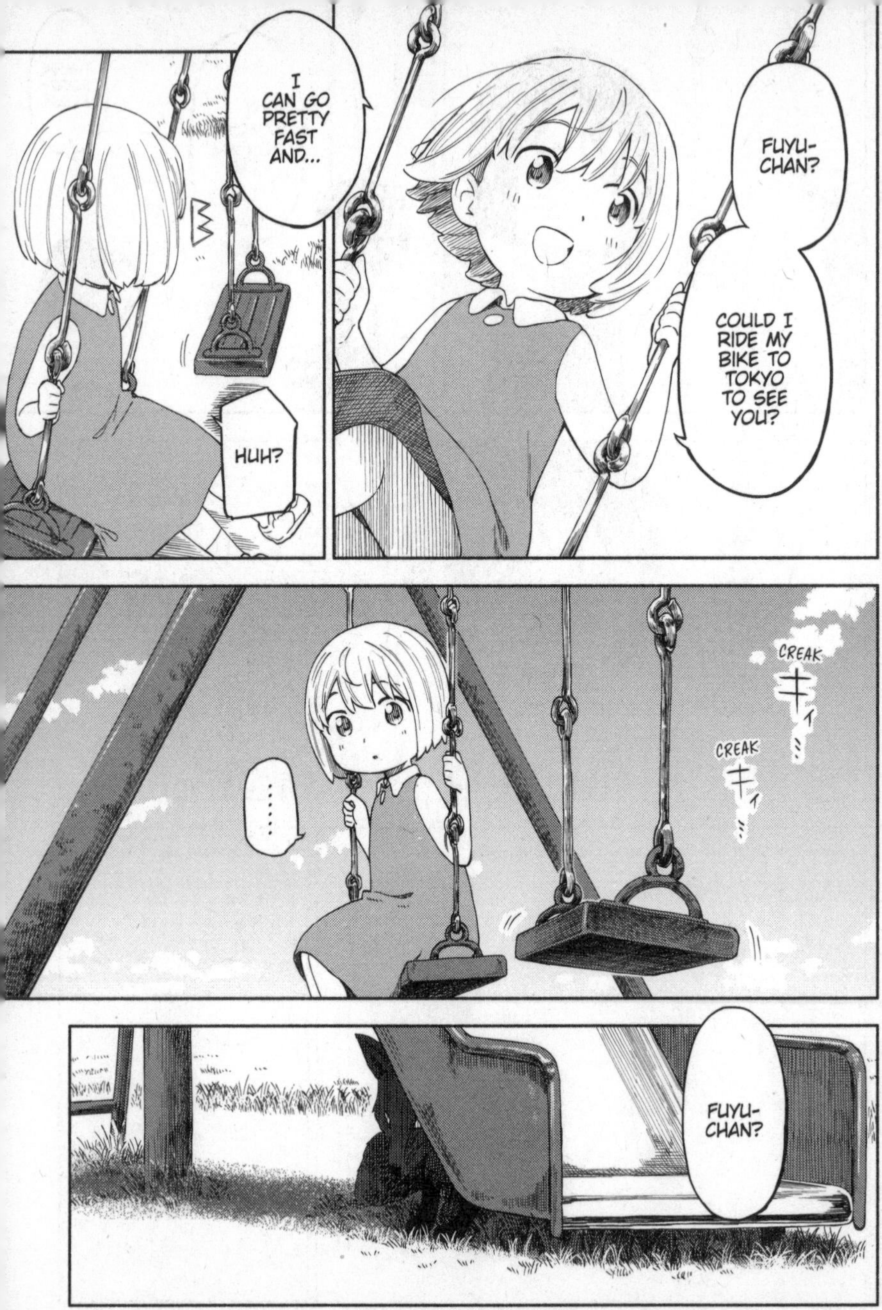
FUYU-CHAN?
COULD I RIDE MY BIKE TO TOKYO TO SEE YOU?
I CAN GO PRETTY FAST AND...
HUH?
CREAK
キィ…
CREAK
キィ…
……
FUYU-CHAN?

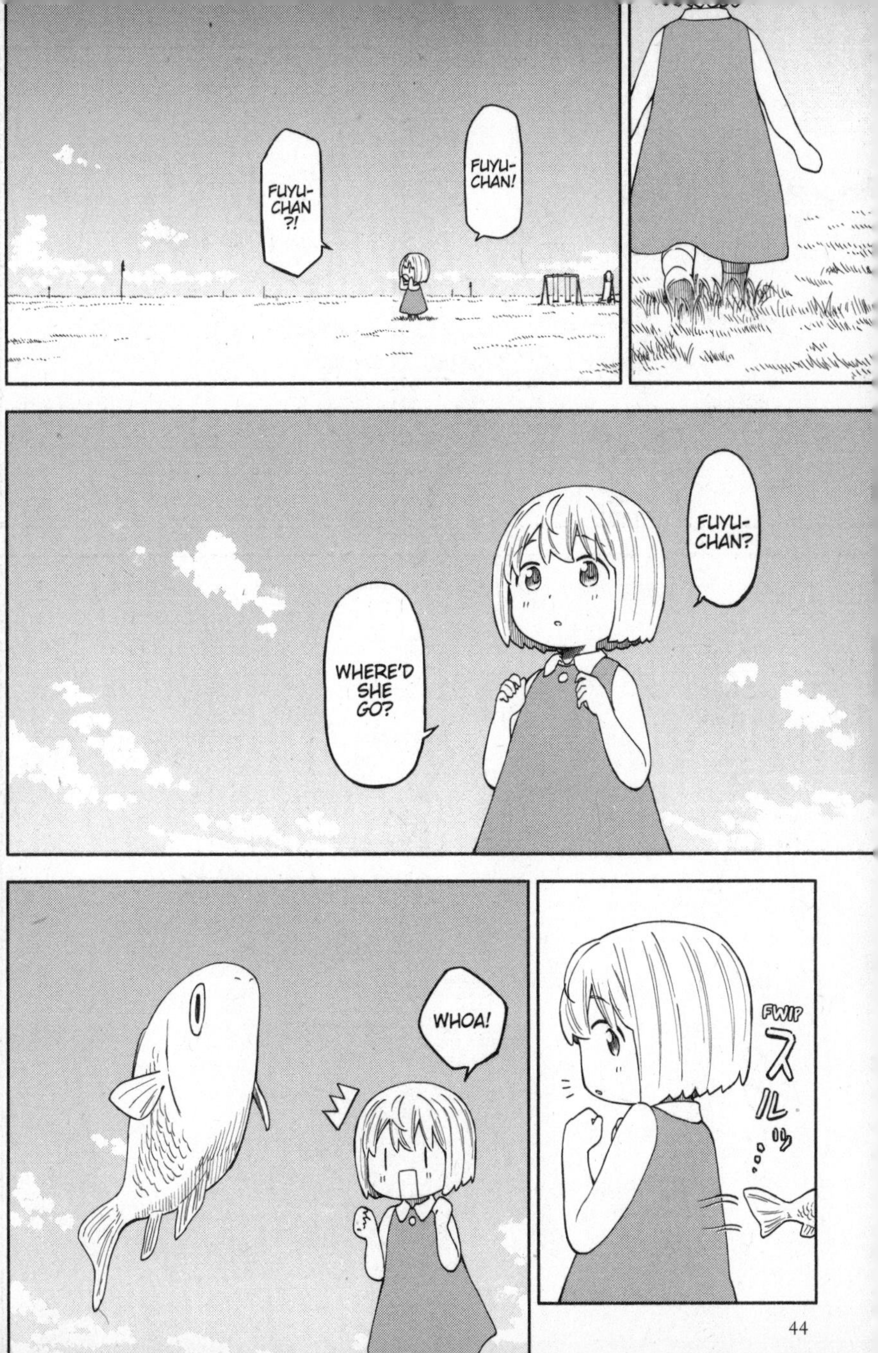
FUYU-CHAN!
FUYU-CHAN?!
FUYU-CHAN?
WHERE'D SHE GO?
FWIP
スルッ
WHOA!

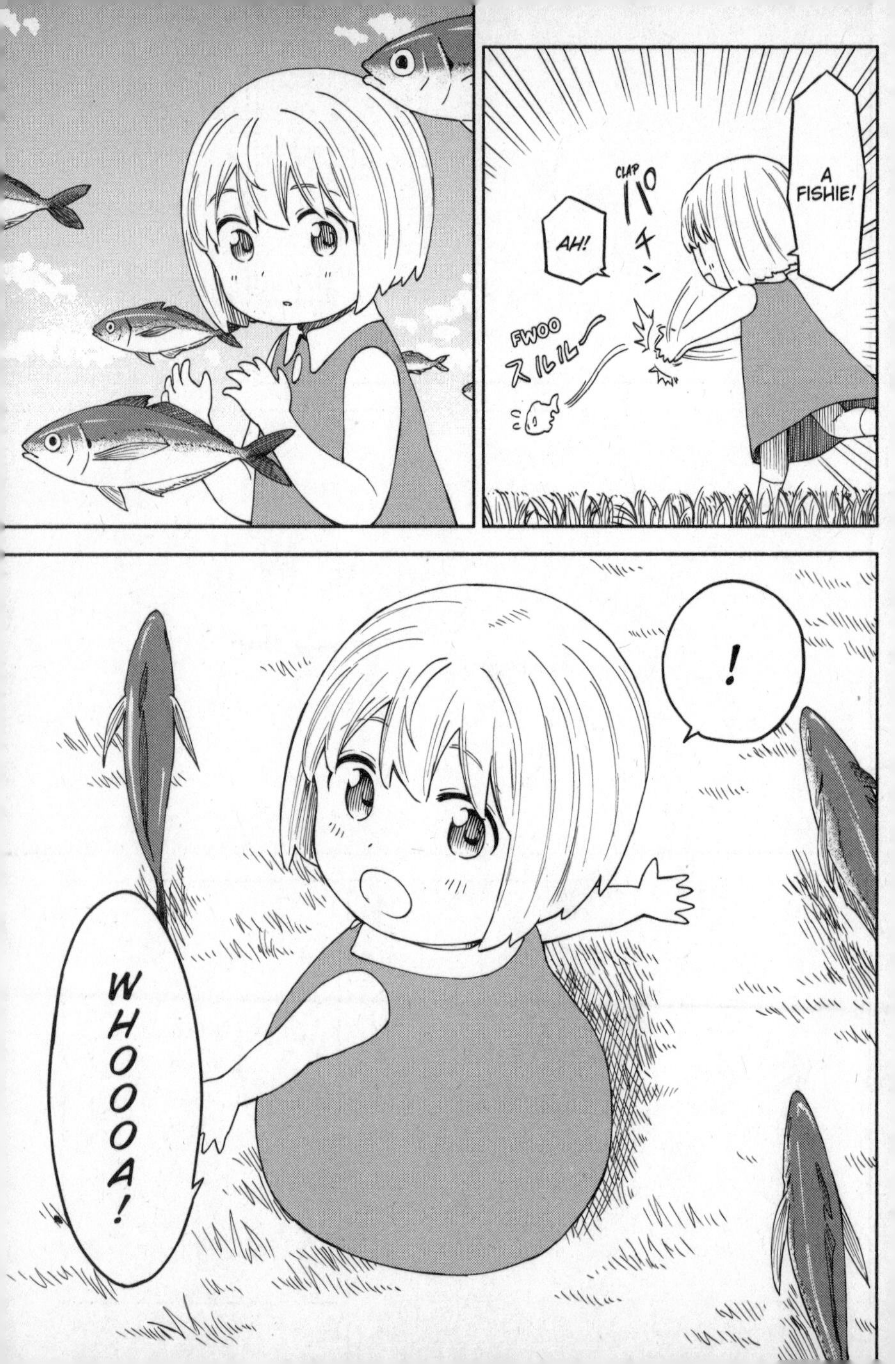
A FISHIE!
CLAP
パチン
AH!
FWOO
スルルー
!
WHOOOOA!

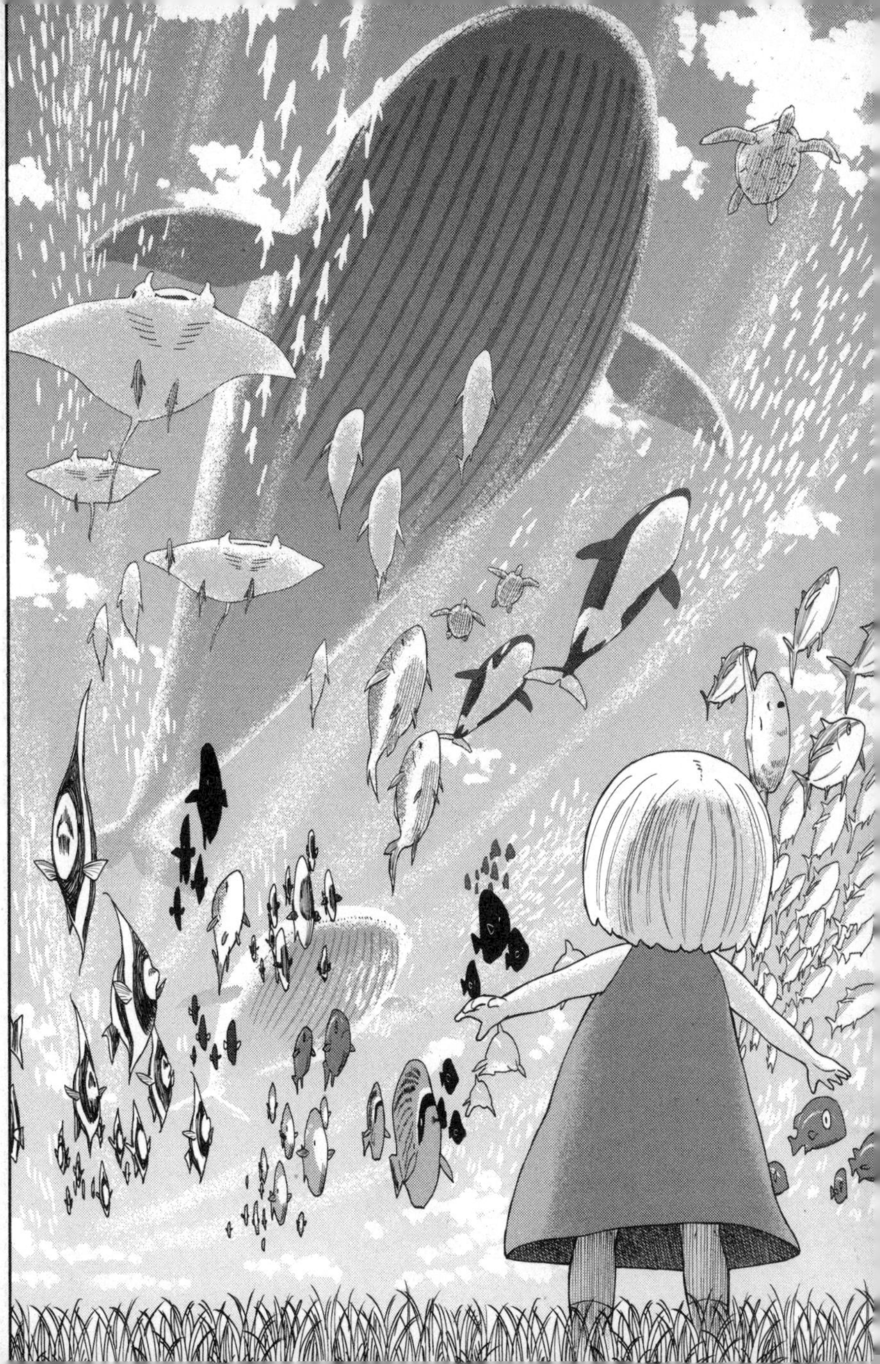

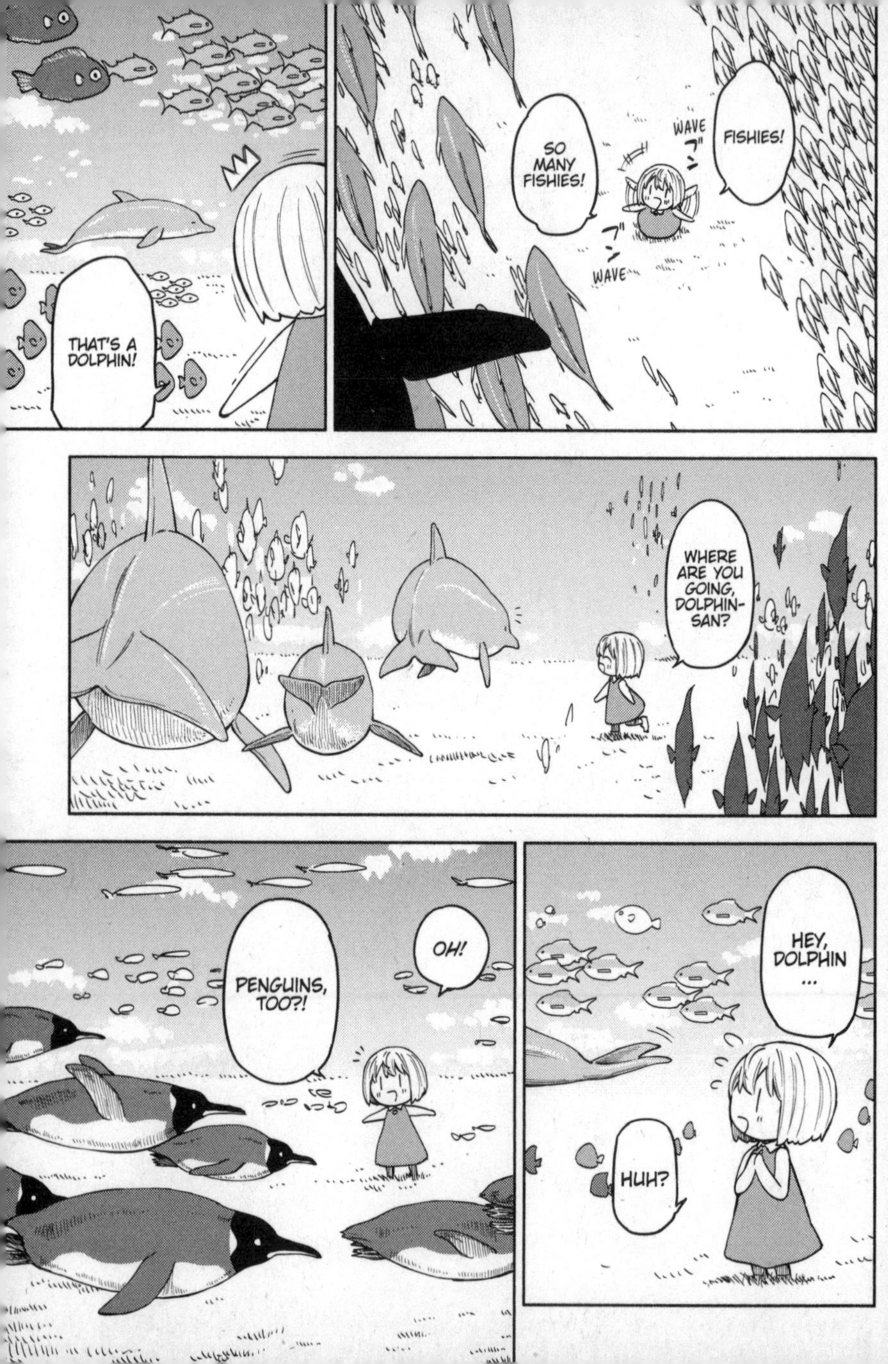
FISHIES!
WAVE
SO MANY FISHIES!
WAVE
THAT'S A DOLPHIN!
WHERE ARE YOU GOING, DOLPHIN-SAN?
HEY, DOLPHIN ...
HUH?
OH!
PENGUINS, TOO?!

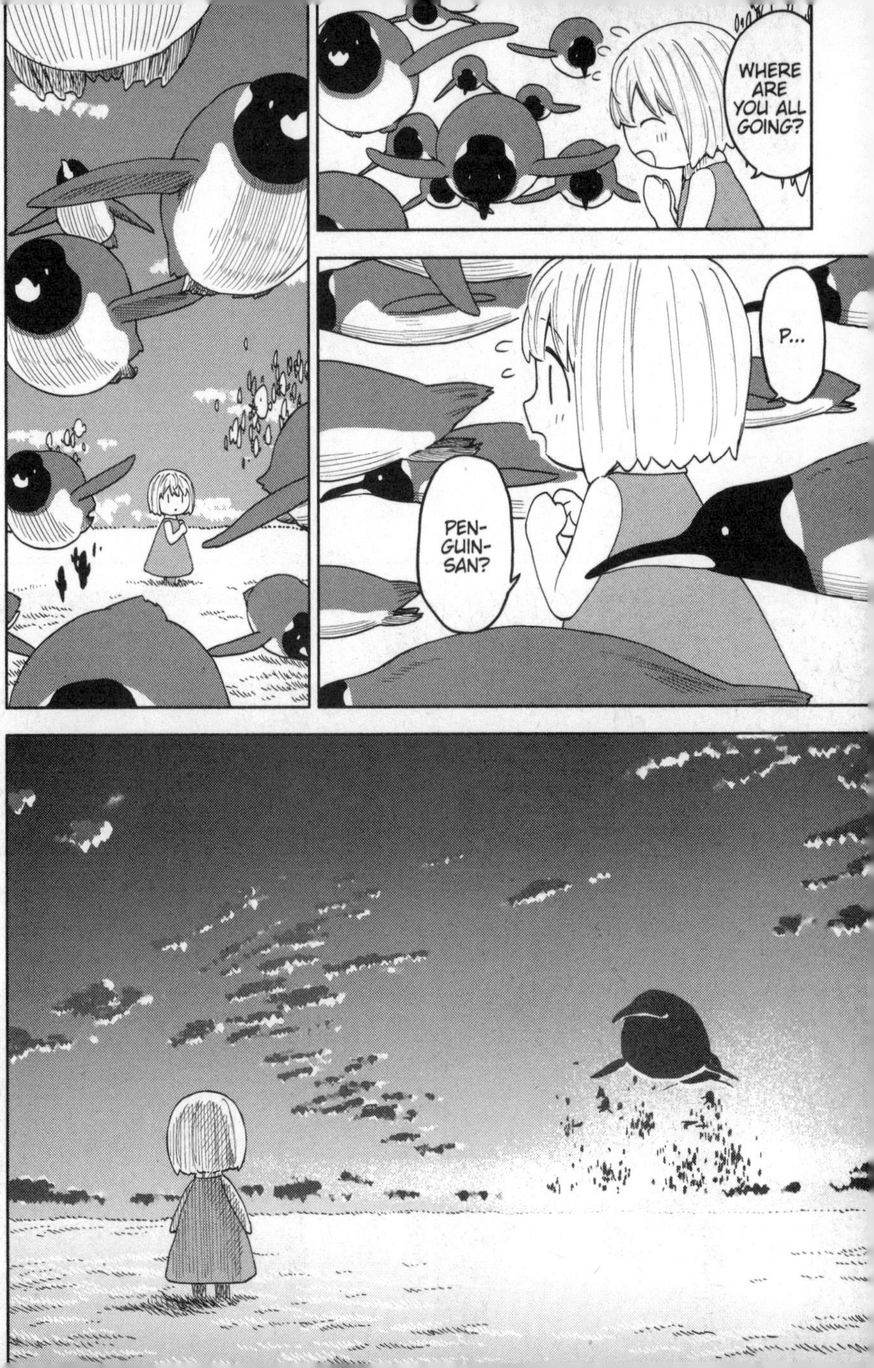
WHERE ARE YOU ALL GOING?
P...
PEN-GUIN-SAN?

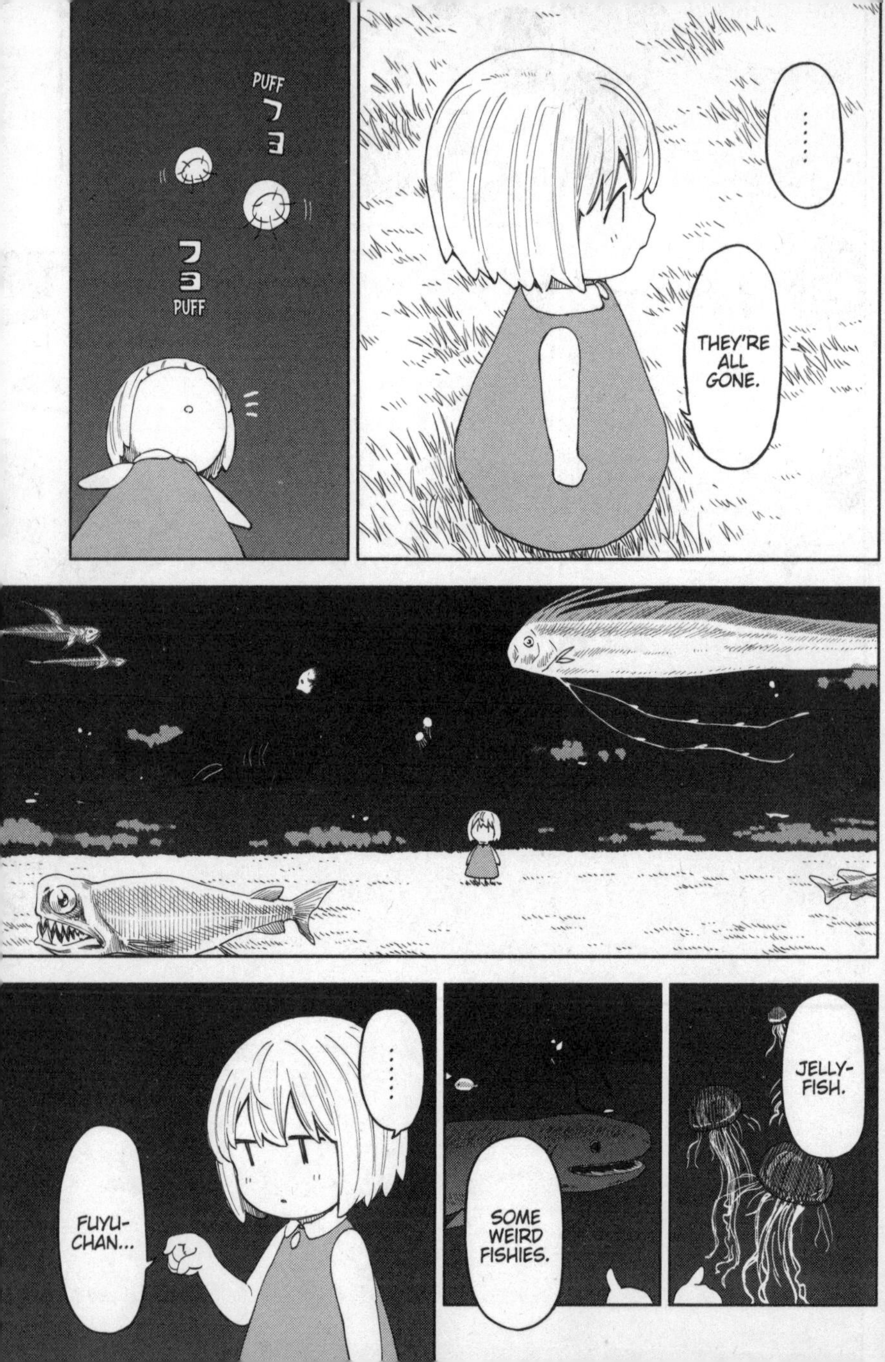
……
THEY'RE ALL GONE.
PUFF
フヨ
フヨ
PUFF
JELLY-FISH.
SOME WEIRD FISHIES.
……
FUYU-CHAN...

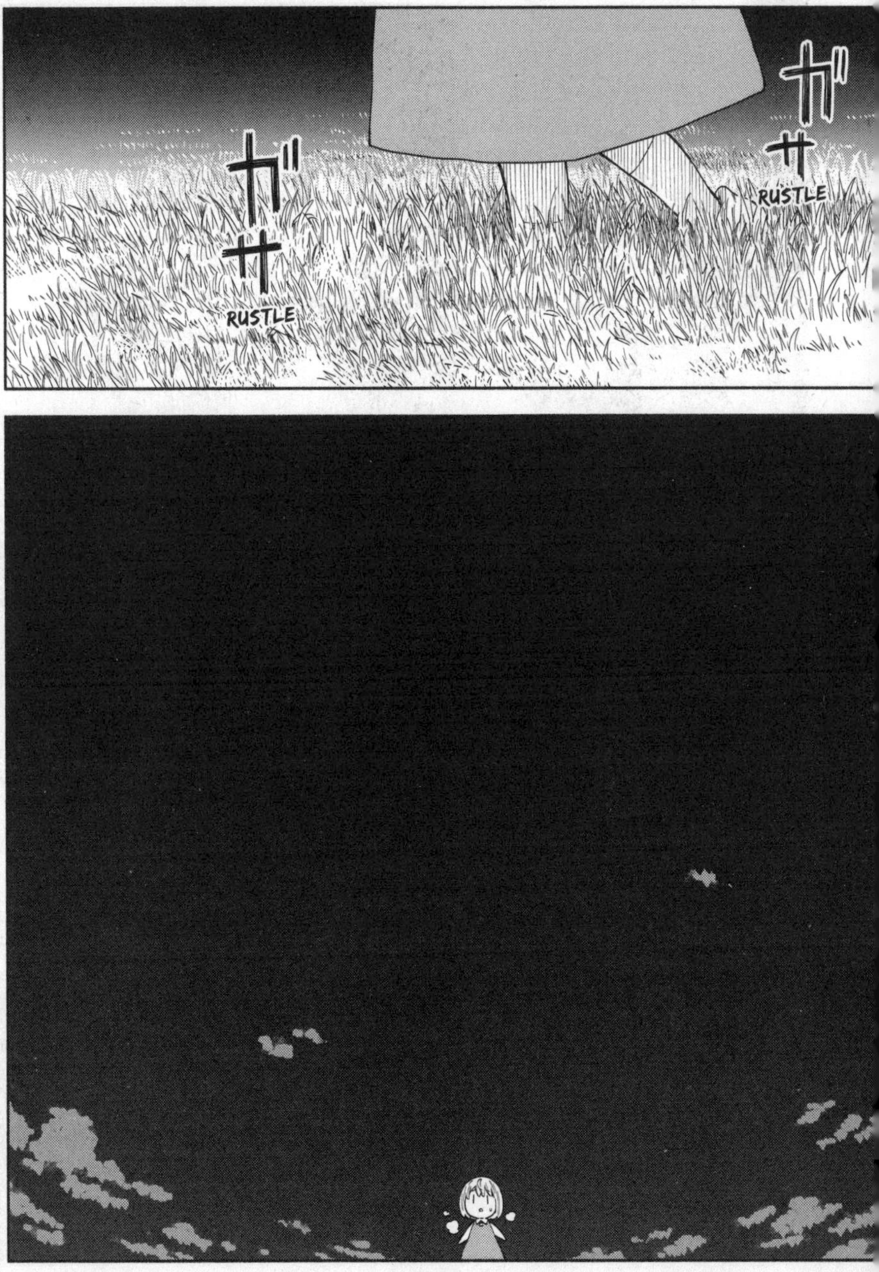
ガサ
RUSTLE
ガサ
RUSTLE

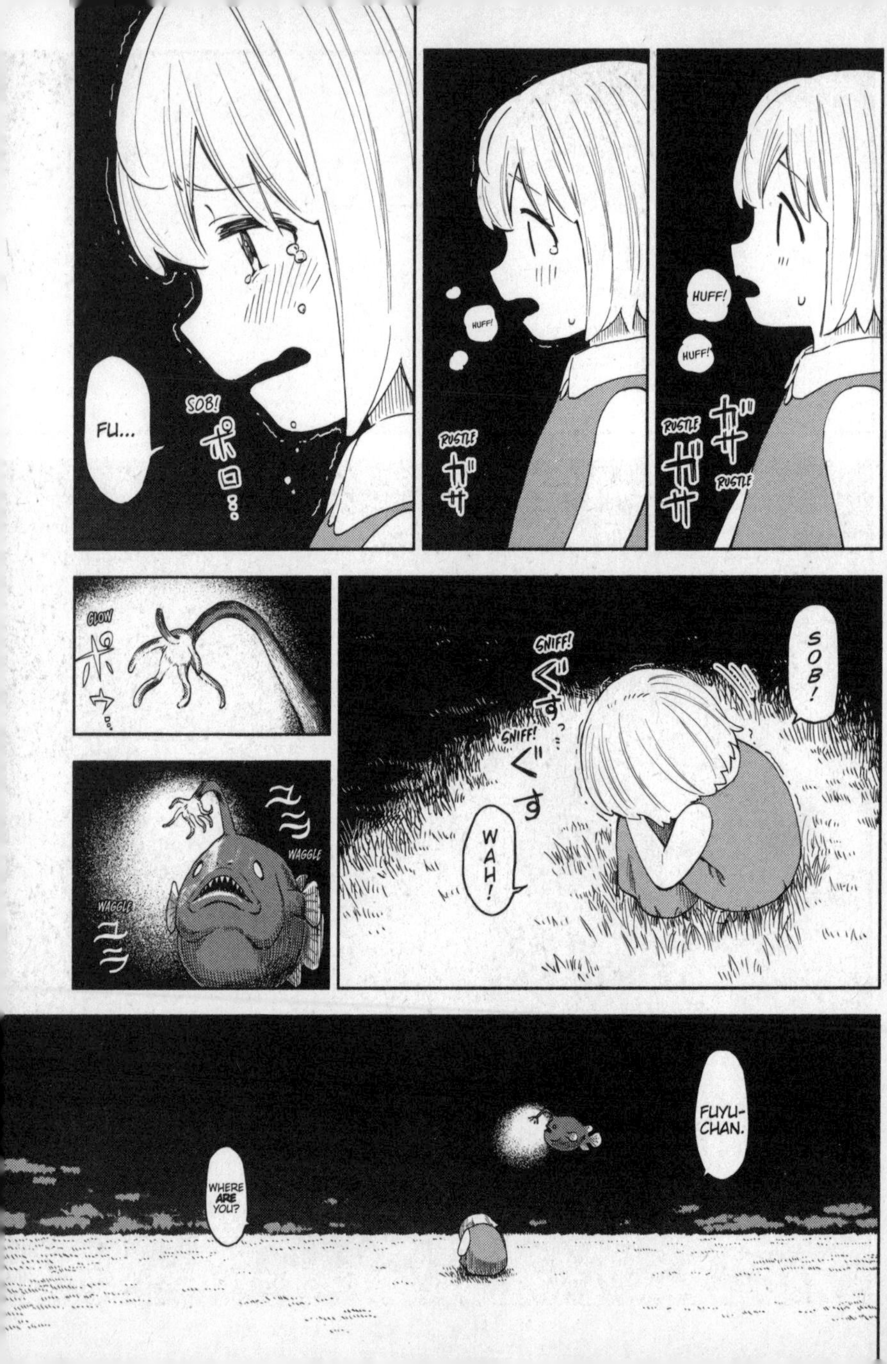

HUFF!
HUFF!
RUSTLE
ガサ
ガサ
RUSTLE
HUFF!
RUSTLE
ガサ
FU...
SOB!
ポロ
SOB!
SNIFF!
ぐすっ
SNIFF!
ぐす
WAH!
GLOW
ポゥ
WAGGLE
ユラ
WAGGLE
ユラ
FUYU-CHAN.
WHERE ARE YOU?

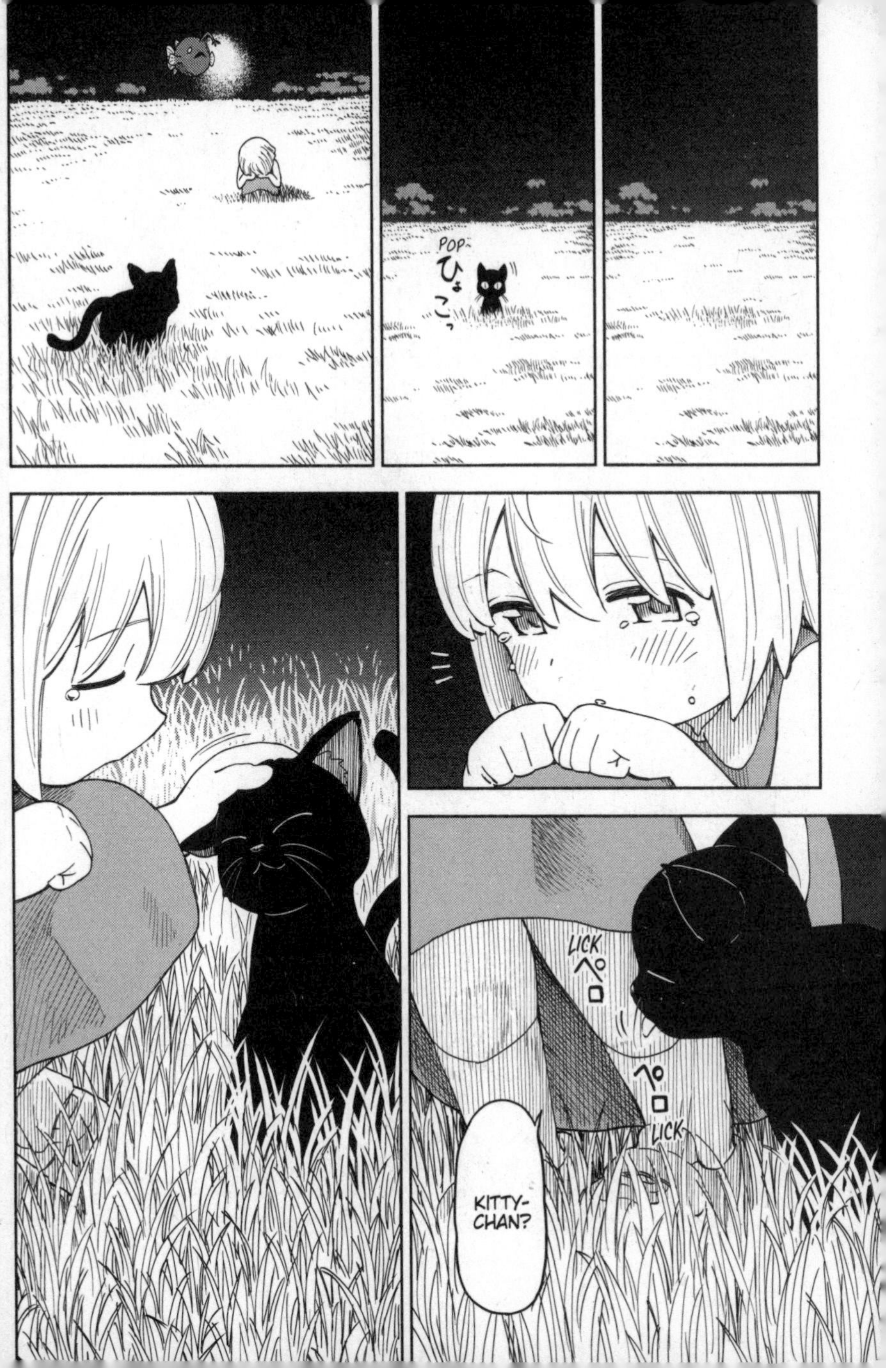
POP
ひょこっ
LICK
ペロ
ペロ
LICK
KITTY-CHAN?

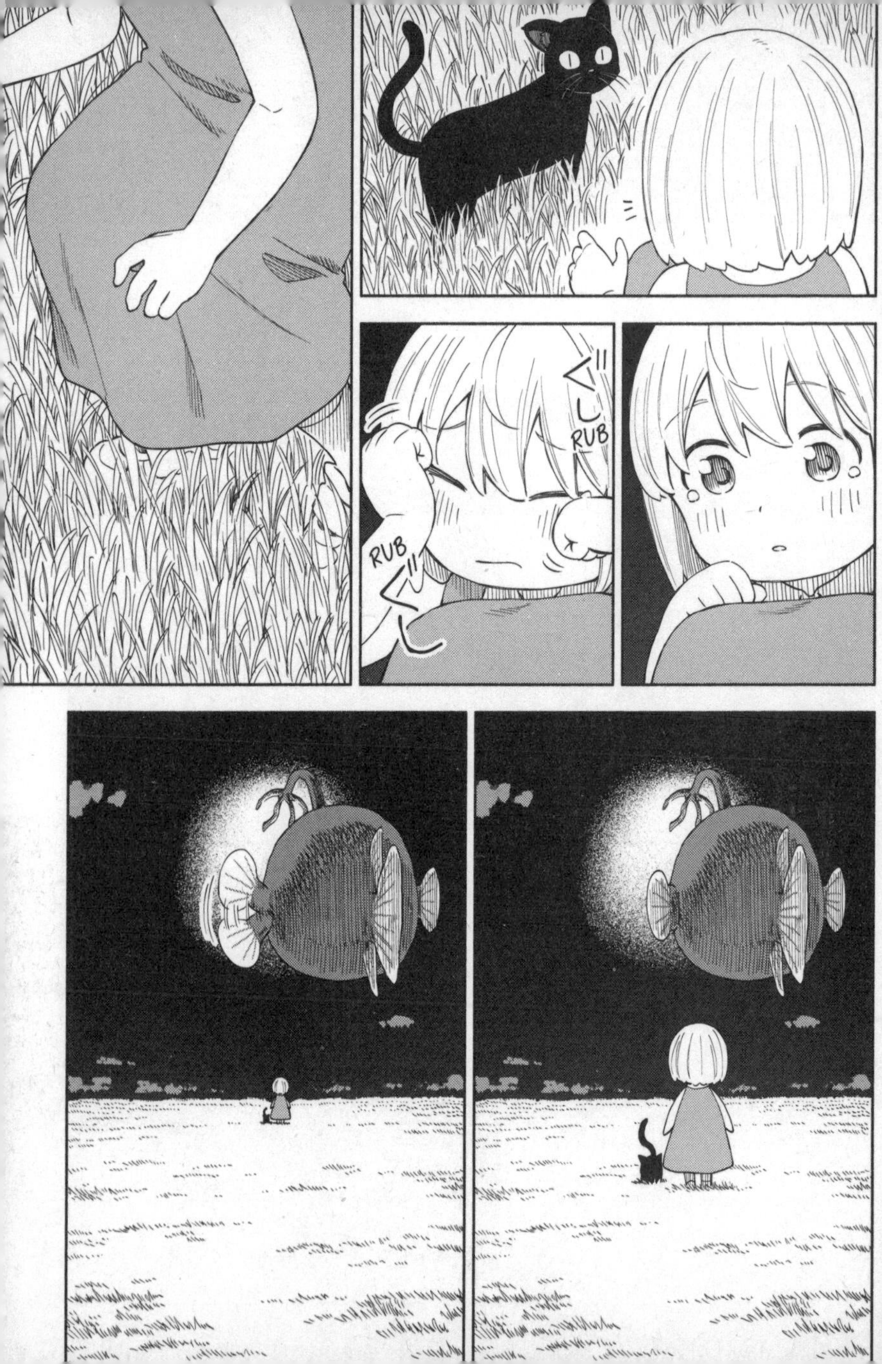
くし
RUB
RUB
くし

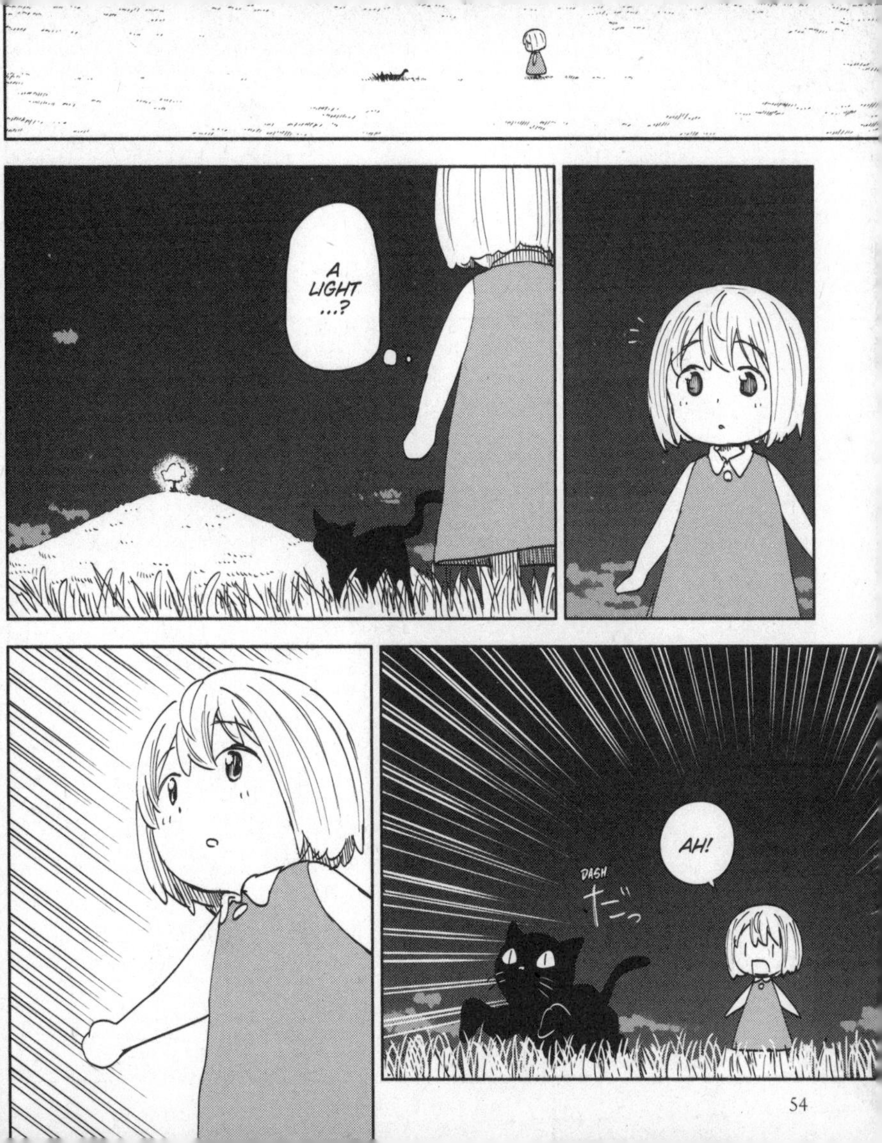
A LIGHT …?
AH!
DASH

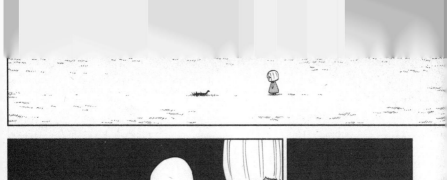

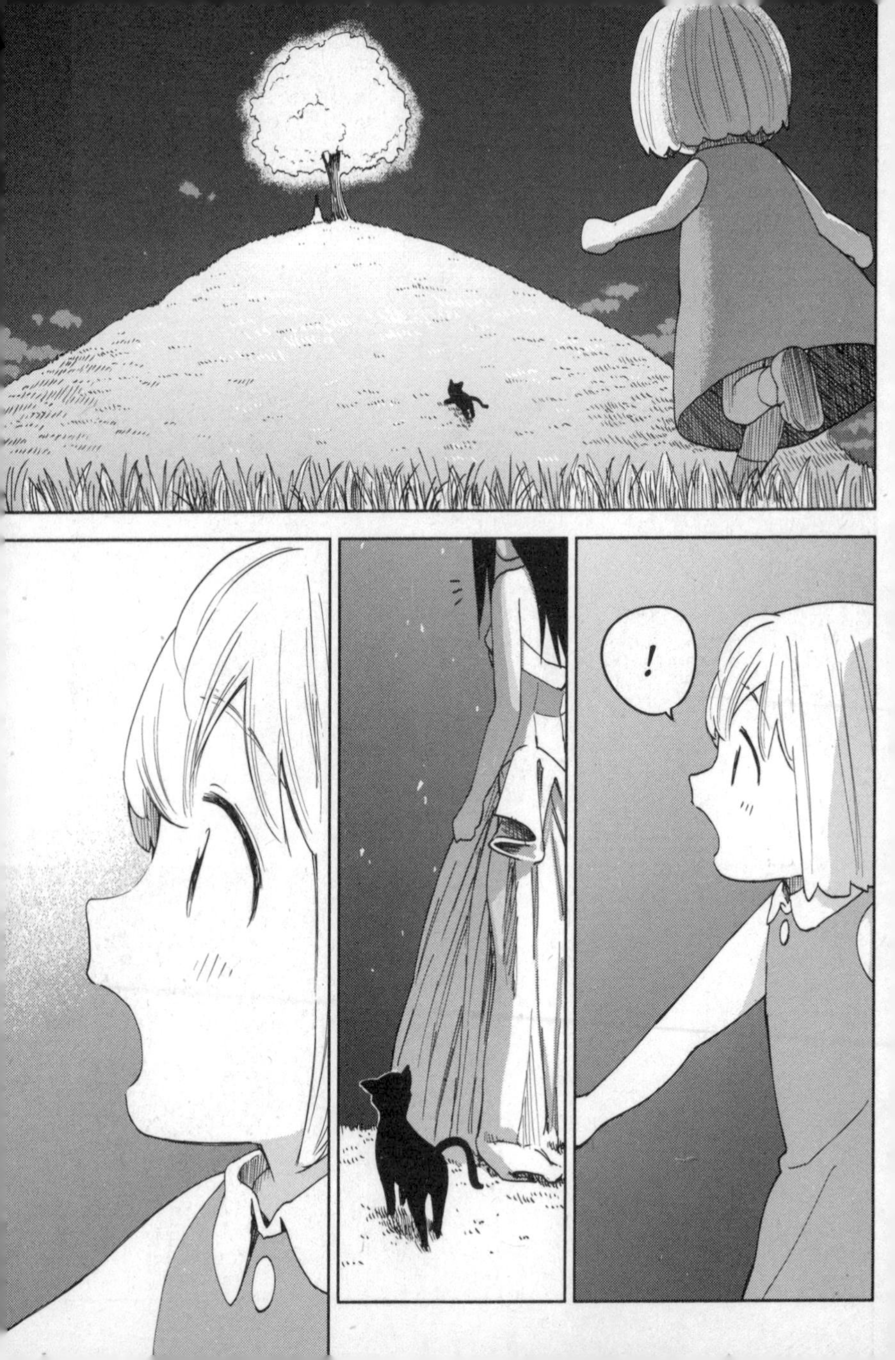
!

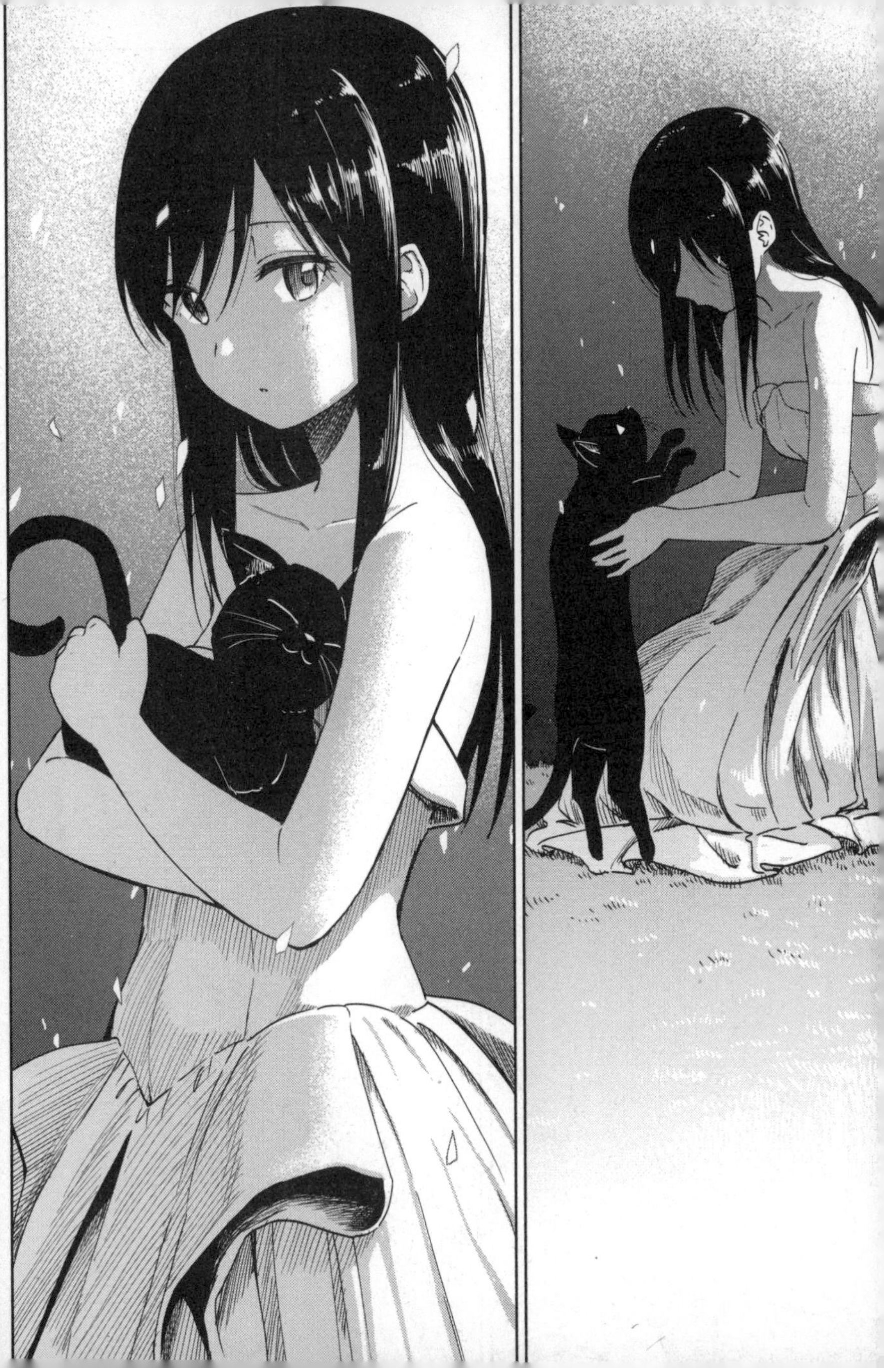

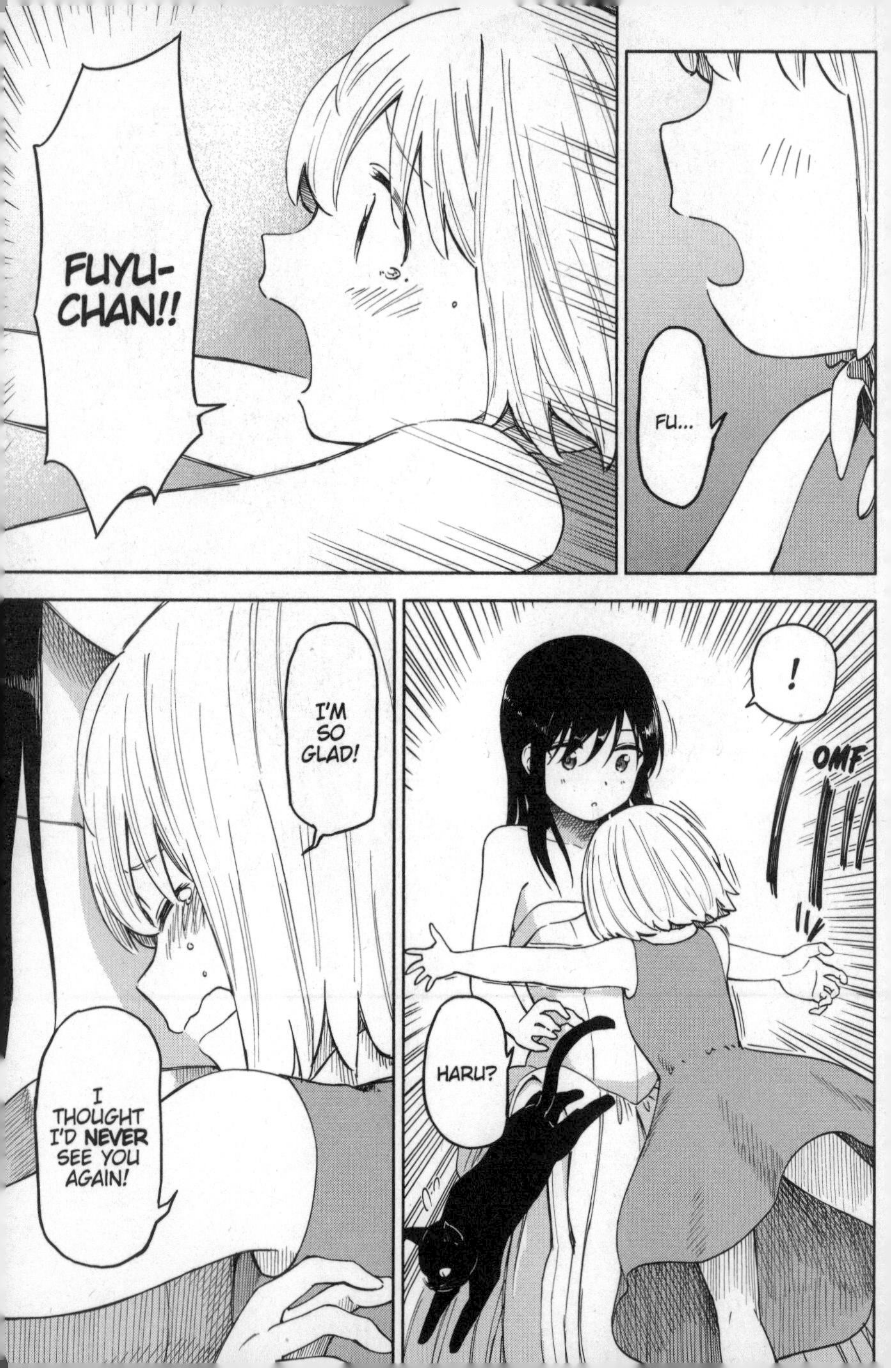
FU...
FUYU-CHAN!!
!
OMF
HARU?
I'M SO GLAD!
I THOUGHT I'D **NEVER** SEE YOU AGAIN!

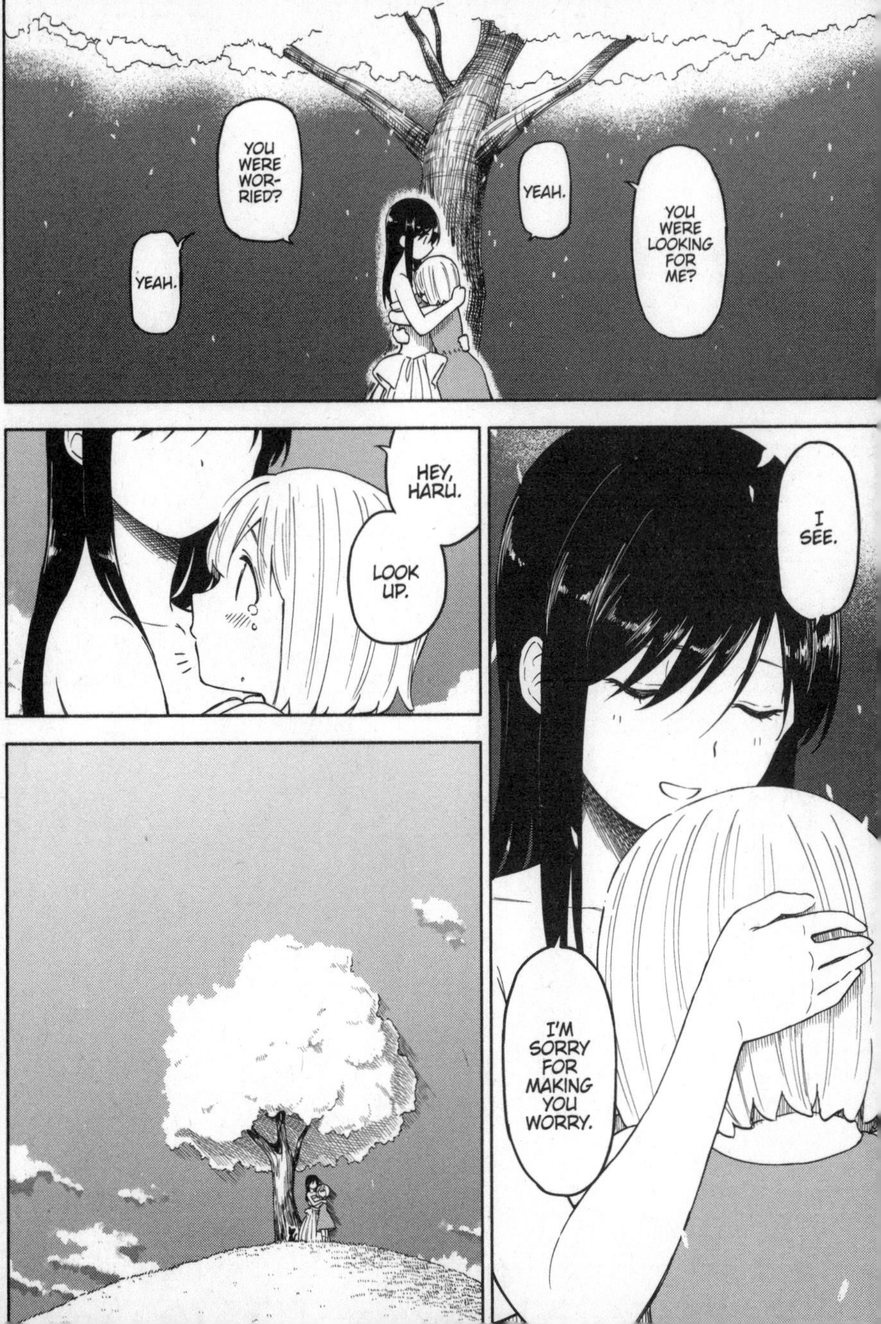
YOU WERE LOOKING FOR ME?
YEAH.
YOU WERE WOR-RIED?
YEAH.
I SEE.
I'M SORRY FOR MAKING YOU WORRY.
HEY, HARU.
LOOK UP.

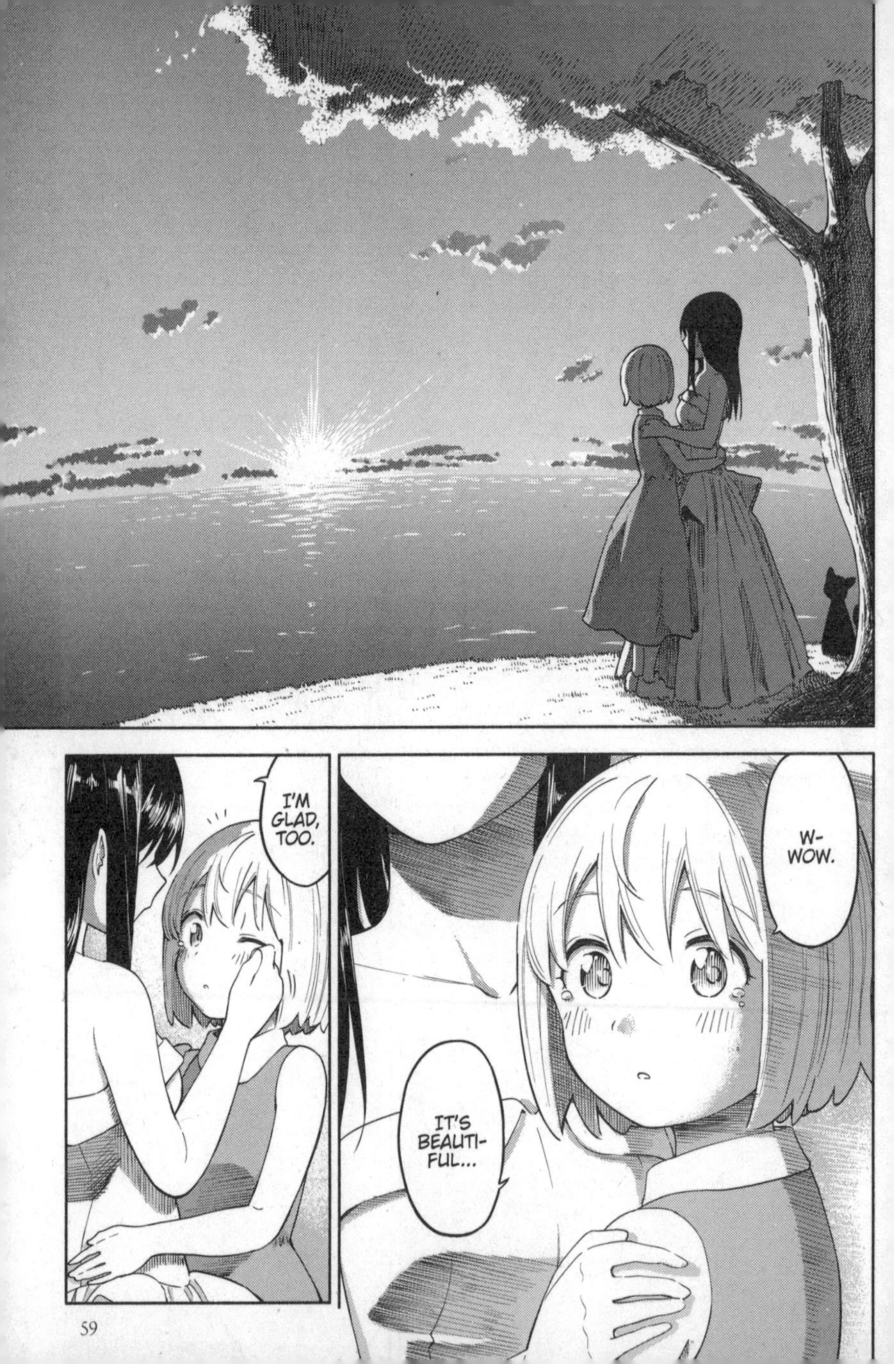
W-WOW.
IT'S BEAUTIFUL...
I'M GLAD, TOO.

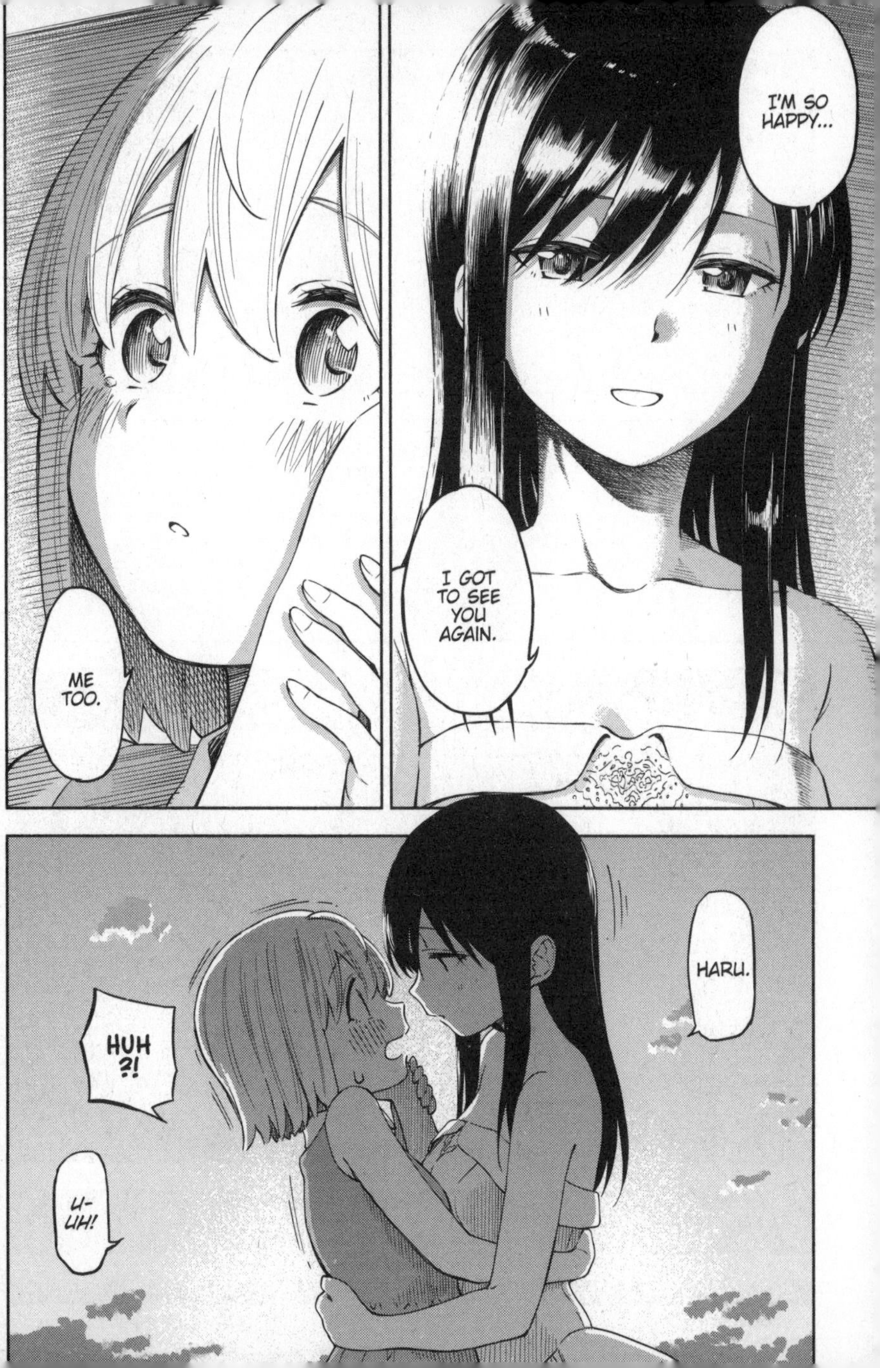
I'M SO HAPPY...
I GOT TO SEE YOU AGAIN.
ME TOO.
HARU.
HUH ?!
U-UH!

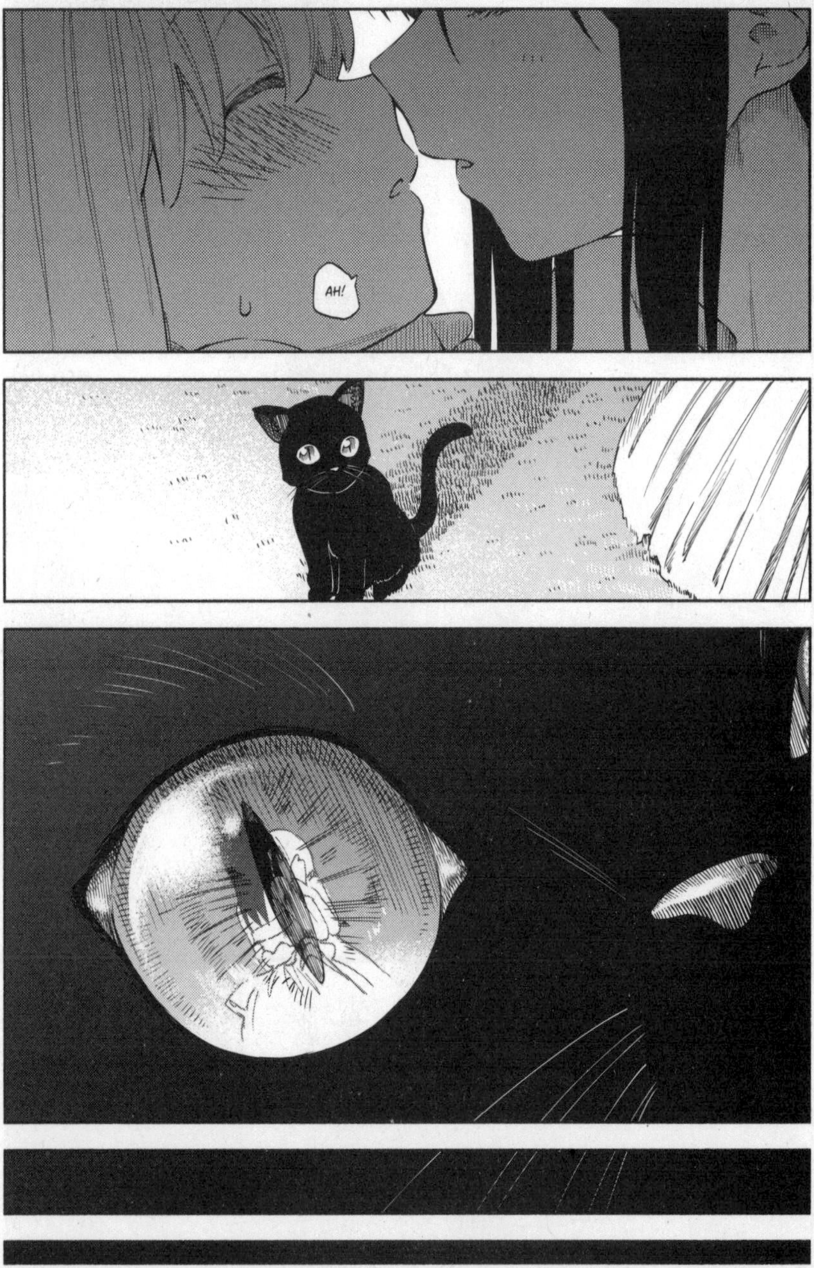
AH!

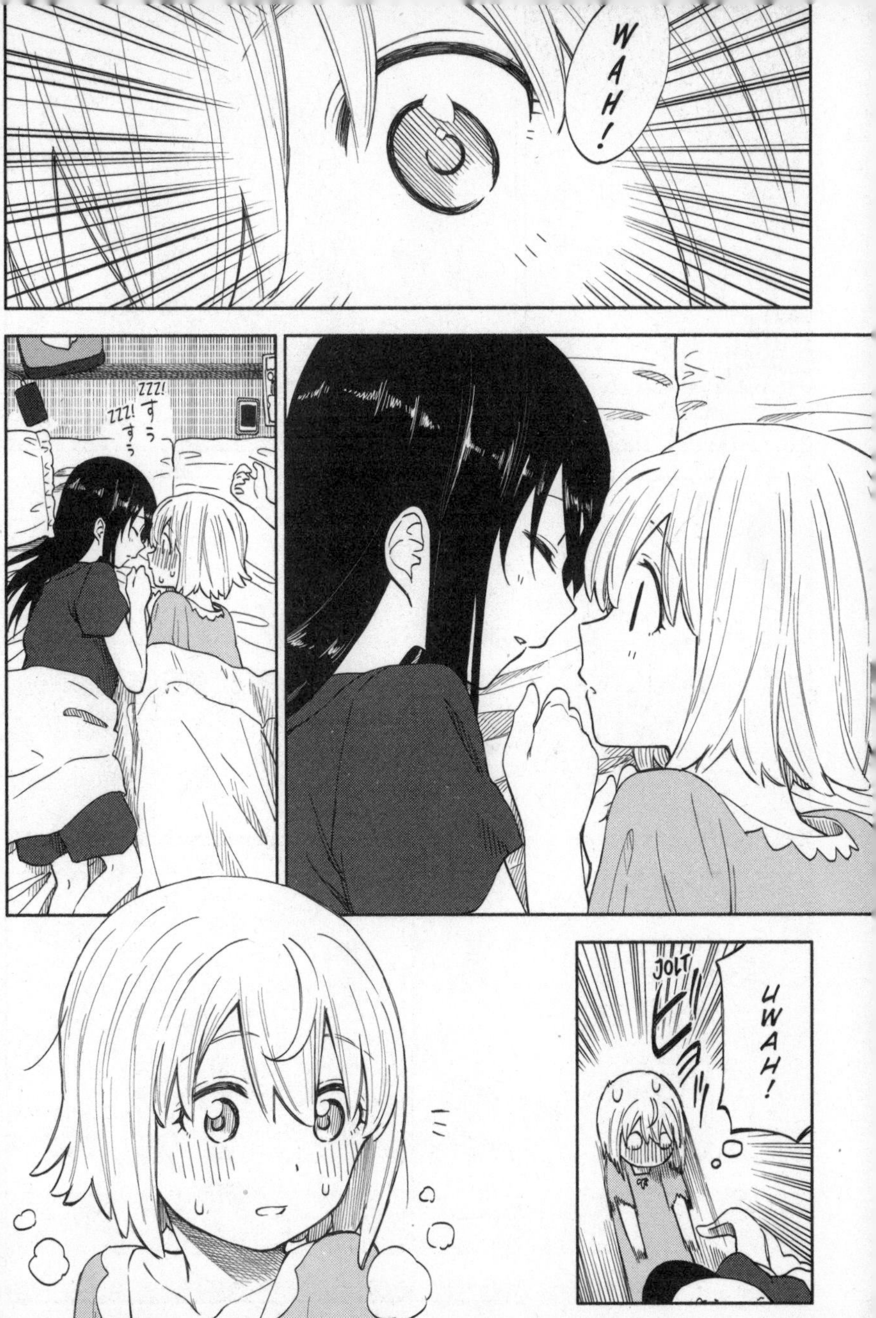
WAH!
ZZZ! すぅ
ZZZ! すぅ
JOLT
UWAH!

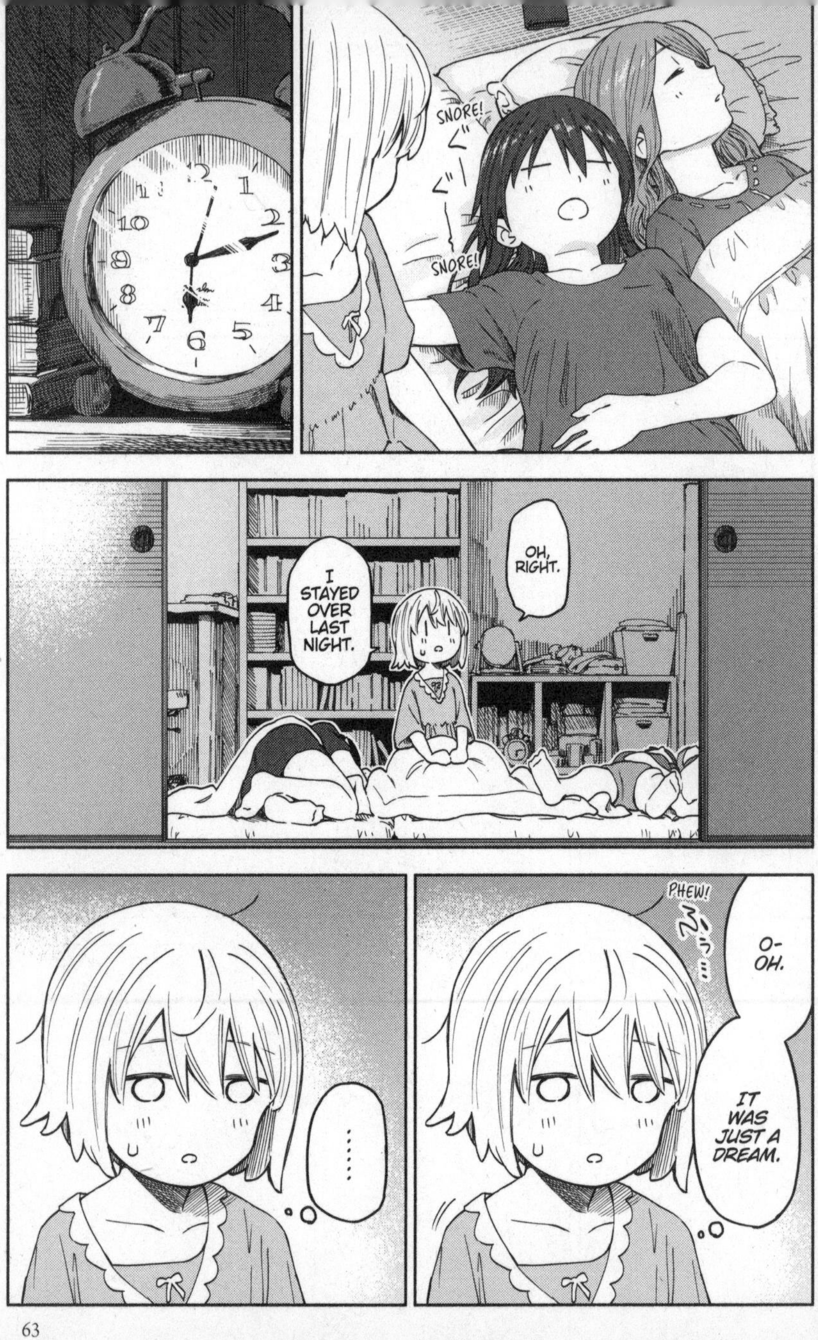
SNORE!
SNORE!
OH, RIGHT.
I STAYED OVER LAST NIGHT.
PHEW!
O- OH.
IT WAS JUST A DREAM.
......

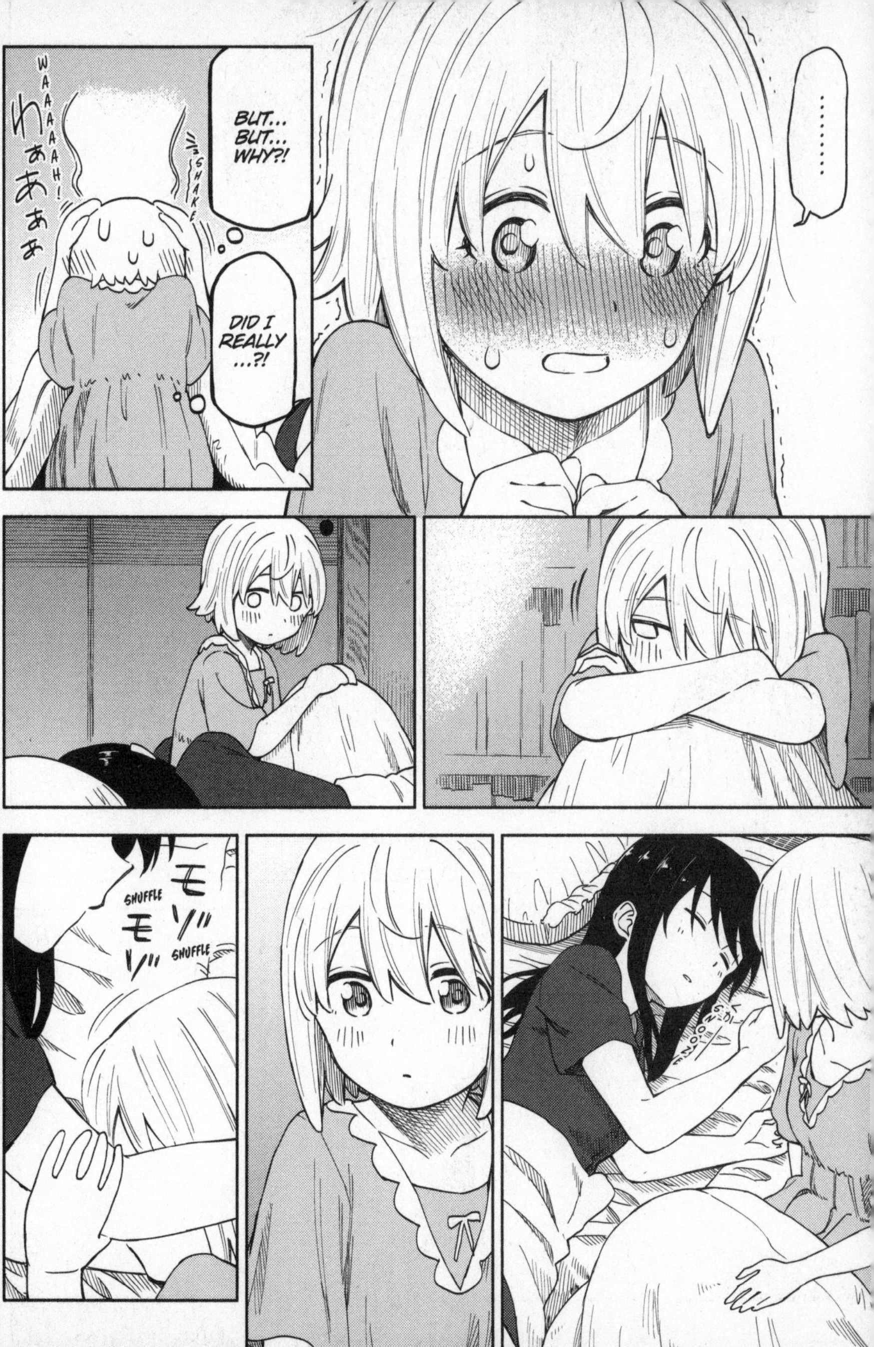
......
BUT... BUT... WHY?!
DID I REALLY ...?!
WAAAAAAH!
わあああ
SHAKE
SNOOZE
モゾモゾ
SHUFFLE SHUFFLE

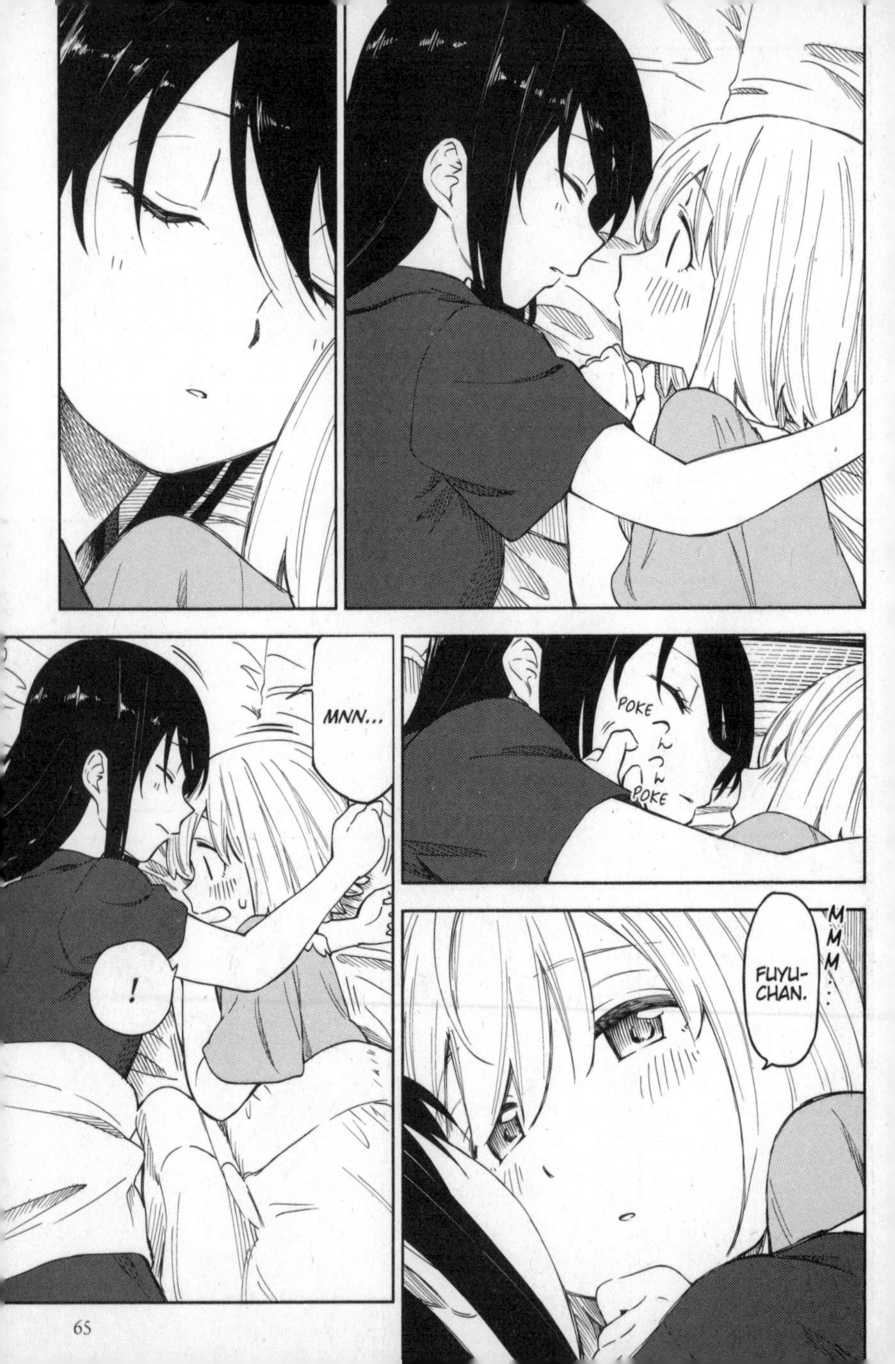
POKE
POKE
MMM...
FUYU-CHAN.
MNN...
!

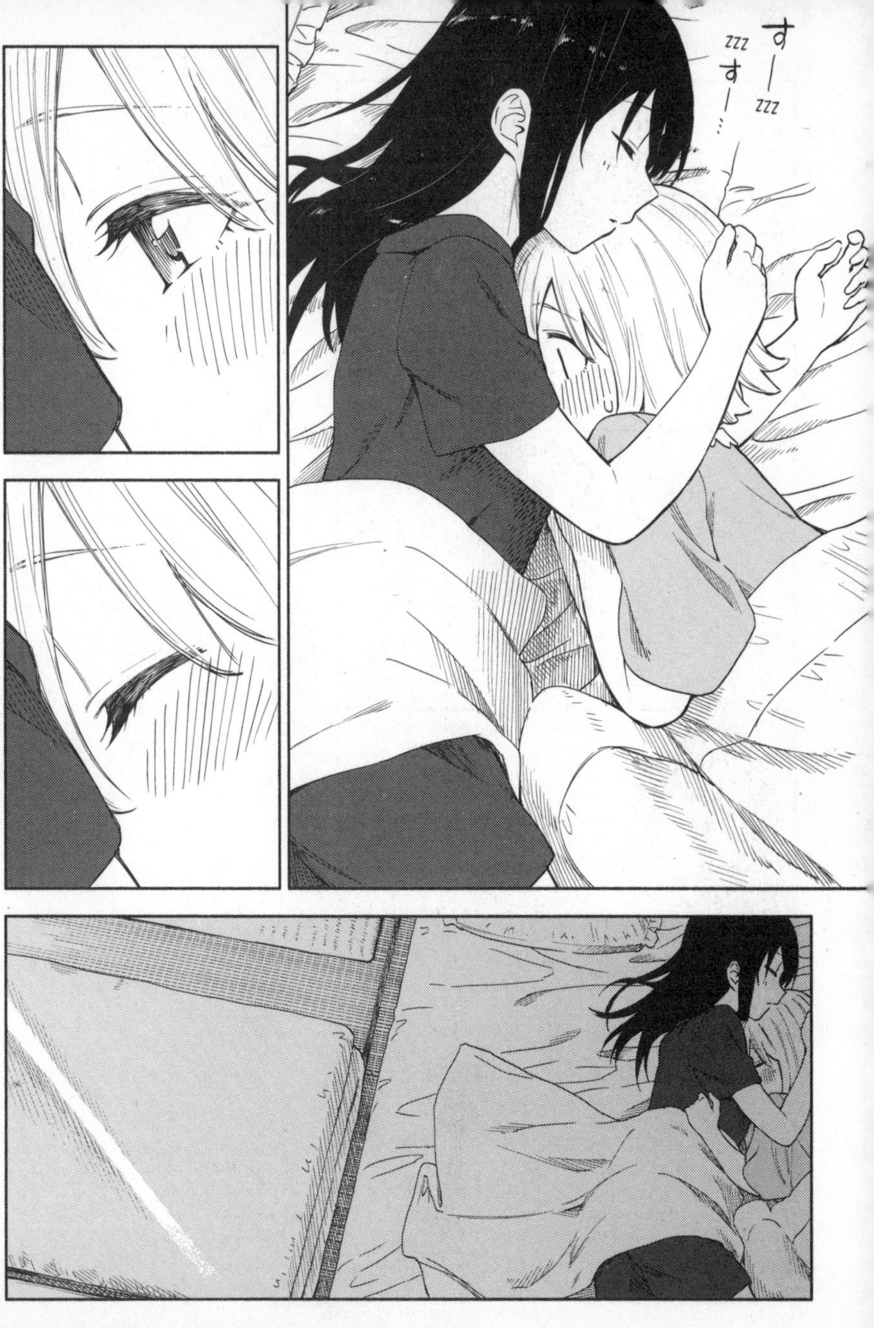
すーzzz すー…

WAKING UP

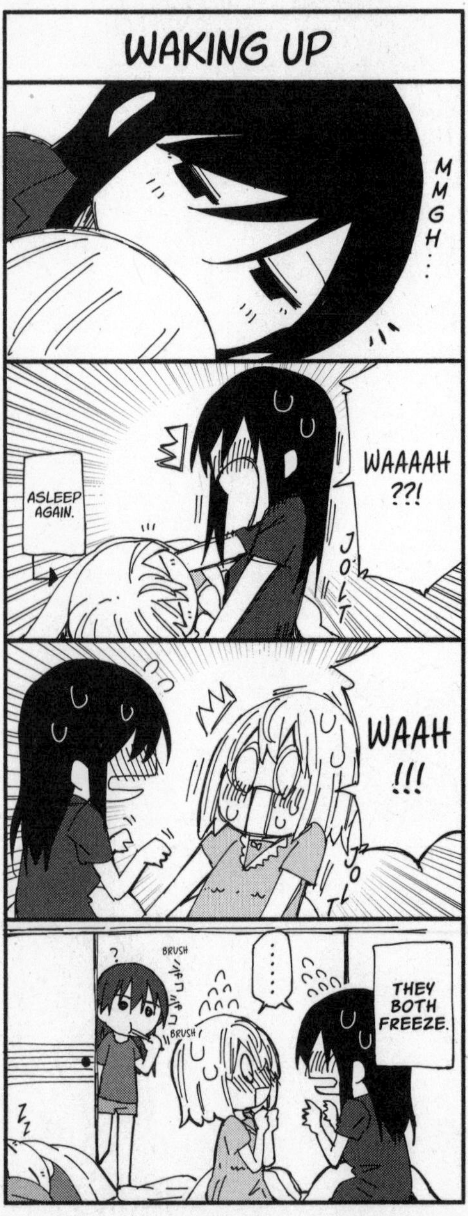
MMGH...
WAAAAH ??!
JOLT
ASLEEP AGAIN.
WAAH !!!
JOLT
THEY BOTH FREEZE.
......
BRUSH
?
BRUSH
ZZ

Our
Wonderful
Days

Tsurezure
Biyori

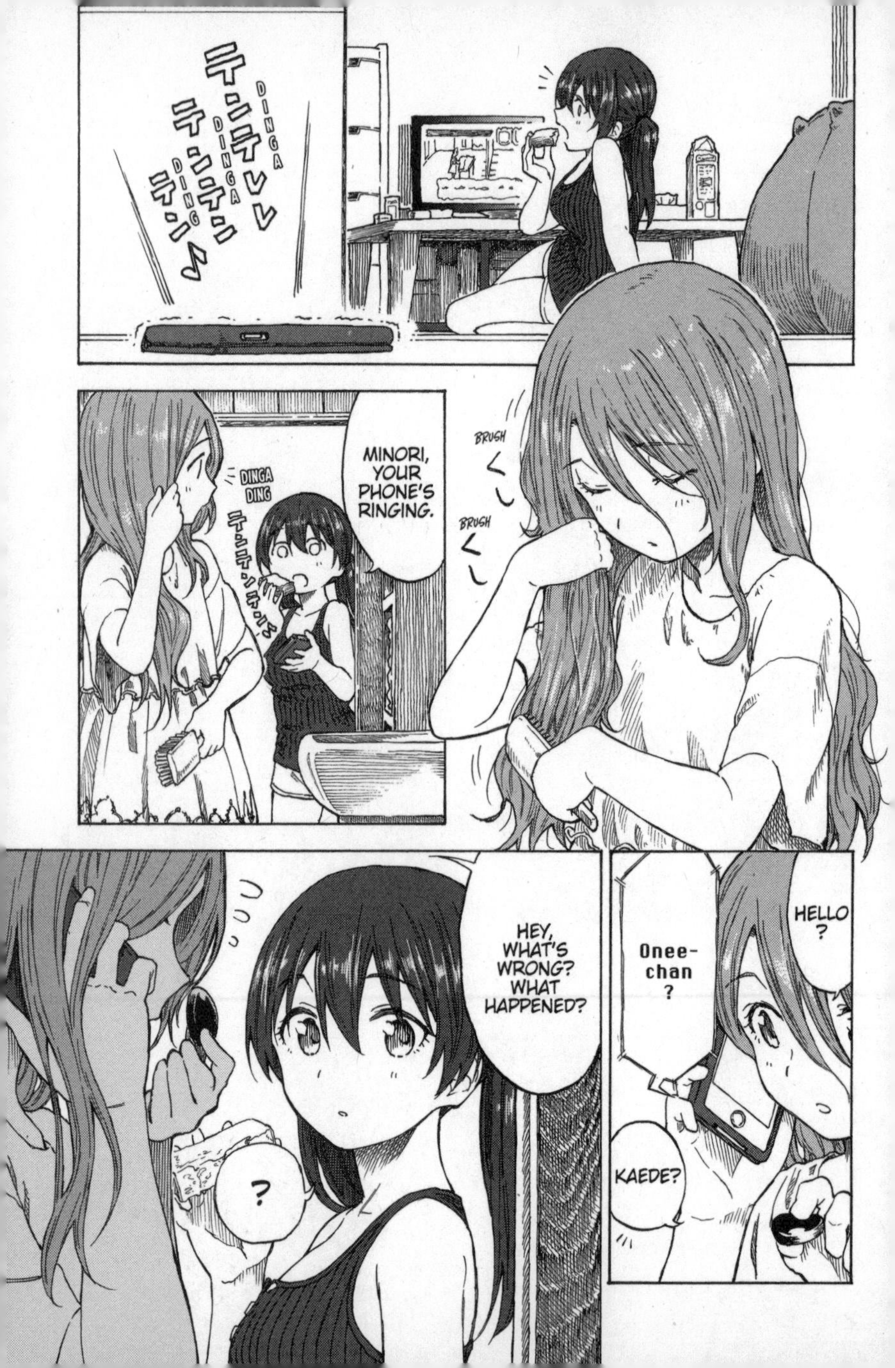
テーンテレレ
DINGA
テーンテーン
DINGA
テーン♪
DING
BRUSH
くし
BRUSH
くし
MINORI, YOUR PHONE'S RINGING.
DINGA DING
テーンテーン
HELLO?
Onee-chan?
KAEDE?
HEY, WHAT'S WRONG? WHAT HAPPENED?
?

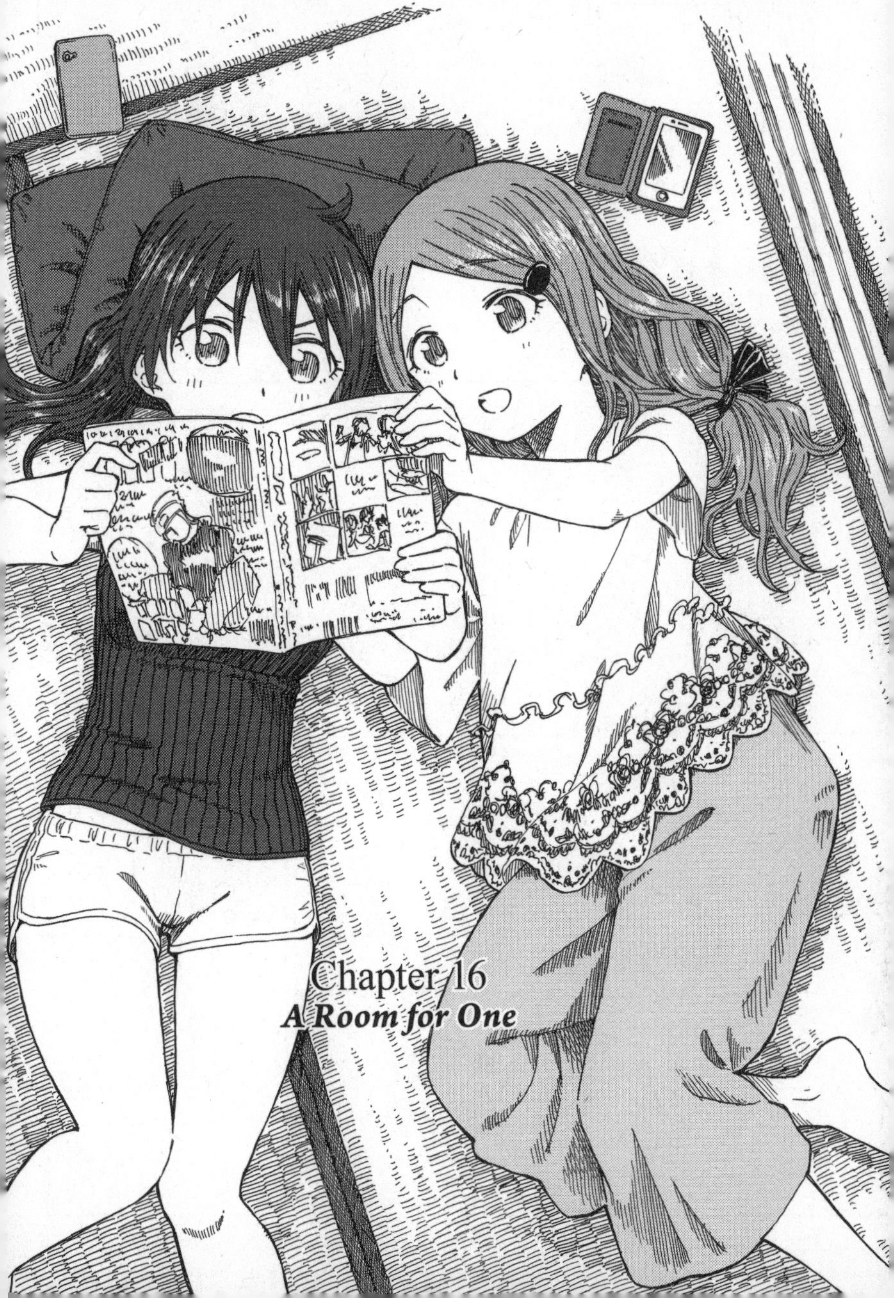
Chapter 16
A Room for One

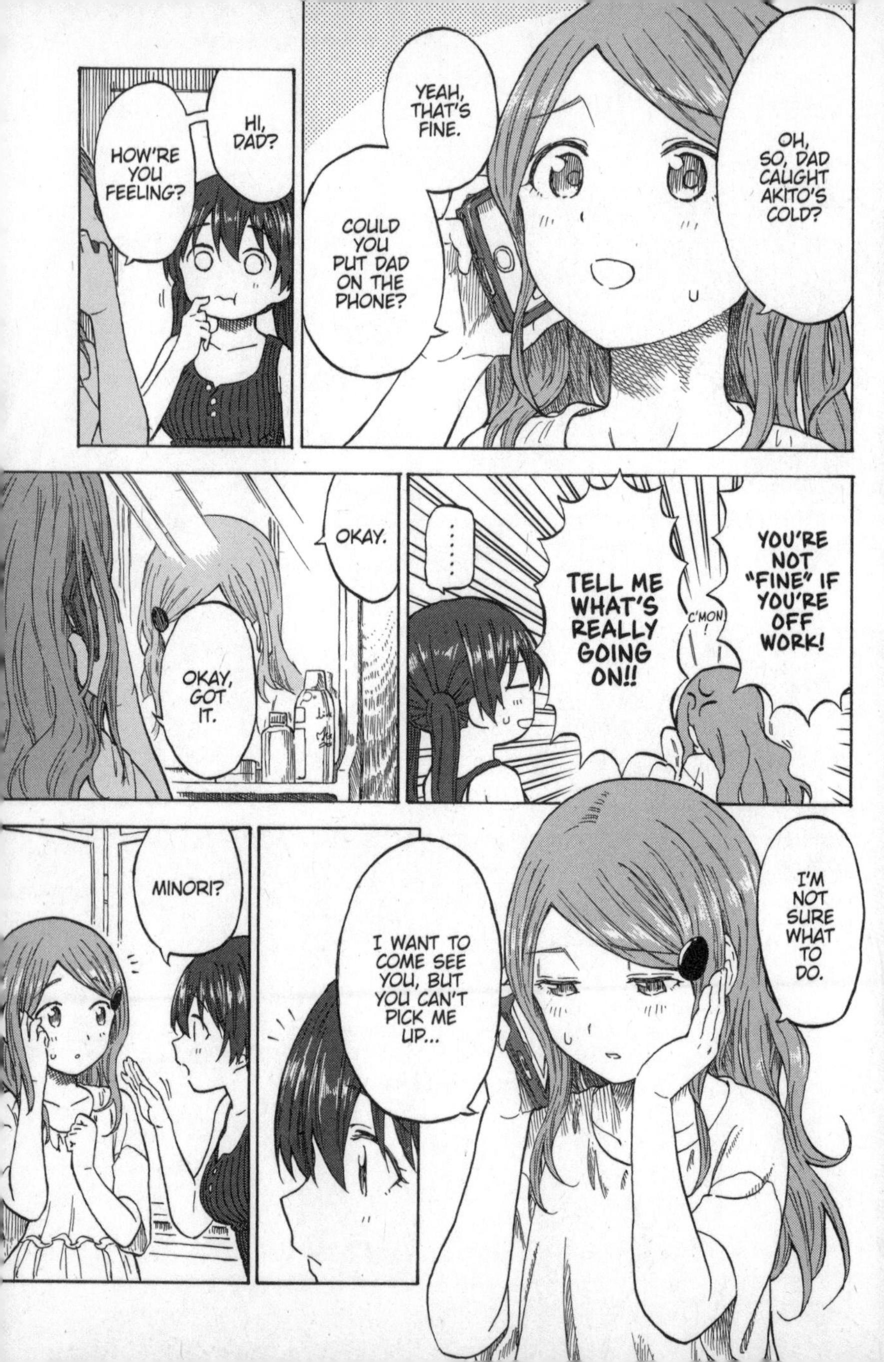
OH, SO, DAD CAUGHT AKITO'S COLD?
YEAH, THAT'S FINE.
COULD YOU PUT DAD ON THE PHONE?
HI, DAD?
HOW'RE YOU FEELING?
YOU'RE NOT "FINE" IF YOU'RE OFF WORK!
C'MON!
TELL ME WHAT'S REALLY GOING ON!!
......
OKAY.
OKAY, GOT IT.
I'M NOT SURE WHAT TO DO.
I WANT TO COME SEE YOU, BUT YOU CAN'T PICK ME UP...
MINORI?

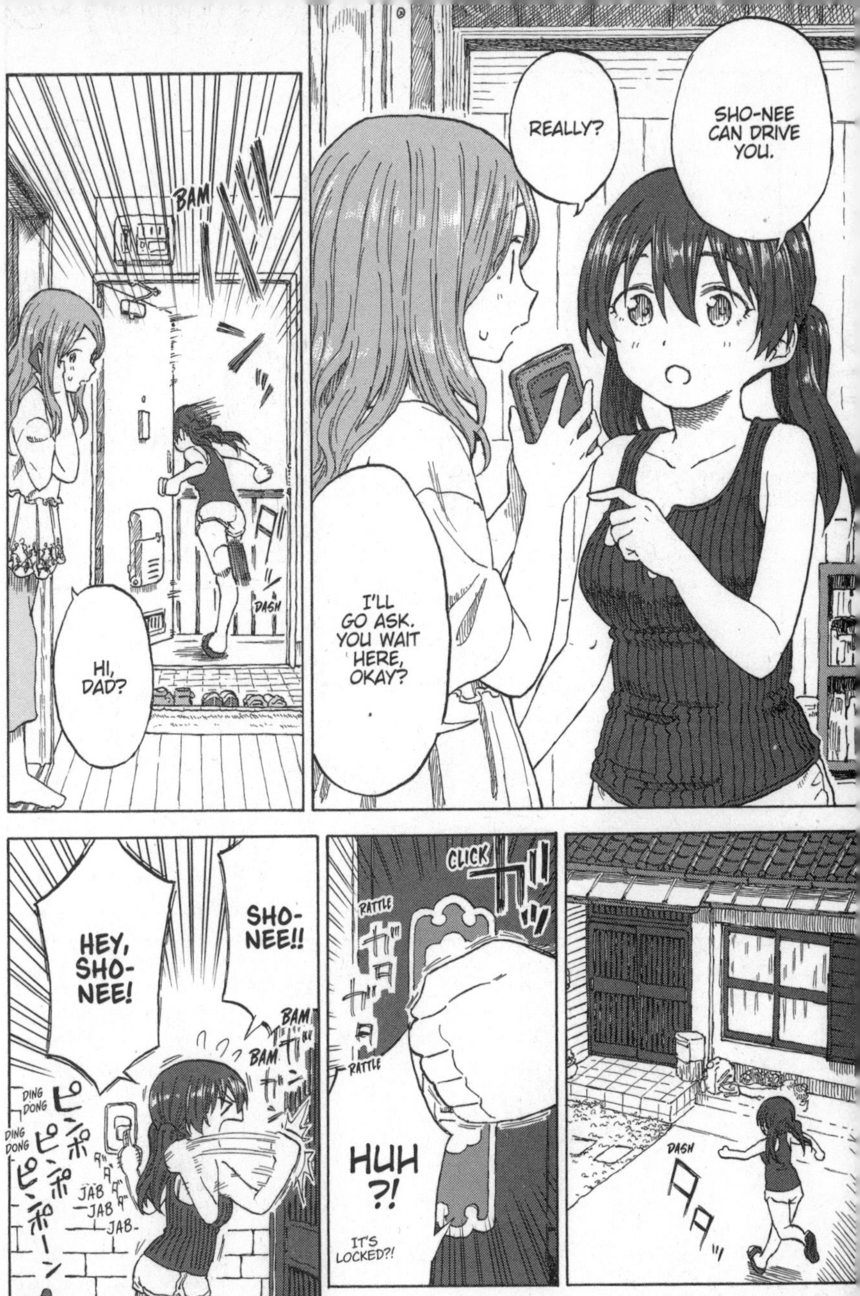
SHO-NEE CAN DRIVE YOU.
REALLY?
I'LL GO ASK. YOU WAIT HERE, OKAY?
BAM
DASH
HI, DAD?
DASH
CLICK
RATTLE
RATTLE
HUH ?!
IT'S LOCKED?!
SHO-NEE!!
HEY, SHO-NEE!
BAM
BAM
DING DONG
DING DONG
ピンポ ピンポ ピンポーン
JAB
JAB
JAB

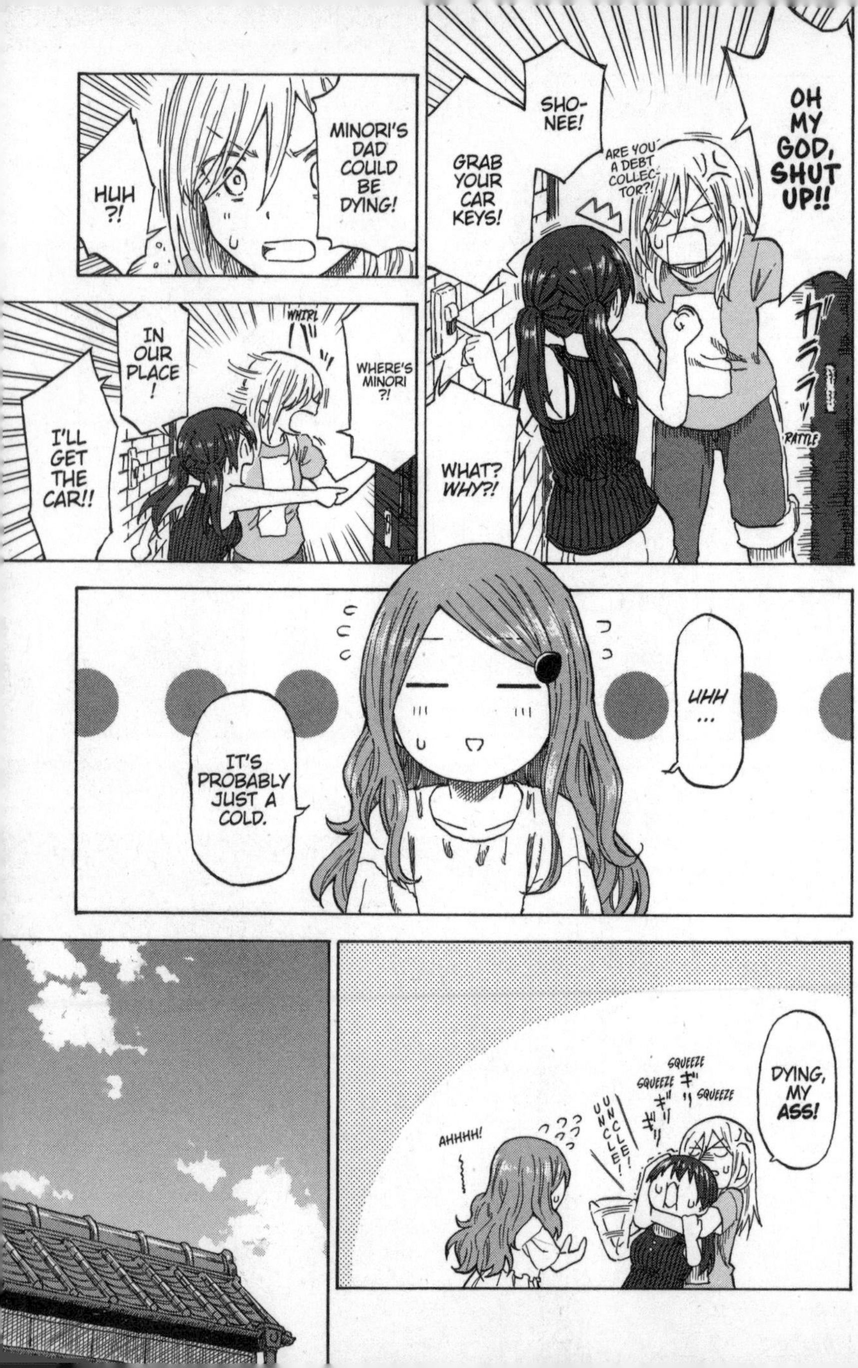
OH MY GOD, SHUT UP!!
SHO-NEE!
ARE YOU A DEBT COLLEC-TOR?!
GRAB YOUR CAR KEYS!
RATTLE
WHAT? WHY?!
MINORI'S DAD COULD BE DYING!
HUH?!
WHERE'S MINORI?!
WHIRL
IN OUR PLACE!
I'LL GET THE CAR!!
UHH...
IT'S PROBABLY JUST A COLD.
DYING, MY ASS!
SQUEEZE
SQUEEZE
SQUEEZE
UNCLE! UNCLE!
AHHHH!

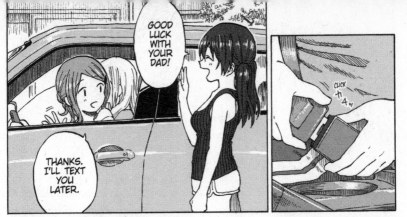

GOOD LUCK WITH YOUR DAD!

THANKS. I'LL TEXT YOU LATER.

CLICK

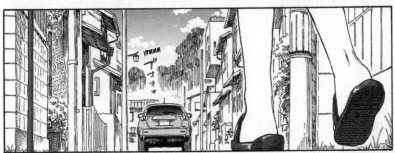

VRMMM

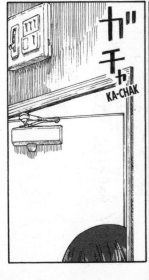

KA-CHAK

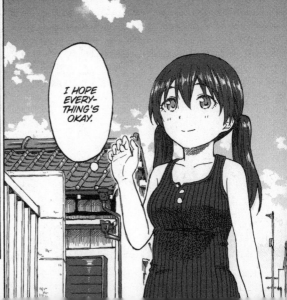

I HOPE EVERY-THING'S OKAY.

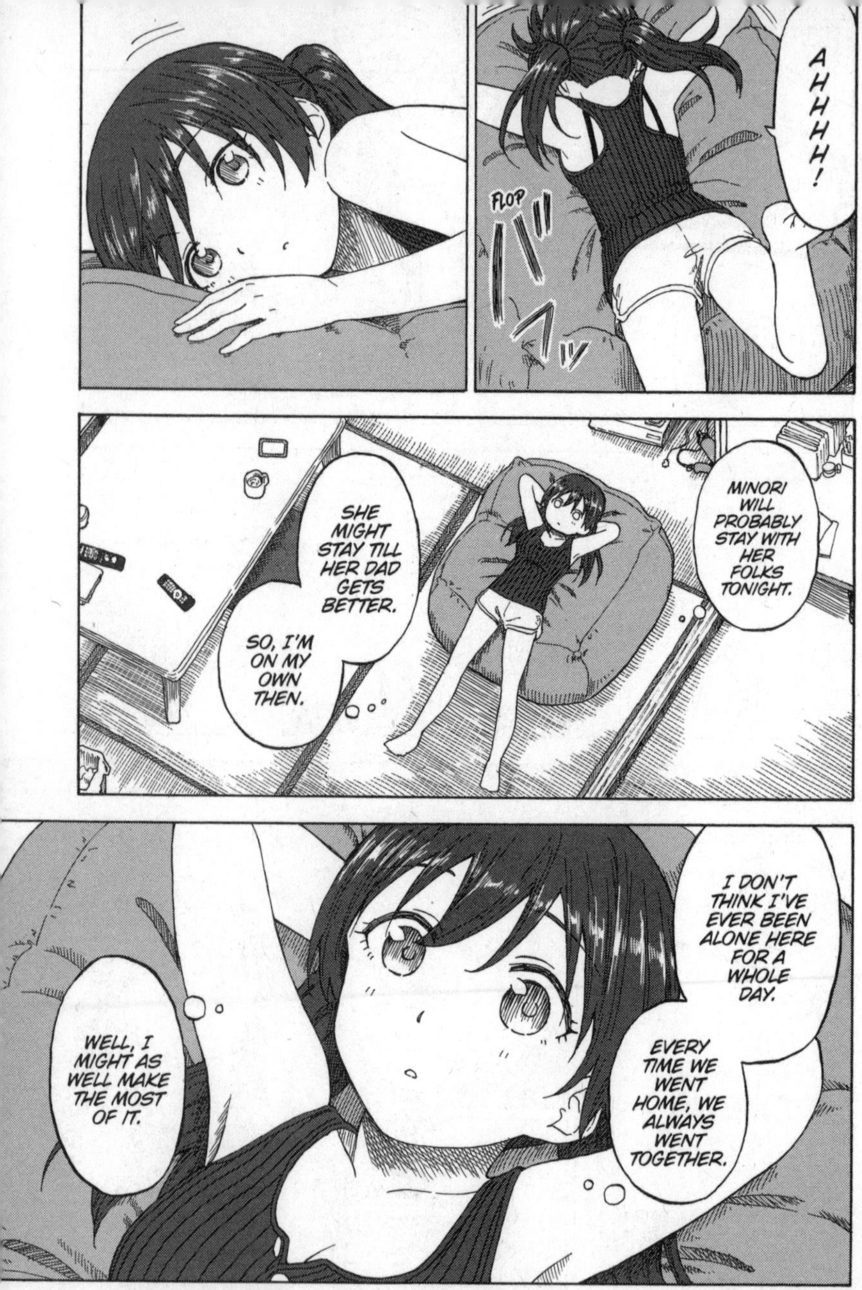
AHHHHH!
FLOP
バッ
MINORI WILL PROBABLY STAY WITH HER FOLKS TONIGHT.
SHE MIGHT STAY TILL HER DAD GETS BETTER.
SO, I'M ON MY OWN THEN.
I DON'T THINK I'VE EVER BEEN ALONE HERE FOR A WHOLE DAY.
EVERY TIME WE WENT HOME, WE ALWAYS WENT TOGETHER.
WELL, I MIGHT AS WELL MAKE THE MOST OF IT.

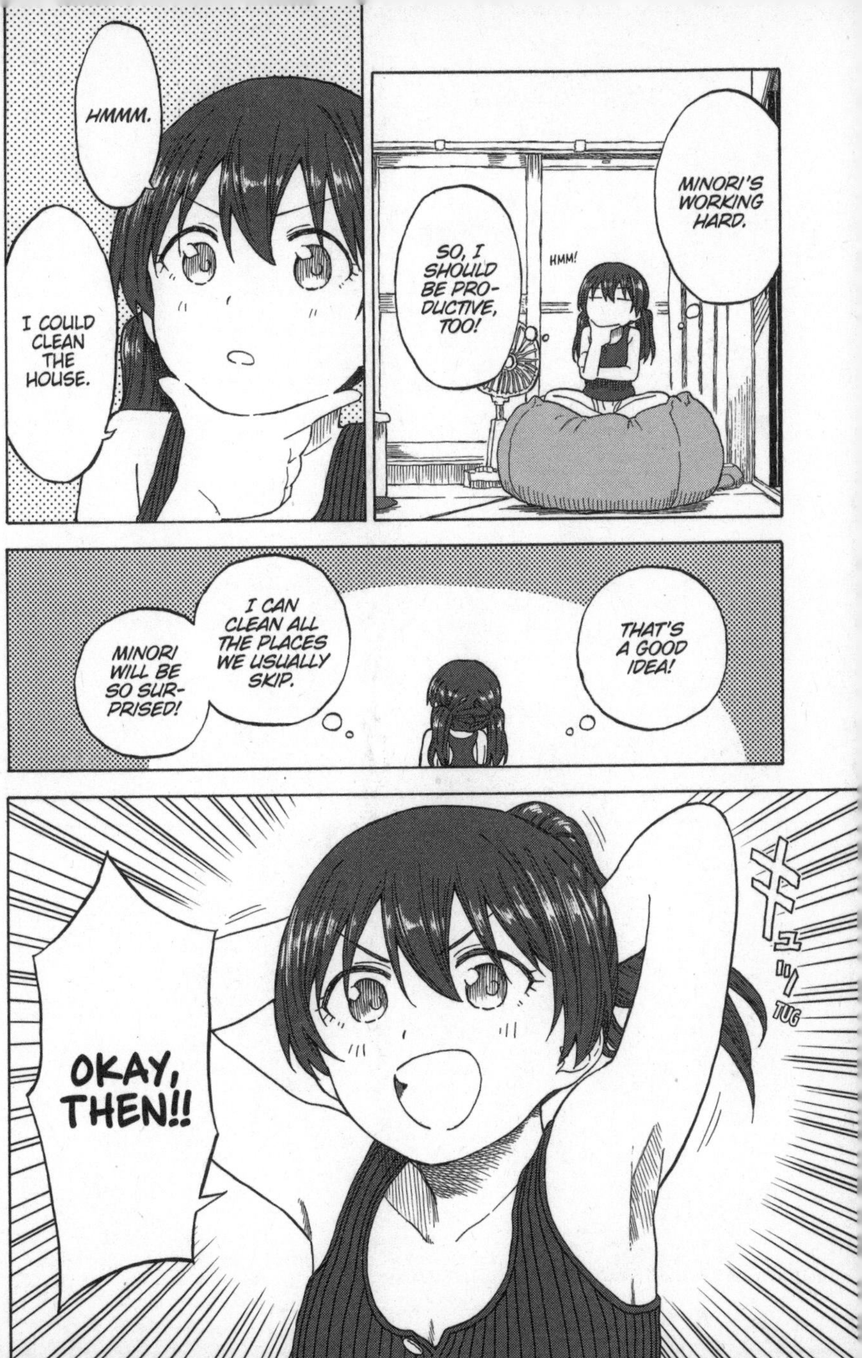
MINORI'S WORKING HARD.
HMM!
SO, I SHOULD BE PRODUCTIVE, TOO!
HMMM.
I COULD CLEAN THE HOUSE.
THAT'S A GOOD IDEA!
I CAN CLEAN ALL THE PLACES WE USUALLY SKIP.
MINORI WILL BE SO SURPRISED!
TUG
OKAY, THEN!!

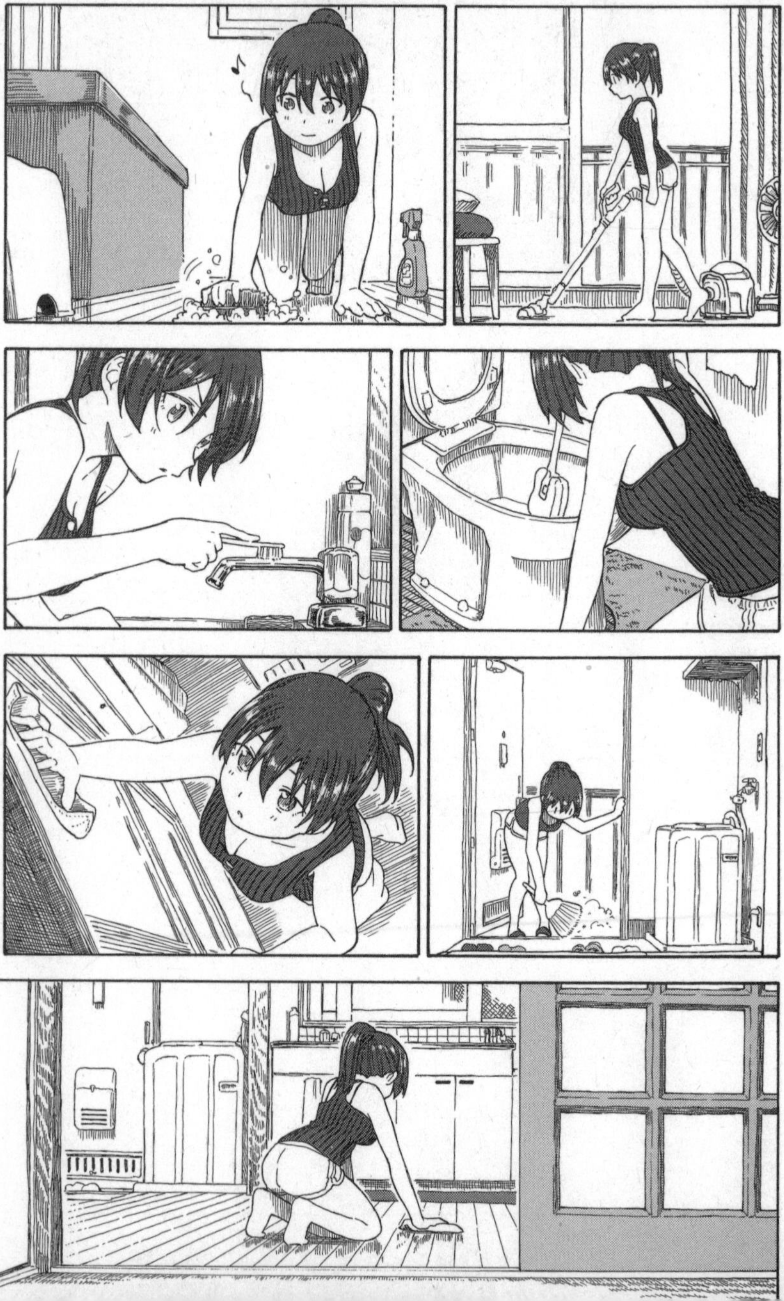

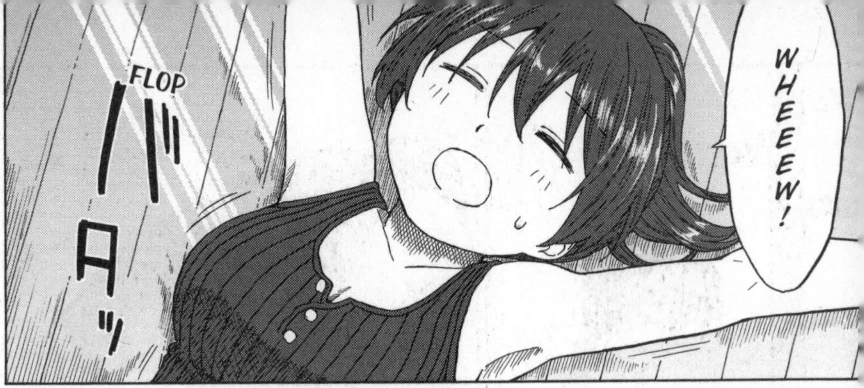
WHEEEW!
FLOP
バタッ

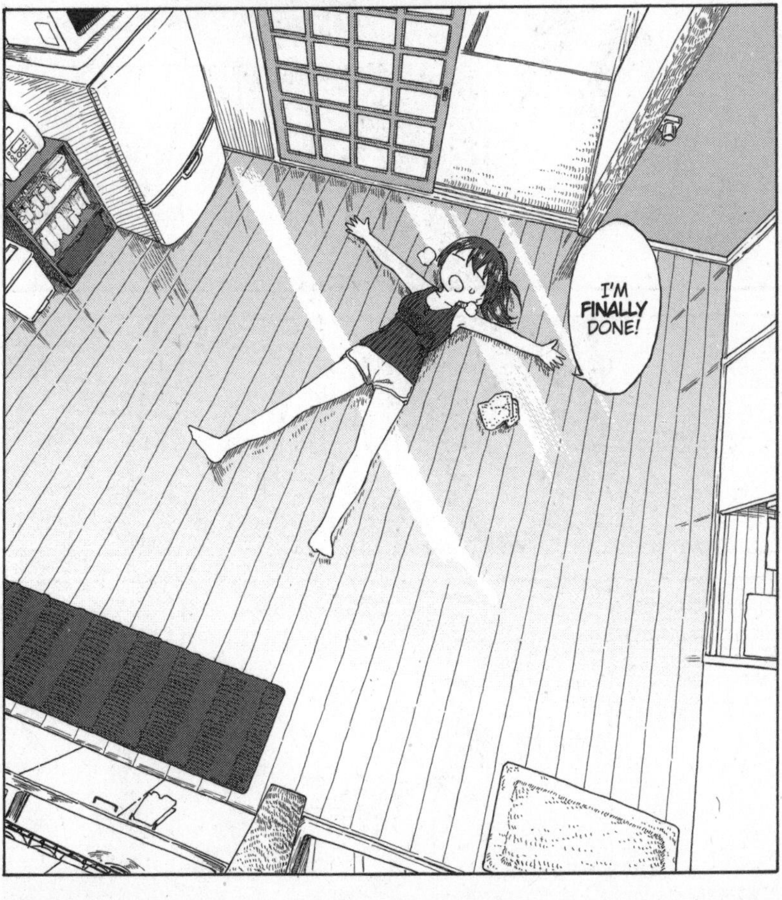
I'M FINALLY DONE!

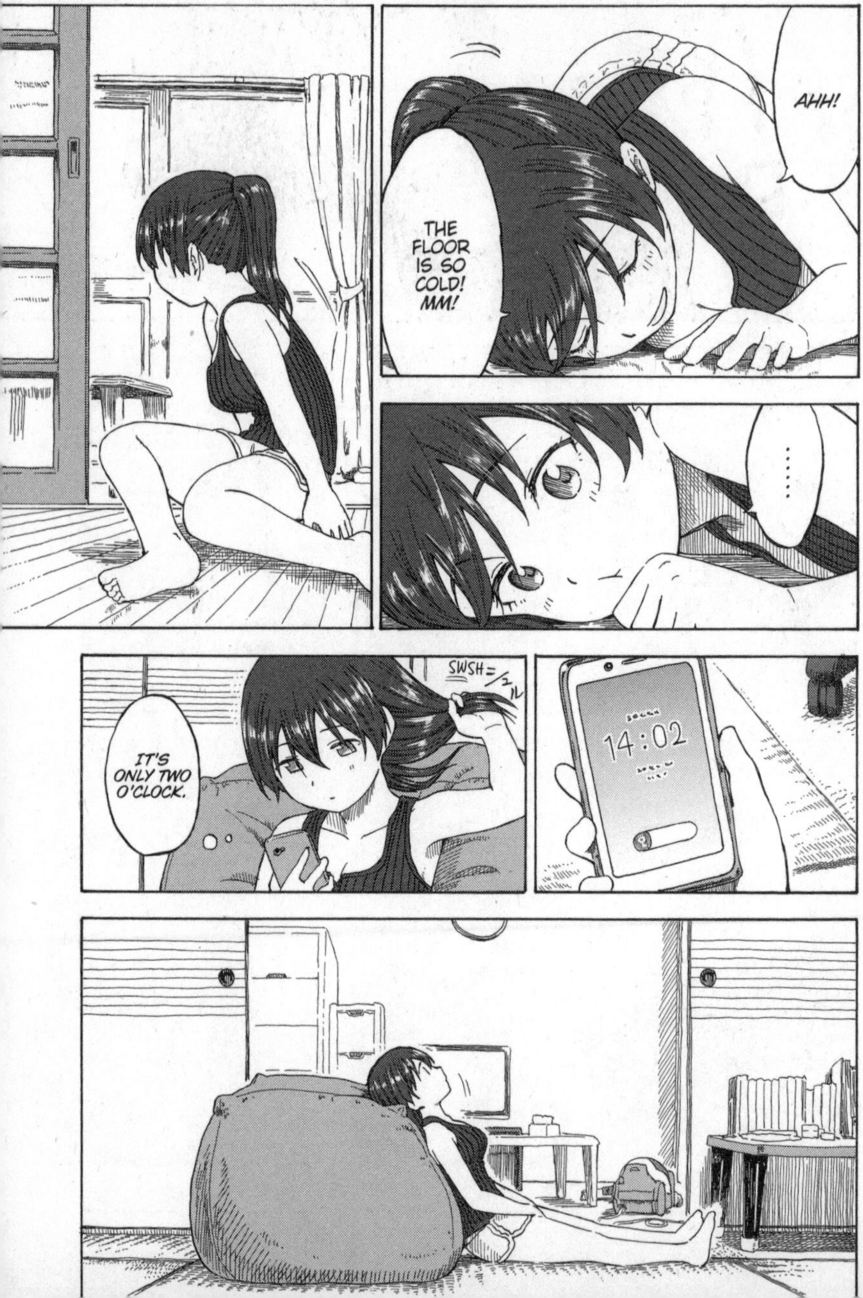
AHH!
THE FLOOR IS SO COLD! MM!
......
14:02
SWSH
IT'S ONLY TWO O'CLOCK.

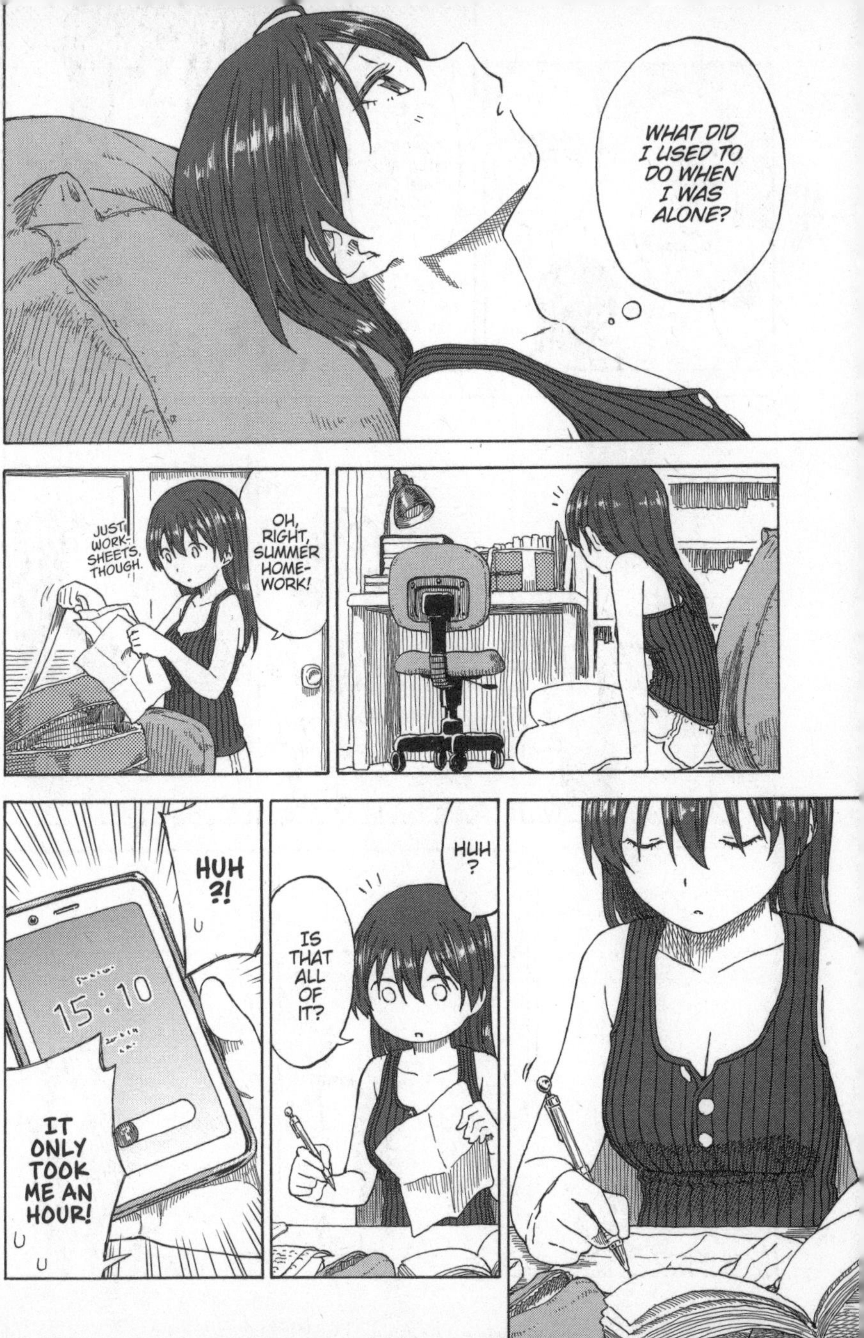
WHAT DID I USED TO DO WHEN I WAS ALONE?
OH, RIGHT, SUMMER HOMEWORK!
JUST WORKSHEETS, THOUGH.
HUH?
IS THAT ALL OF IT?
HUH ?!
15:10
IT ONLY TOOK ME AN HOUR!

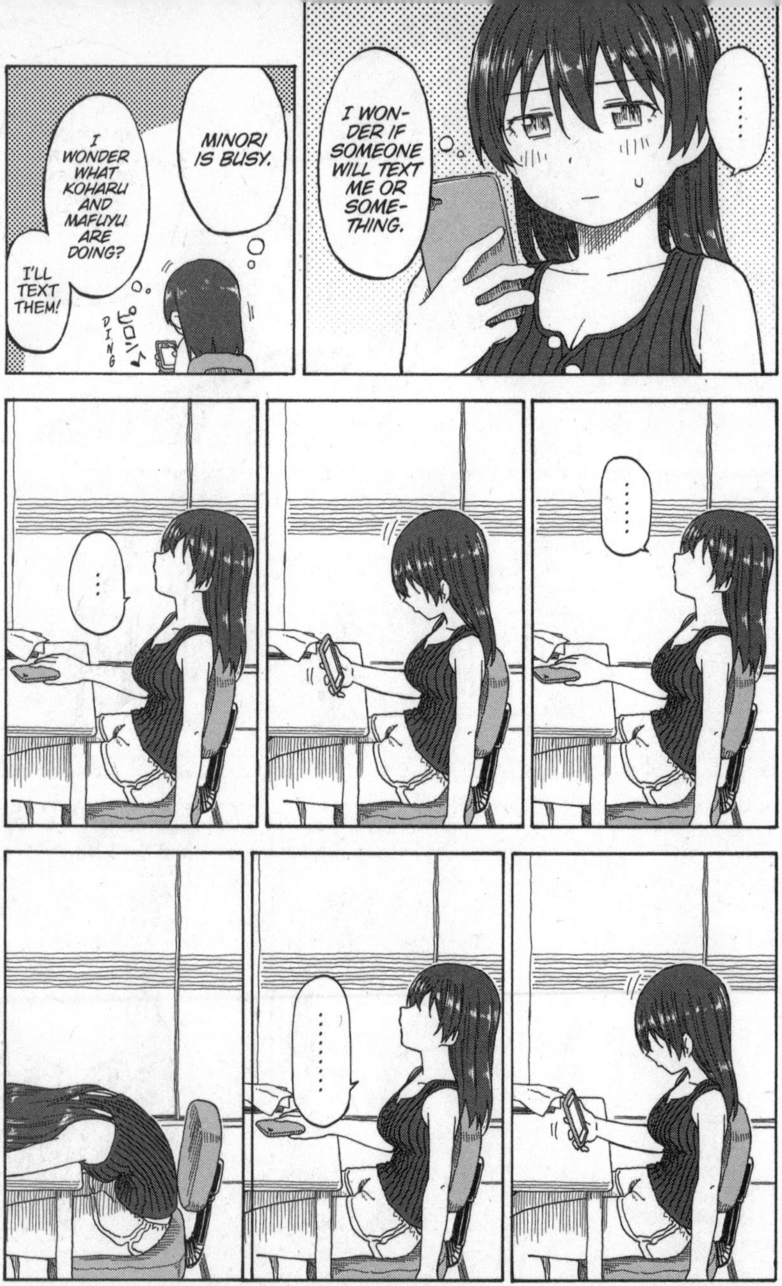
......
I WONDER IF SOMEONE WILL TEXT ME OR SOMETHING.
MINORI IS BUSY.
I WONDER WHAT KOHARU AND MAFUYU ARE DOING?
I'LL TEXT THEM!
ピロン♪
DING
......
...
....

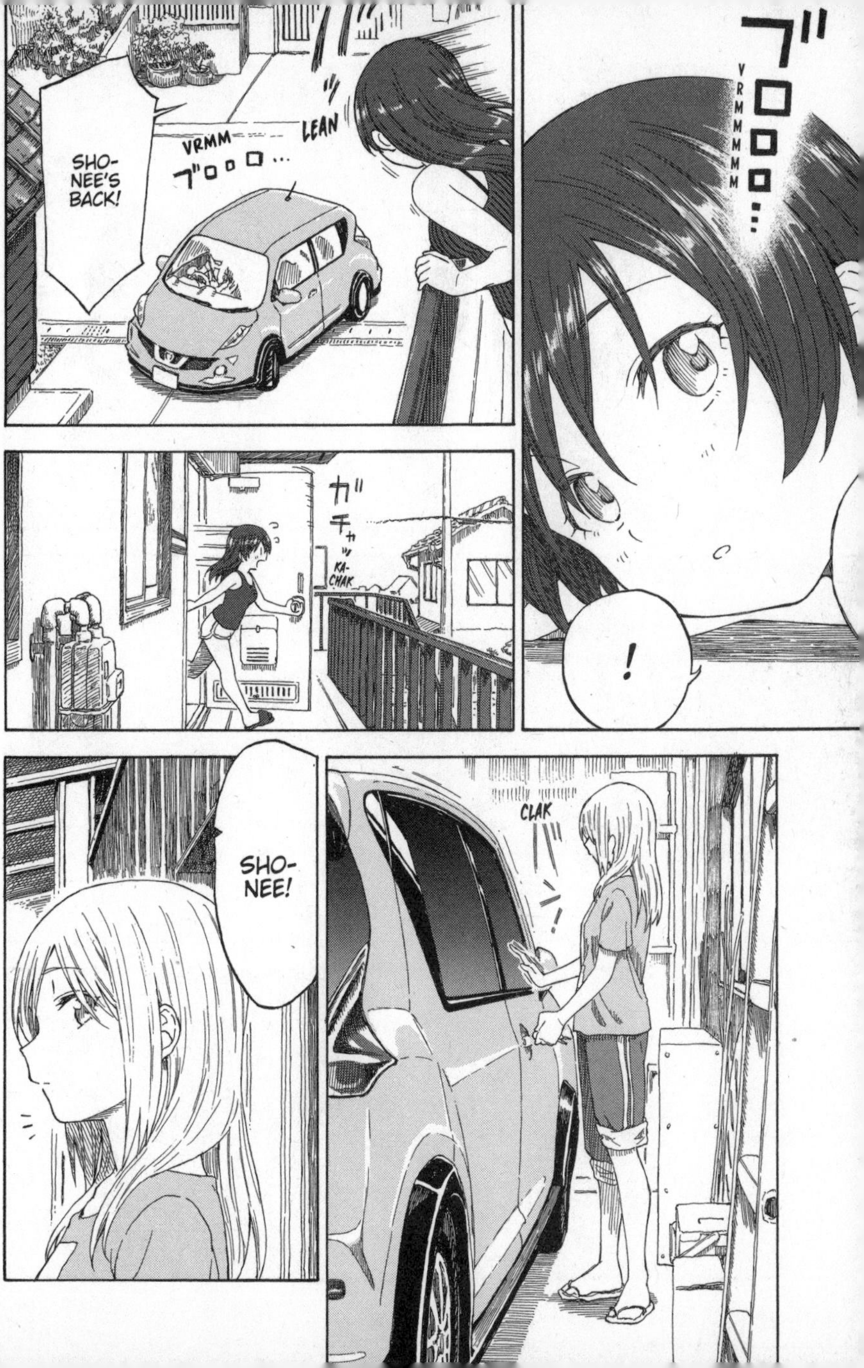
ブロロロ…
VRMMMMMM
!
VRMM
ブロロロ…
ッ
LEAN
SHO-NEE'S BACK!
ガチャッ
KA-CHAK
CLAK
SHO-NEE!

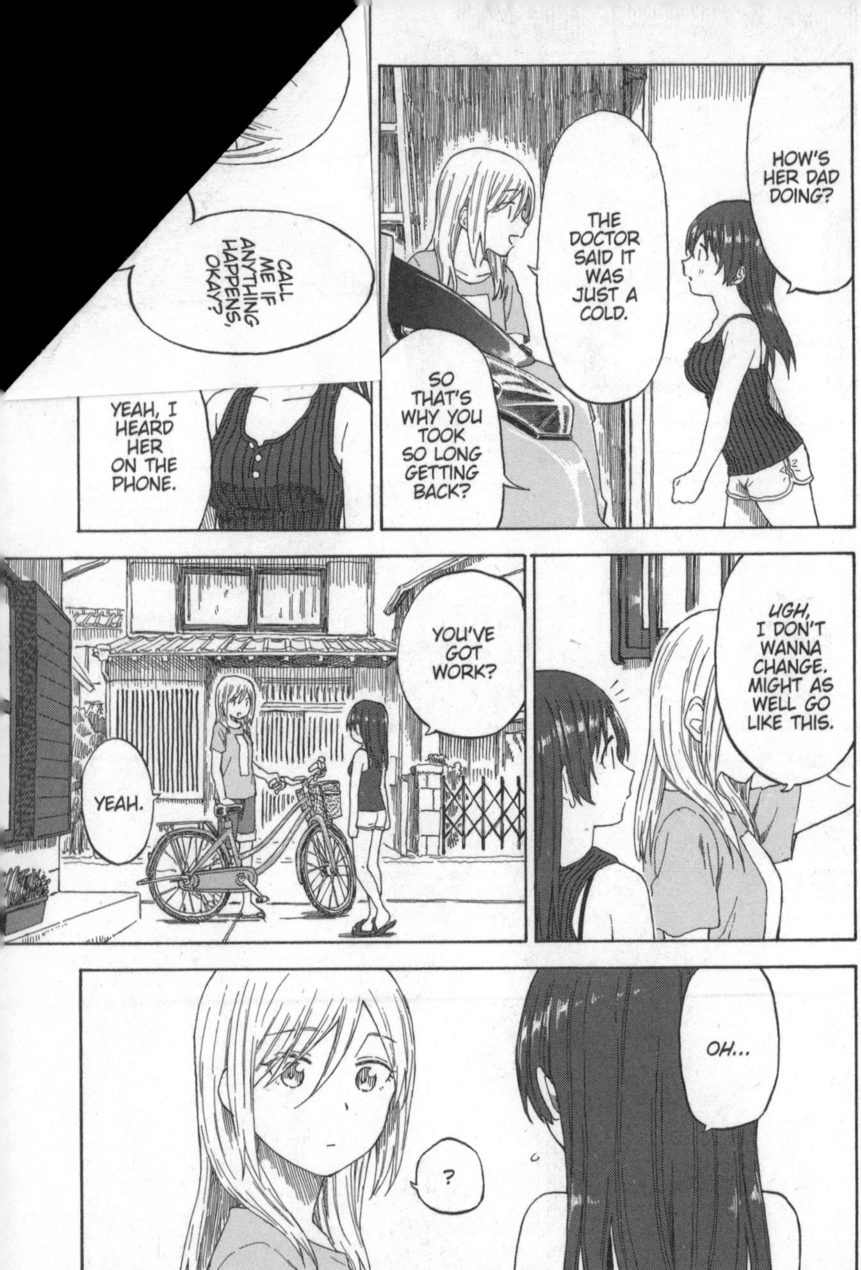
HOW'S HER DAD DOING?
THE DOCTOR SAID IT WAS JUST A COLD.
SO THAT'S WHY YOU TOOK SO LONG GETTING BACK?
CALL ME IF ANYTHING HAPPENS, OKAY?
YEAH, I HEARD HER ON THE PHONE.
UGH, I DON'T WANNA CHANGE. MIGHT AS WELL GO LIKE THIS.
YOU'VE GOT WORK?
YEAH.
OH...
?

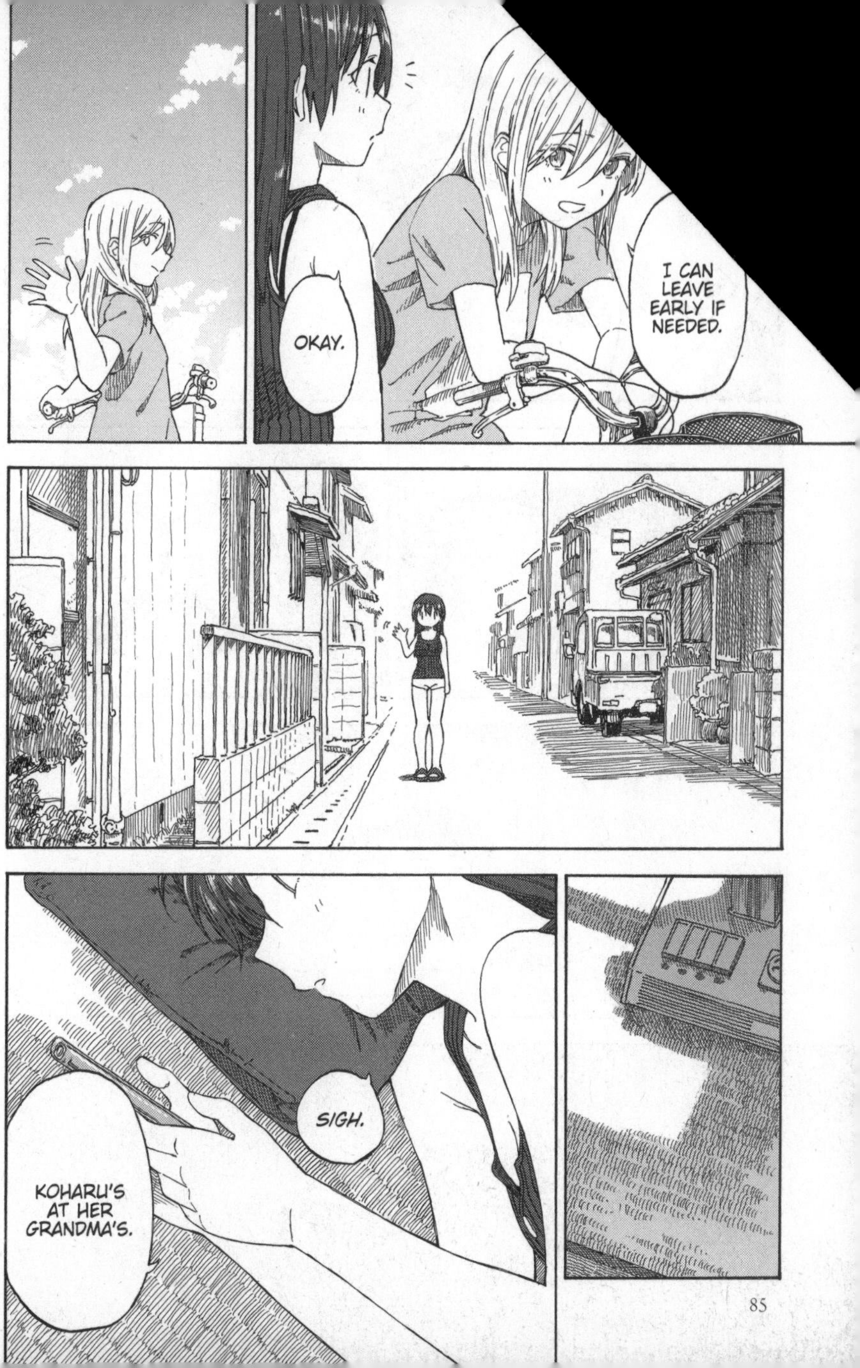
I CAN LEAVE EARLY IF NEEDED.
OKAY.
SIGH.
KOHARU'S AT HER GRANDMA'S.

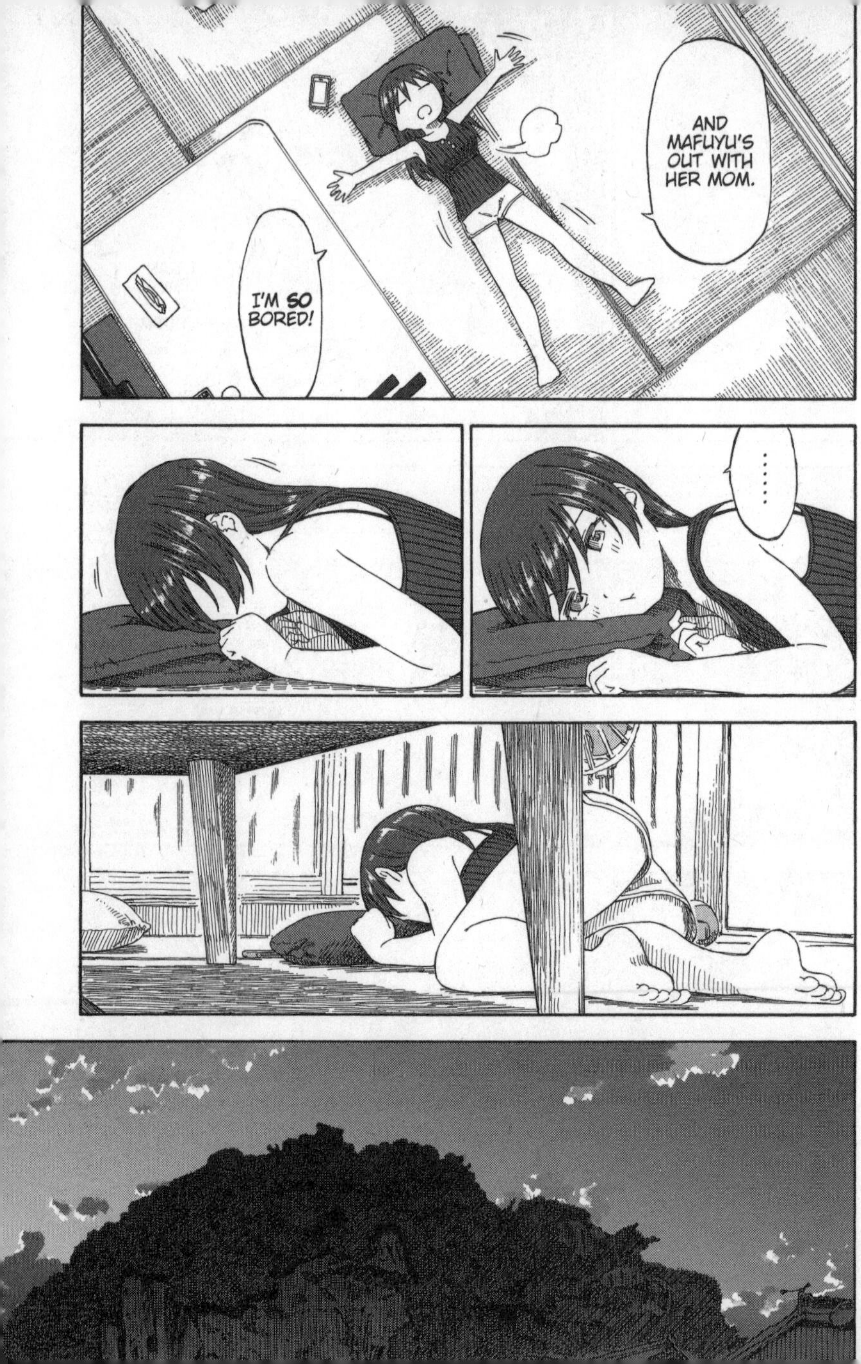
AND MAFUYU'S OUT WITH HER MOM.
I'M SO BORED!
......

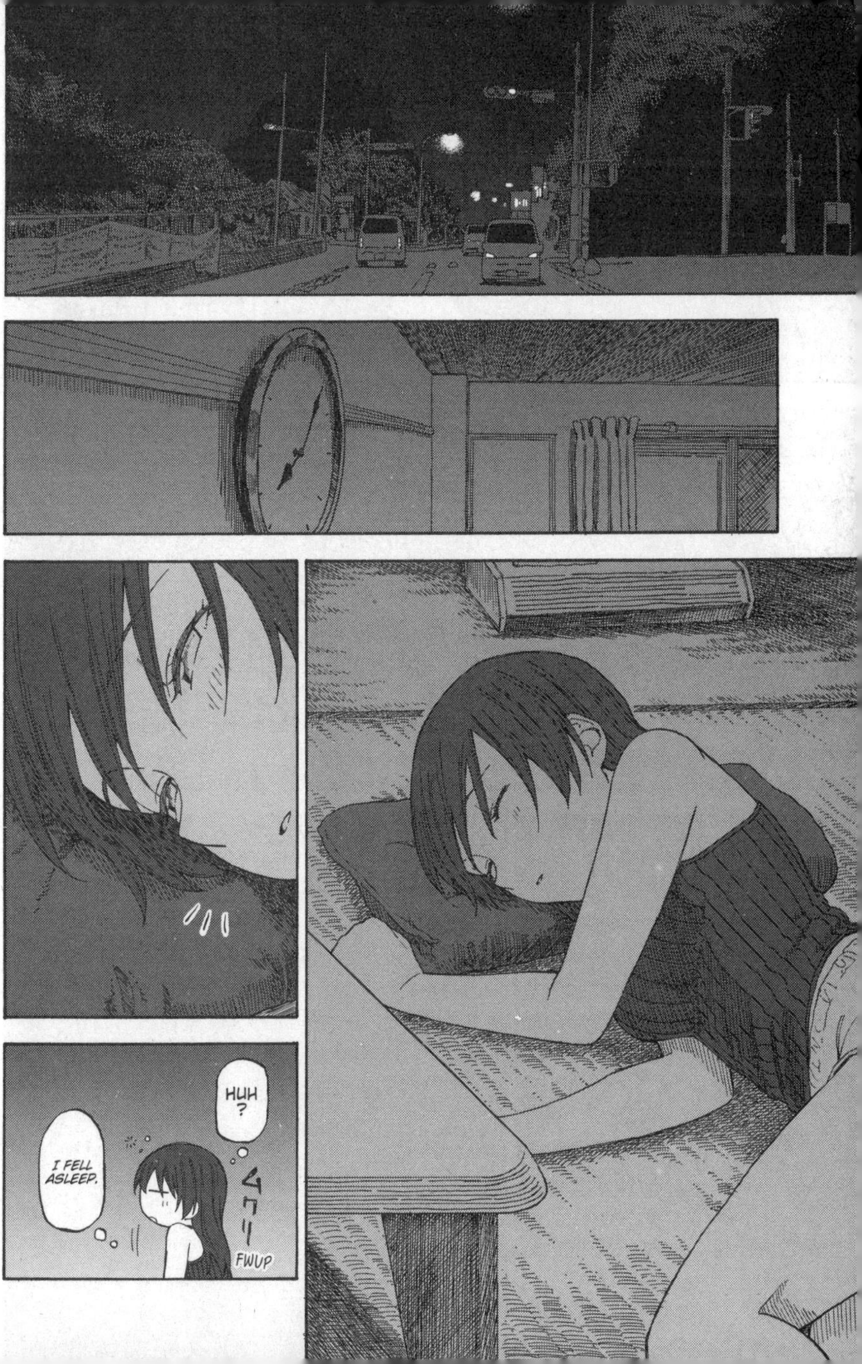
HUH?
ムクリ
FWUP
I FELL ASLEEP.

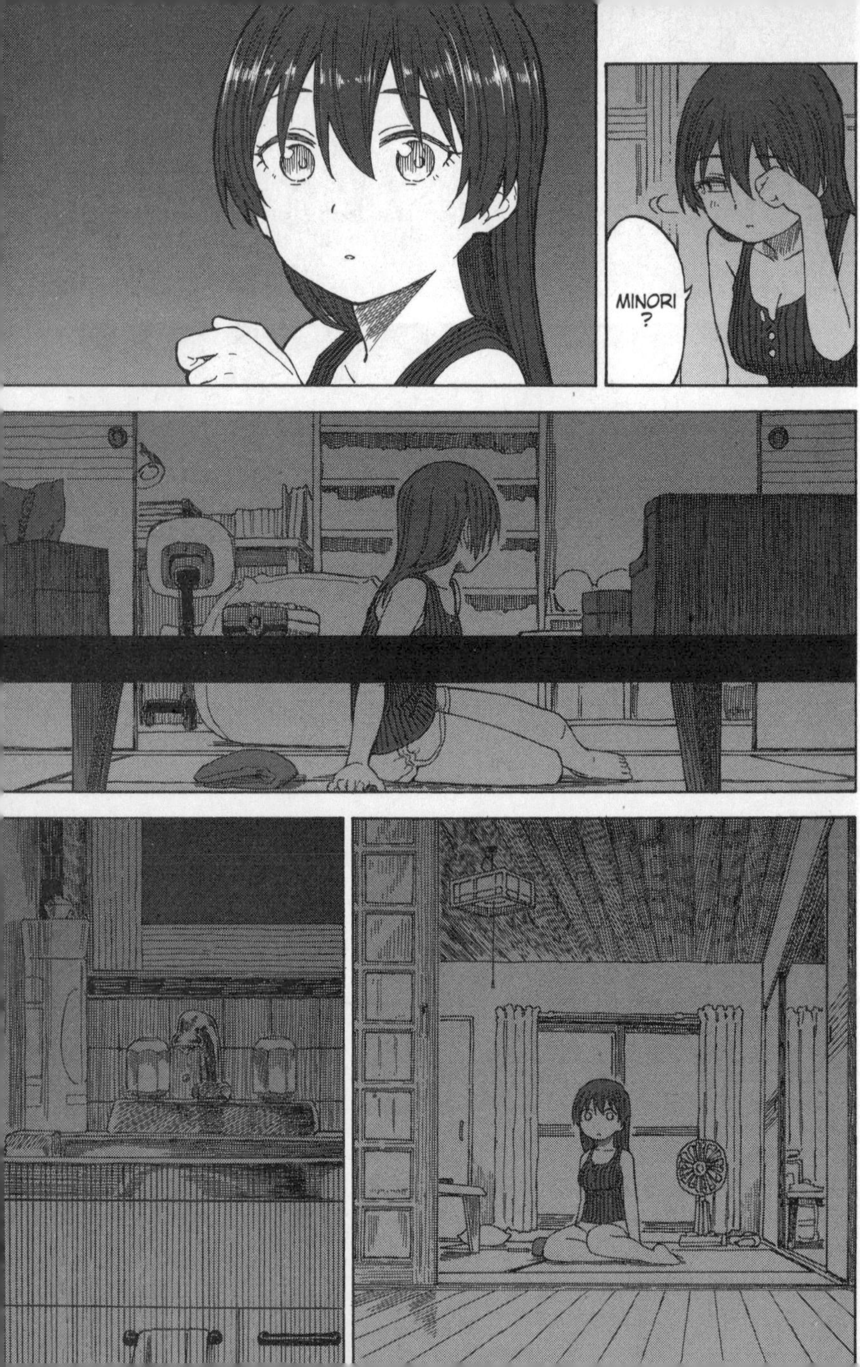
MINORI ?

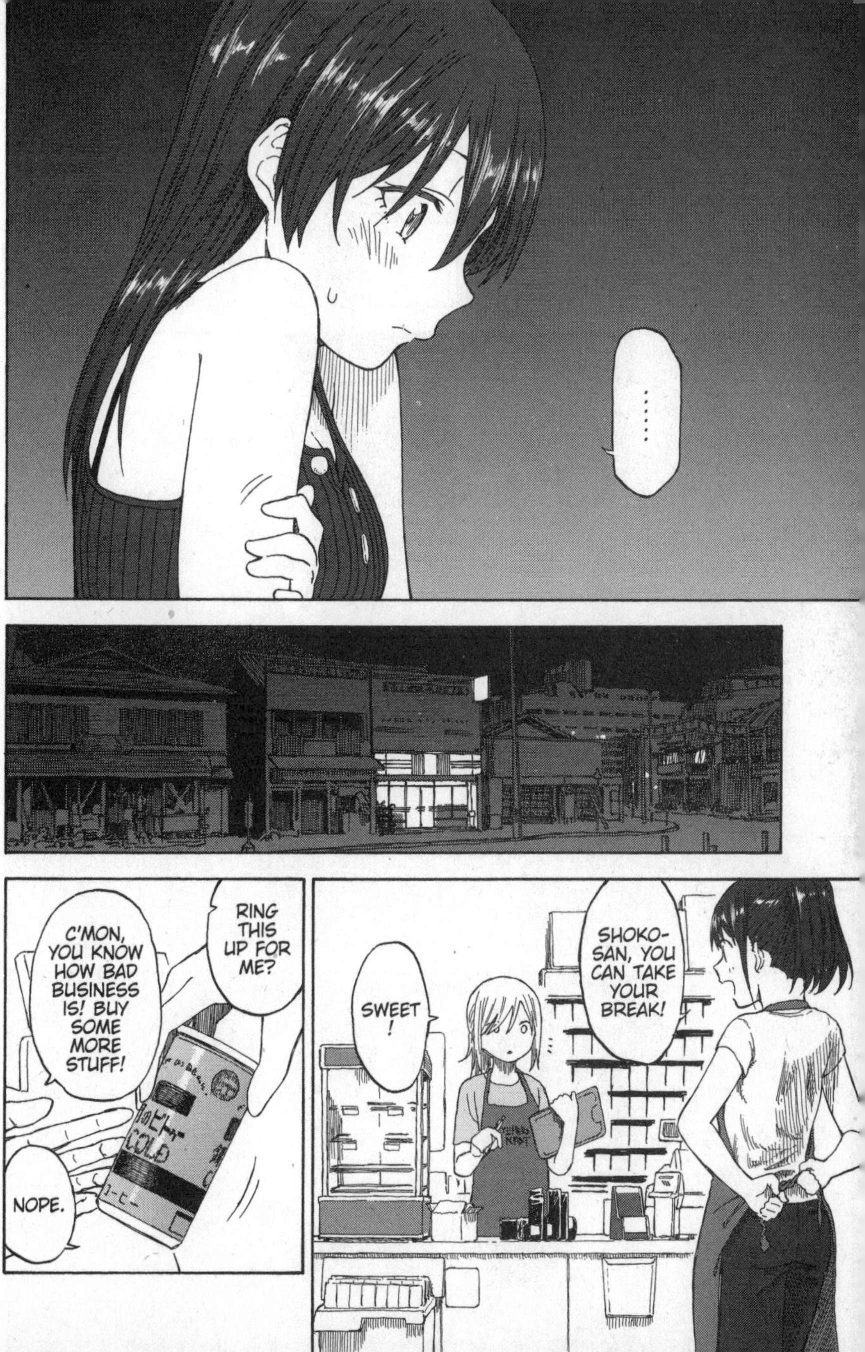
……
SHOKO-SAN, YOU CAN TAKE YOUR BREAK!
SWEET!
RING THIS UP FOR ME?
C'MON, YOU KNOW HOW BAD BUSINESS IS! BUY SOME MORE STUFF!
NOPE.

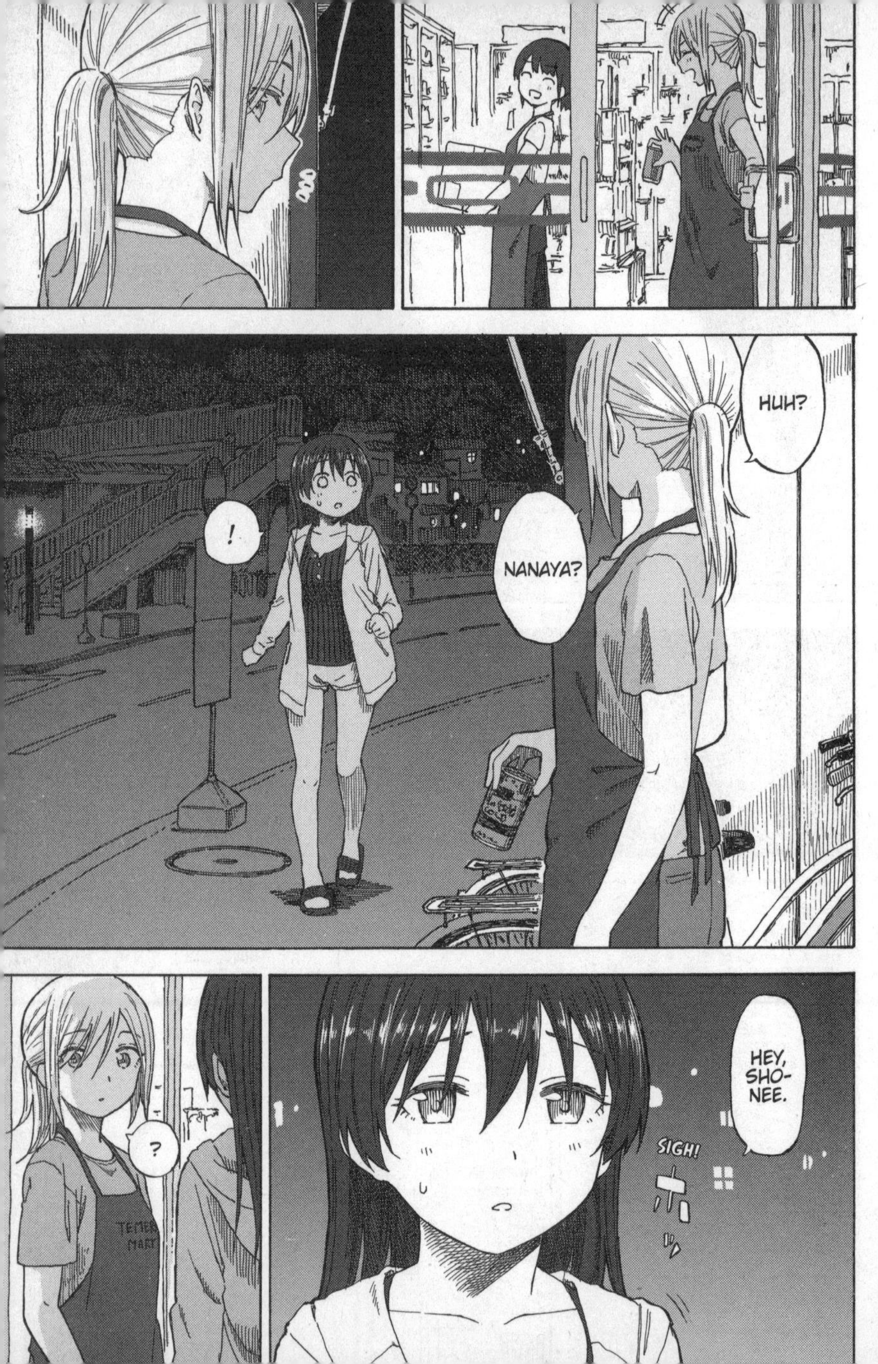
HUH?
NANAYA?
!
HEY, SHO-NEE.
SIGH!
?

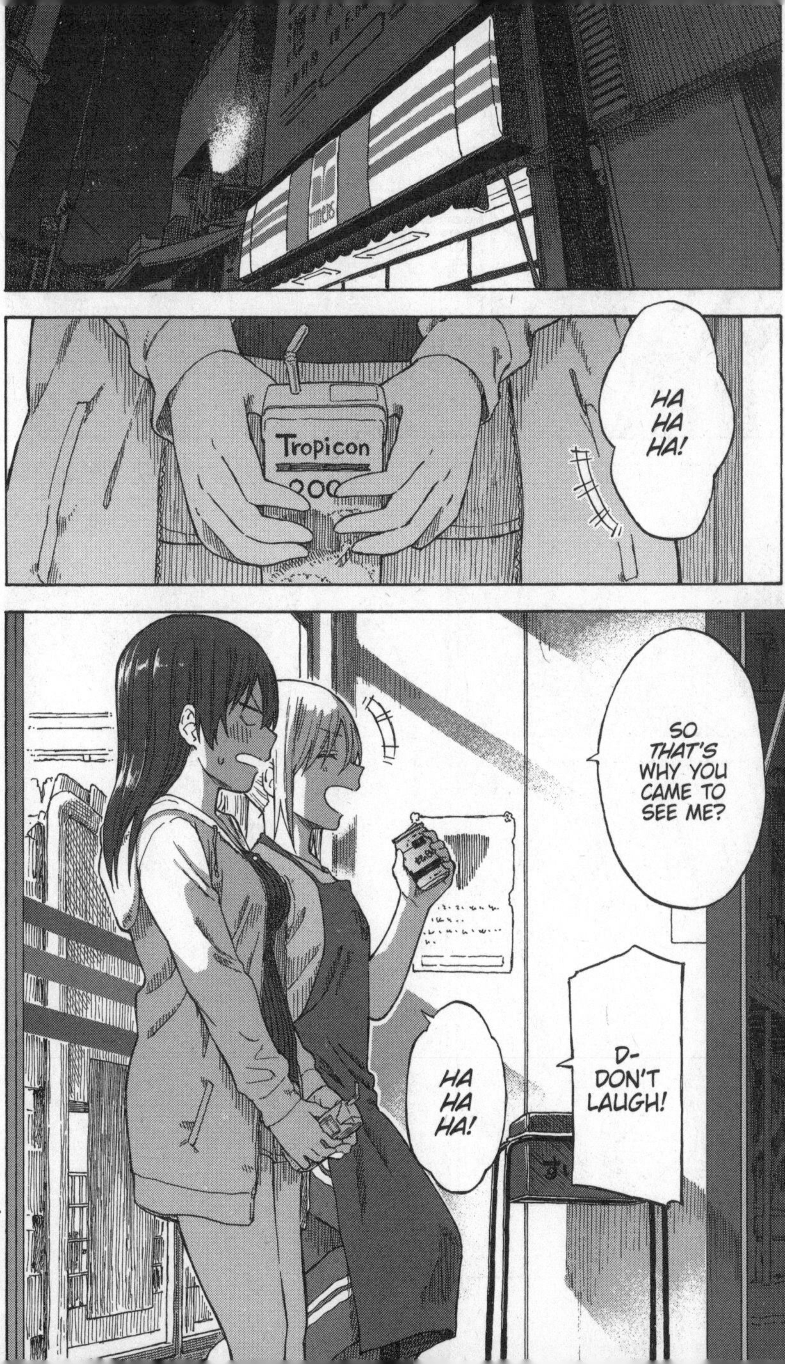
Tropicon
HA HA HA!
SO THAT'S WHY YOU CAME TO SEE ME?
D- DON'T LAUGH!
HA HA HA!

Label: Ashtray

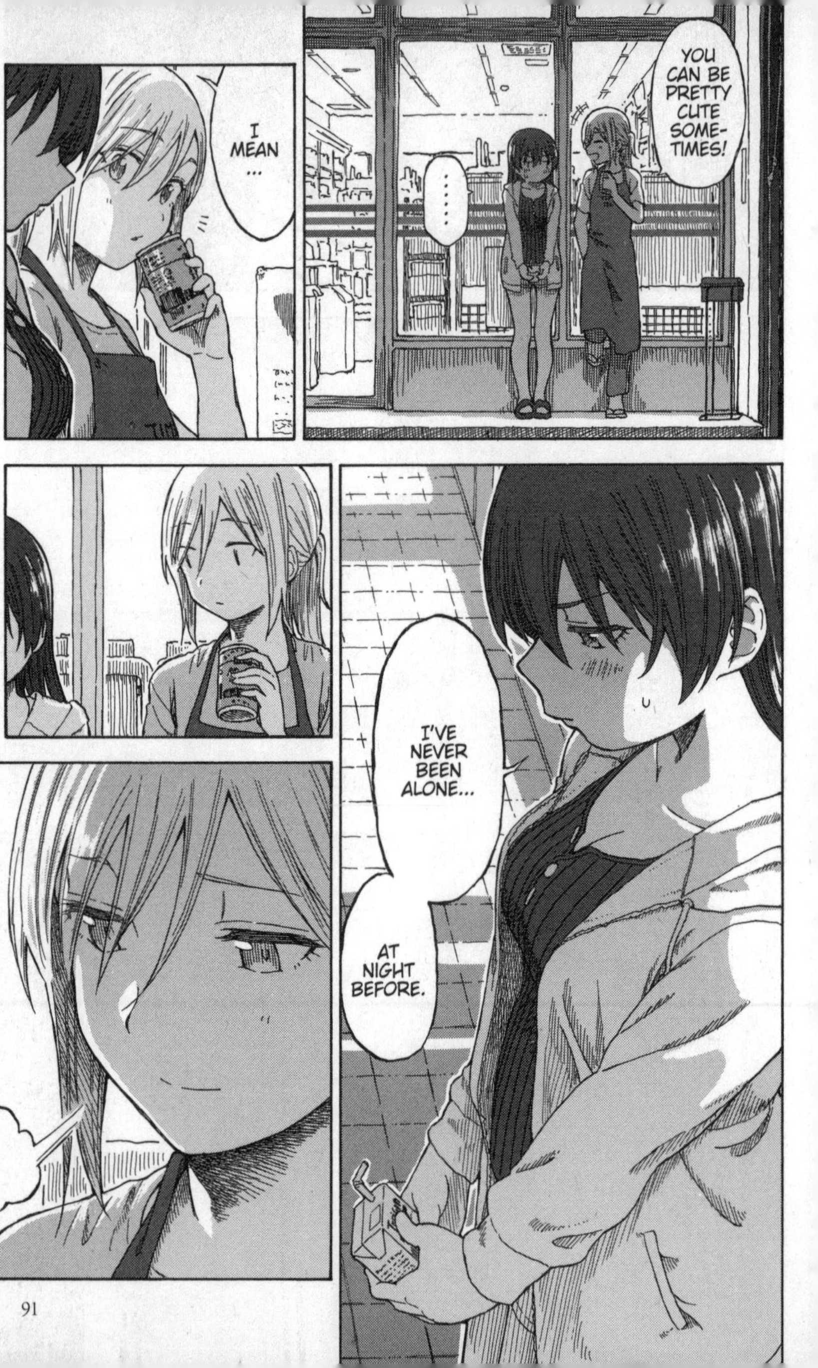
YOU CAN BE PRETTY CUTE SOME-TIMES!
......
I MEAN ...
I'VE NEVER BEEN ALONE...
AT NIGHT BEFORE.

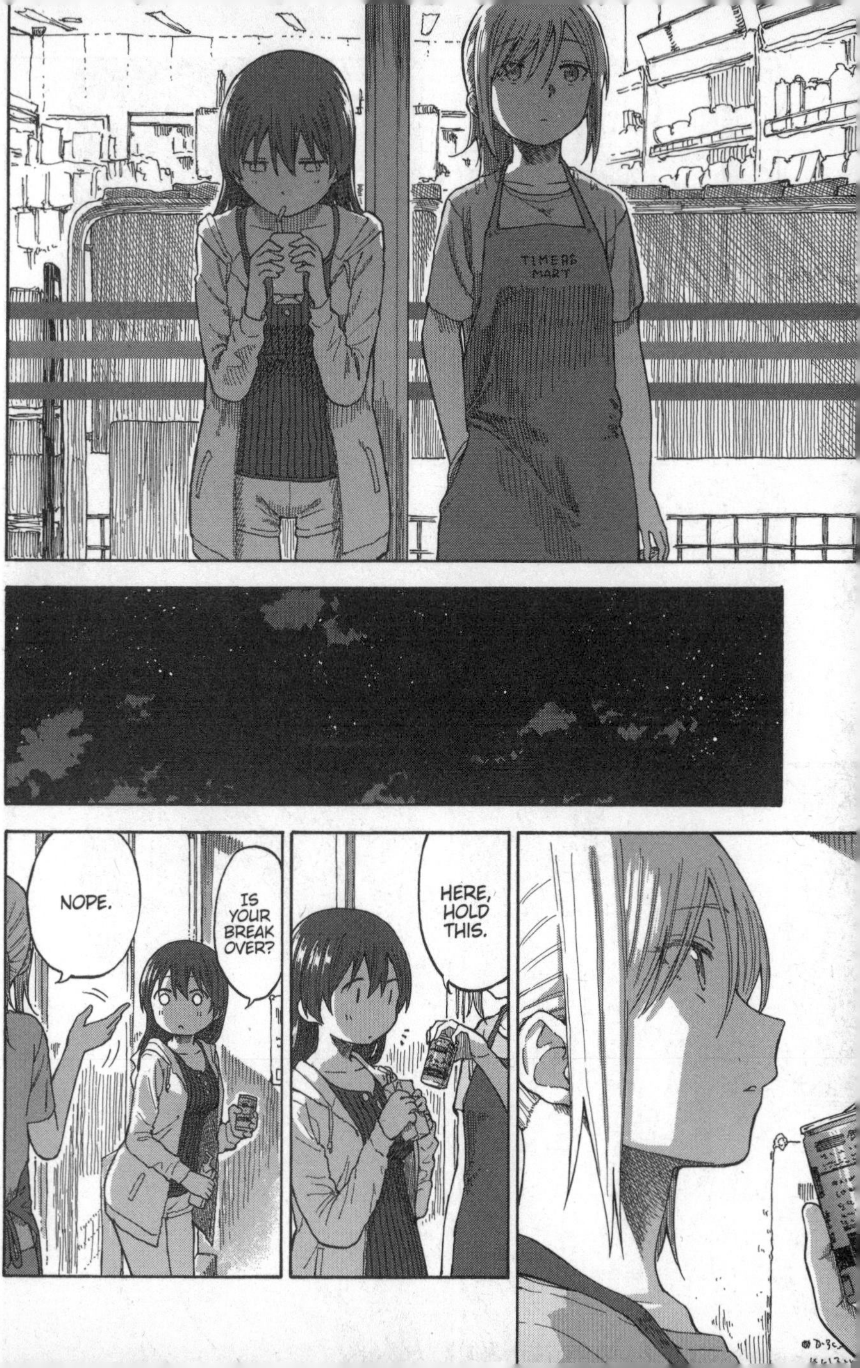
TIMERS MART
HERE, HOLD THIS.
IS YOUR BREAK OVER?
NOPE.

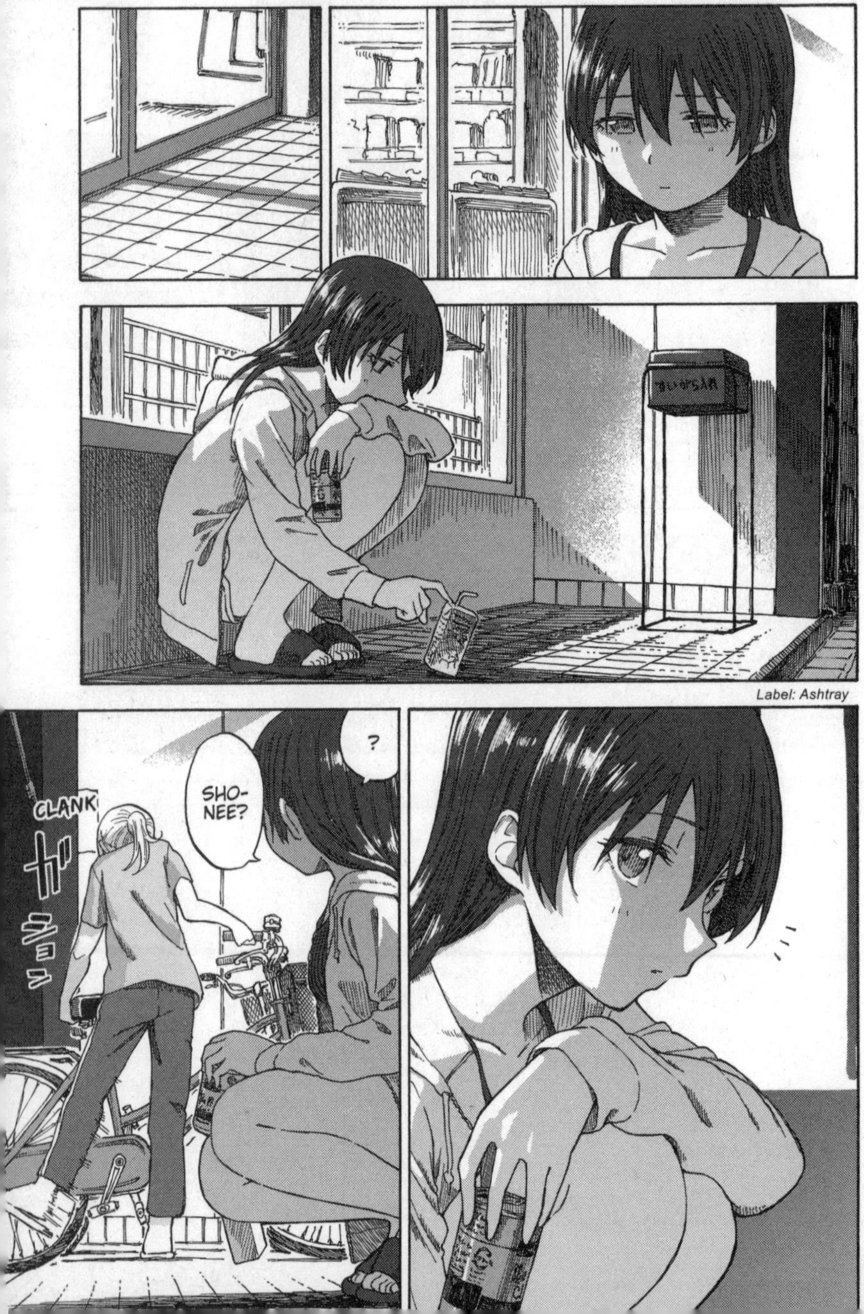
Label: Ashtray
?
SHO-NEE?
CLANK

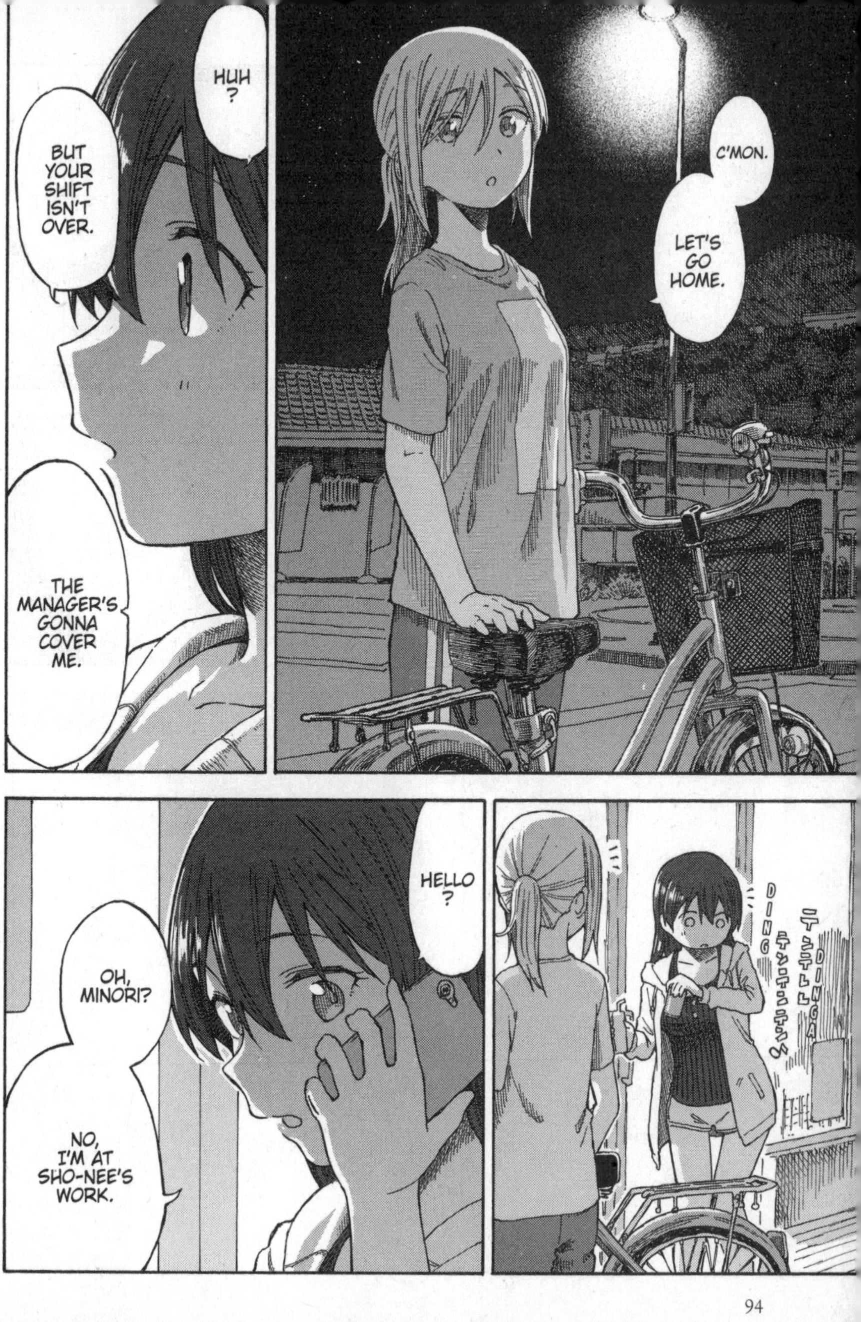
C'MON.
LET'S GO HOME.
HUH?
BUT YOUR SHIFT ISN'T OVER.
THE MANAGER'S GONNA COVER ME.
DINGA
DING
HELLO?
OH, MINORI?
NO, I'M AT SHO-NEE'S WORK.

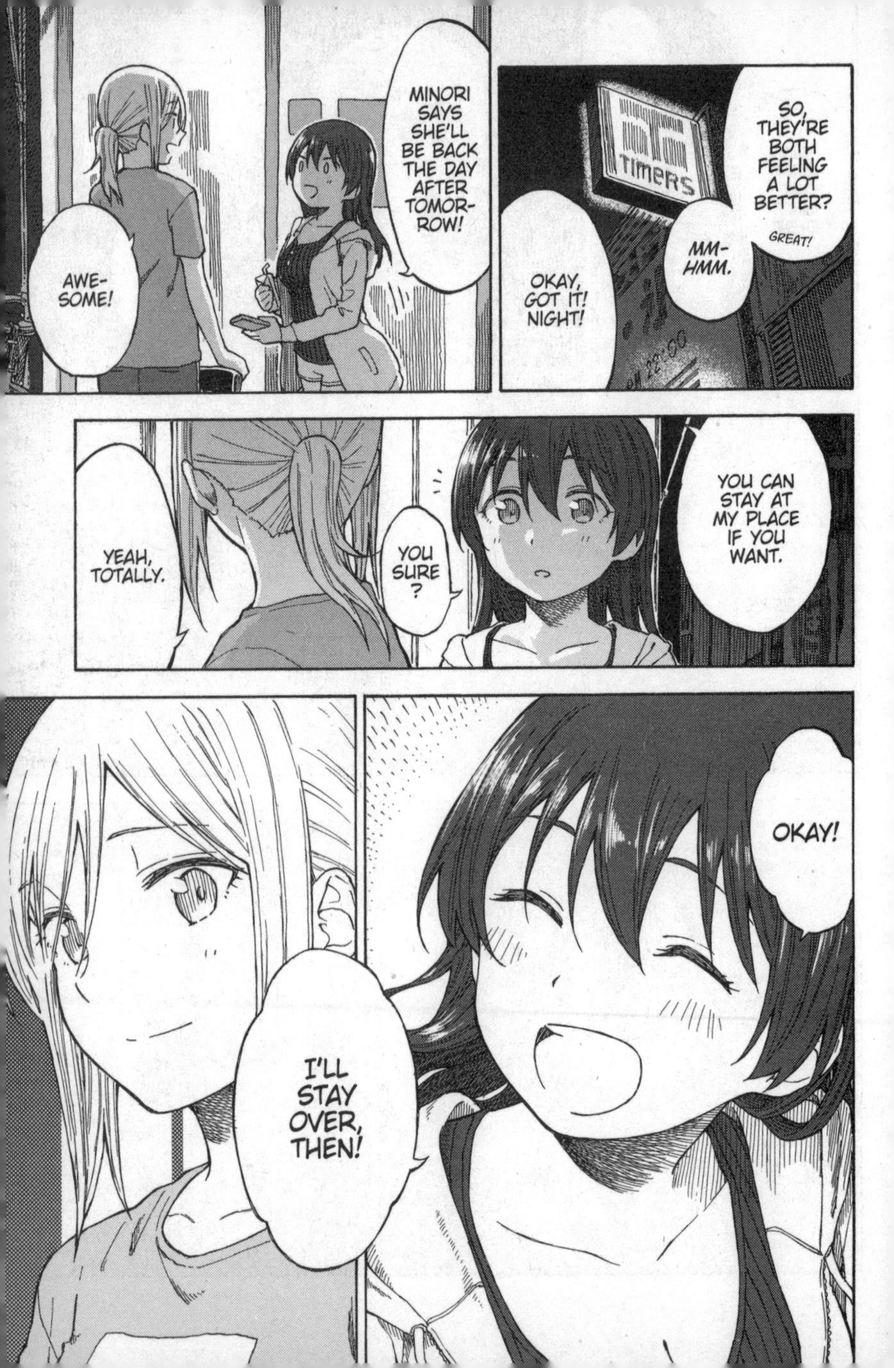
TIMERS
SO, THEY'RE BOTH FEELING A LOT BETTER?
GREAT!
MM-HMM.
OKAY, GOT IT! NIGHT!
MINORI SAYS SHE'LL BE BACK THE DAY AFTER TOMORROW!
AWE-SOME!
YOU CAN STAY AT MY PLACE IF YOU WANT.
YOU SURE?
YEAH, TOTALLY.
OKAY!
I'LL STAY OVER, THEN!

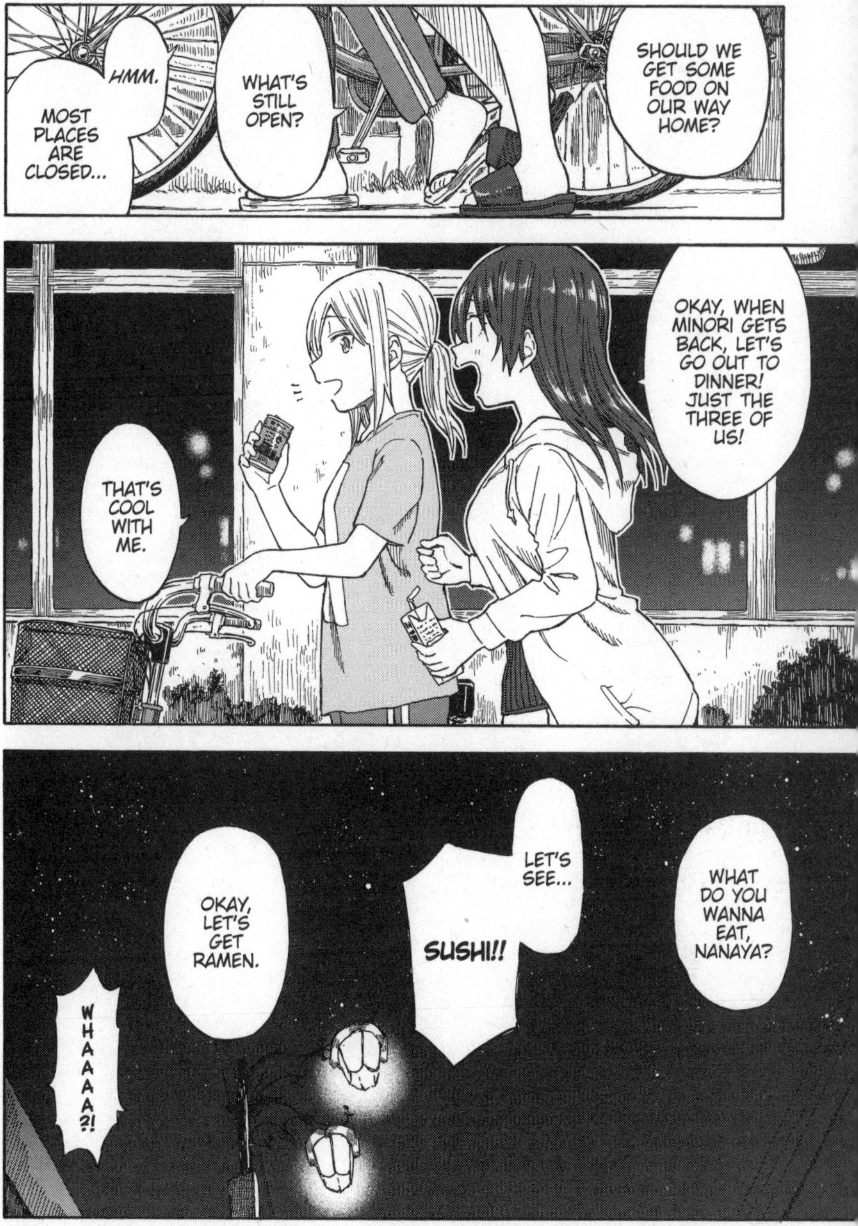
SHOULD WE GET SOME FOOD ON OUR WAY HOME?
WHAT'S STILL OPEN?
HMM.
MOST PLACES ARE CLOSED...
OKAY, WHEN MINORI GETS BACK, LET'S GO OUT TO DINNER! JUST THE THREE OF US!
THAT'S COOL WITH ME.
WHAT DO YOU WANNA EAT, NANAYA?
LET'S SEE...
SUSHI!!
OKAY, LET'S GET RAMEN.
WHAAAAA?!

Our Wonderful Days

story & art by Kei Hamuro

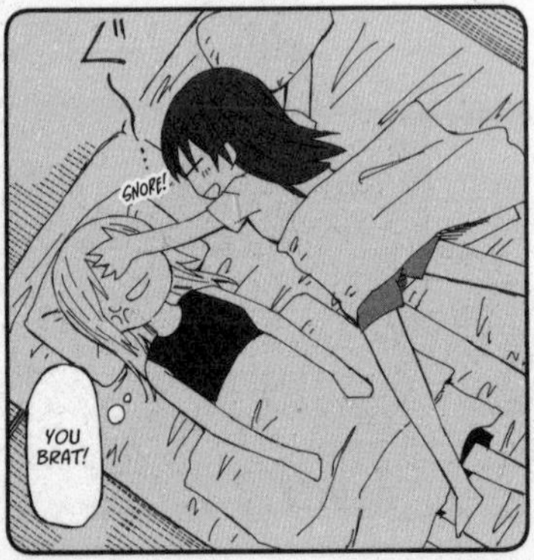
SNORE!
YOU BRAT!

ONE DAY WITH NANAYA AND MINORI

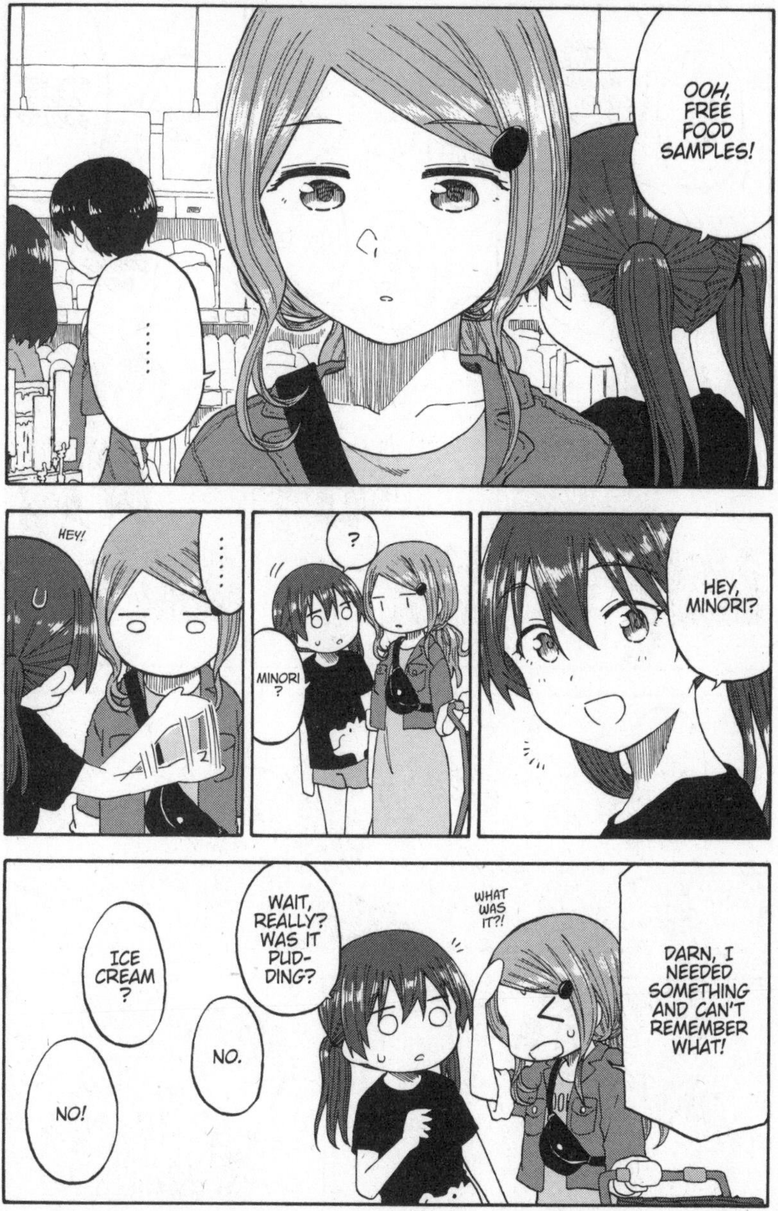

OOH, FREE FOOD SAMPLES!
......
HEY, MINORI?
?
MINORI?
......
HEY!
DARN, I NEEDED SOMETHING AND CAN'T REMEMBER WHAT!
WHAT WAS IT?!
WAIT, REALLY? WAS IT PUD-DING?
NO.
ICE CREAM?
NO!

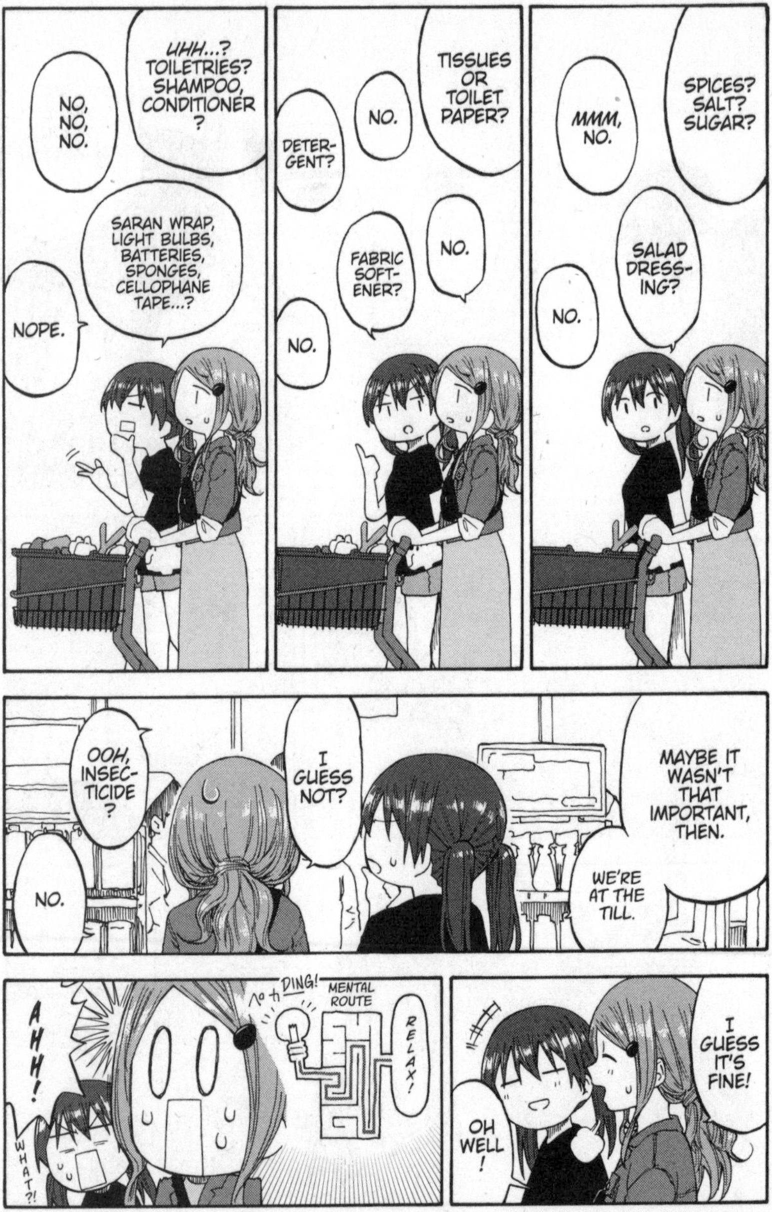
SPICES? SALT? SUGAR?
MMM, NO.
SALAD DRESS-ING?
NO.
TISSUES OR TOILET PAPER?
NO.
DETER-GENT?
NO.
FABRIC SOFT-ENER?
NO.
UHH...? TOILETRIES? SHAMPOO, CONDITIONER?
NO, NO, NO.
SARAN WRAP, LIGHT BULBS, BATTERIES, SPONGES, CELLOPHANE TAPE...?
NOPE.
MAYBE IT WASN'T THAT IMPORTANT, THEN.
WE'RE AT THE TILL.
I GUESS NOT?
OOH, INSEC-TICIDE?
NO.
I GUESS IT'S FINE!
OH WELL!
RELAX!
MENTAL ROUTE
DING!
AHH!
WHAT?!

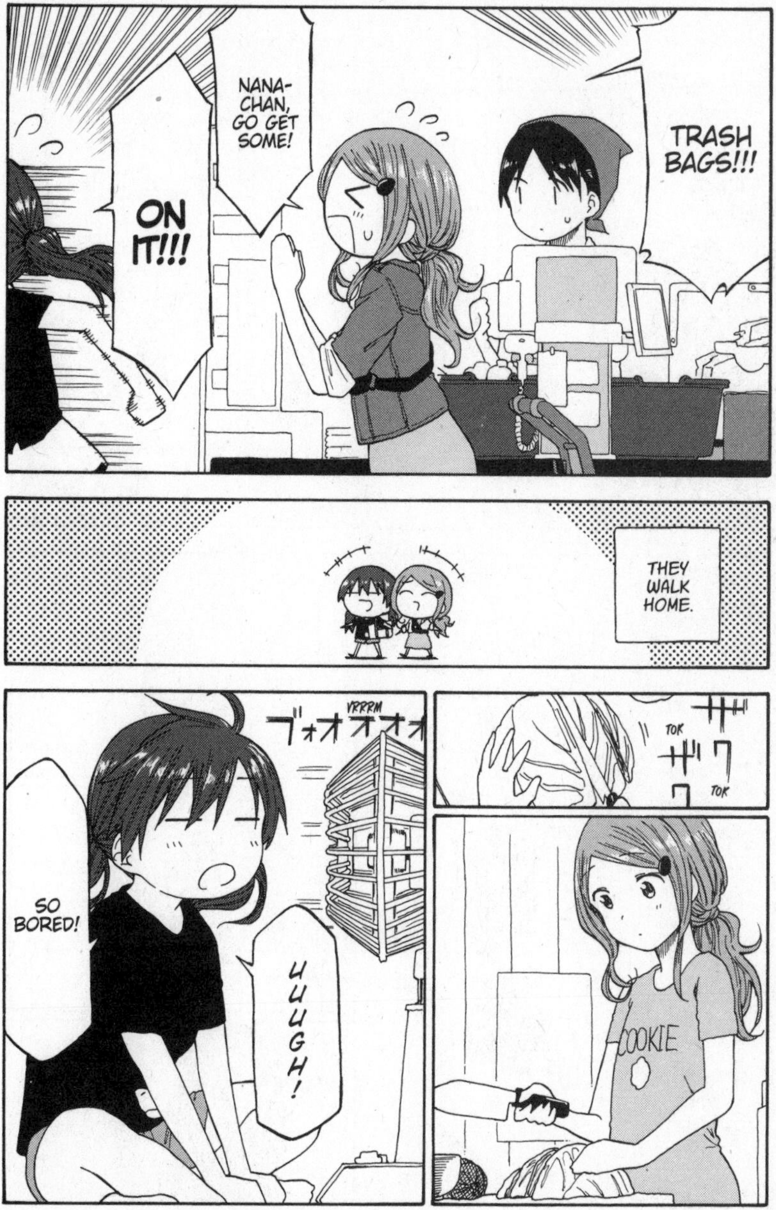
TRASH BAGS!!!
NANA-CHAN, GO GET SOME!
ON IT!!!
THEY WALK HOME.
ザク
TOK
ザク
TOK
ブォオオオオ
VRRRM
UUUGH!
SO BORED!

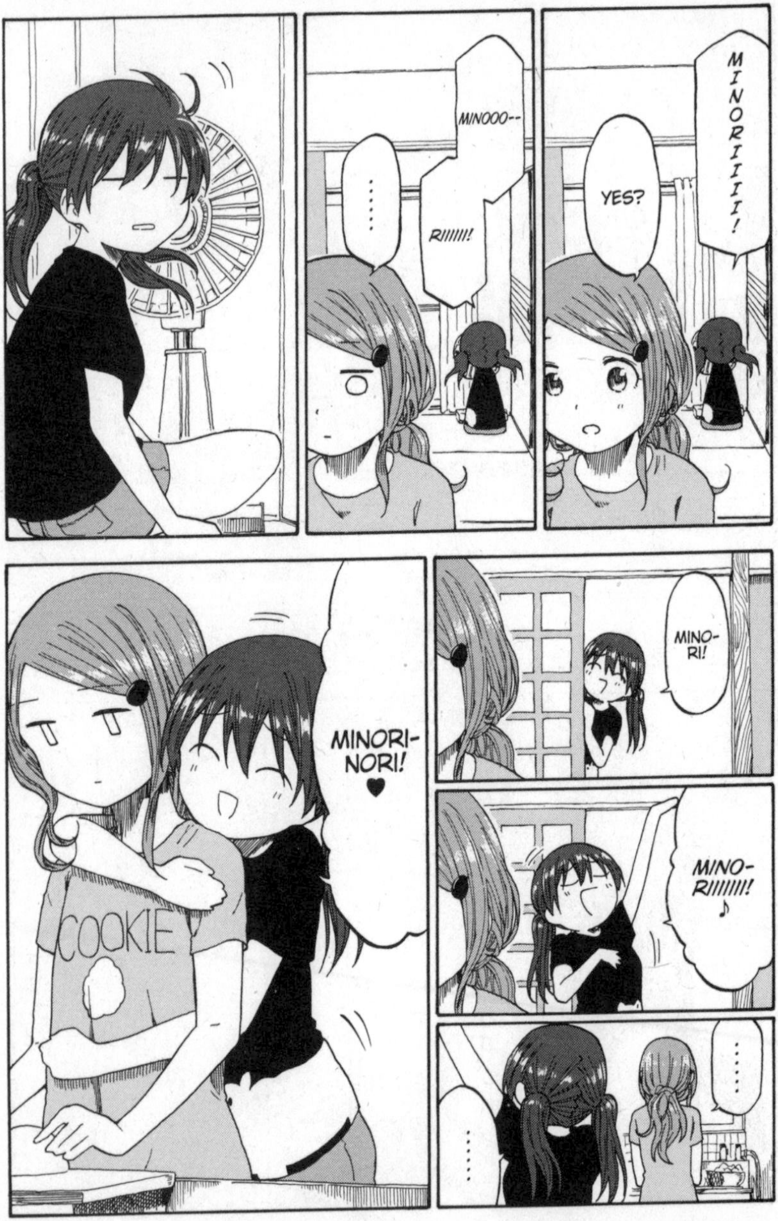
MINORIIIII!
YES?
MINOOO-- RIIIIII!
......
MINO-RI!
MINO-RIIIIIII! ♪
......
......
MINORI-NORI! ♥

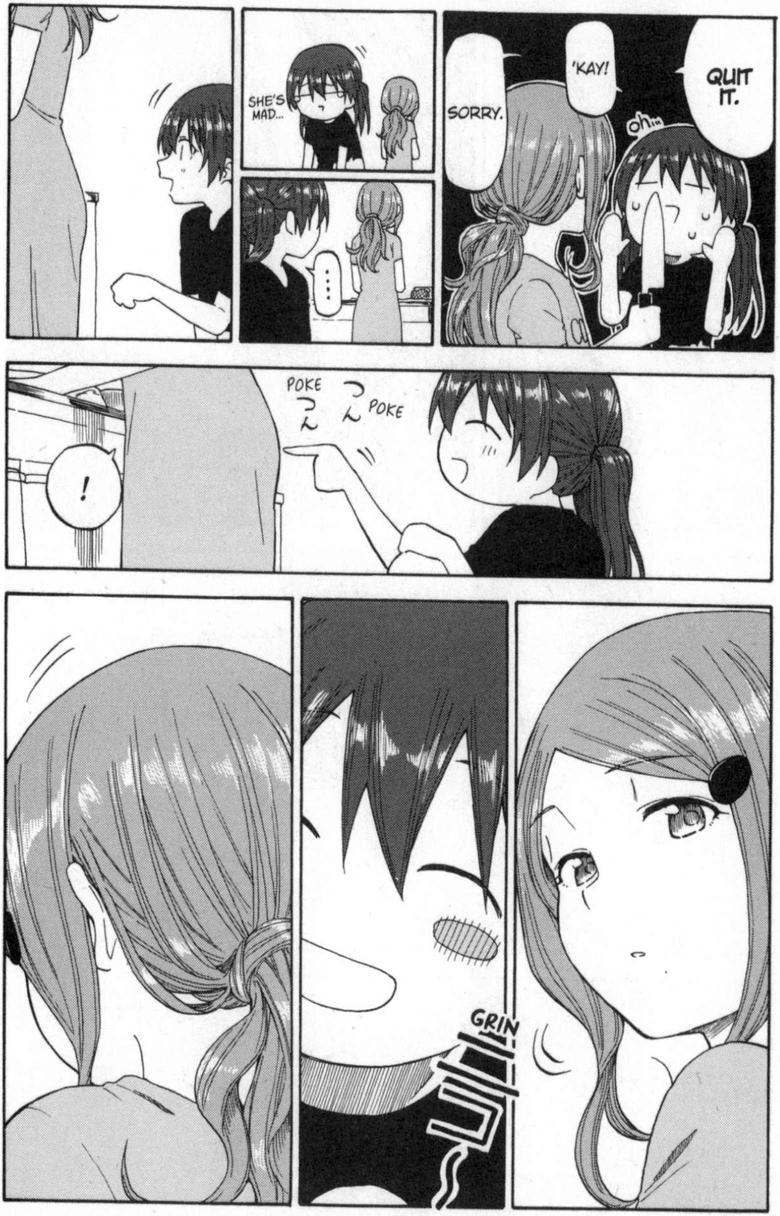
QUIT IT.
'KAY!
oh...
SORRY.
SHE'S MAD...
....
POKE
つん
POKE
つん
!
GRIN

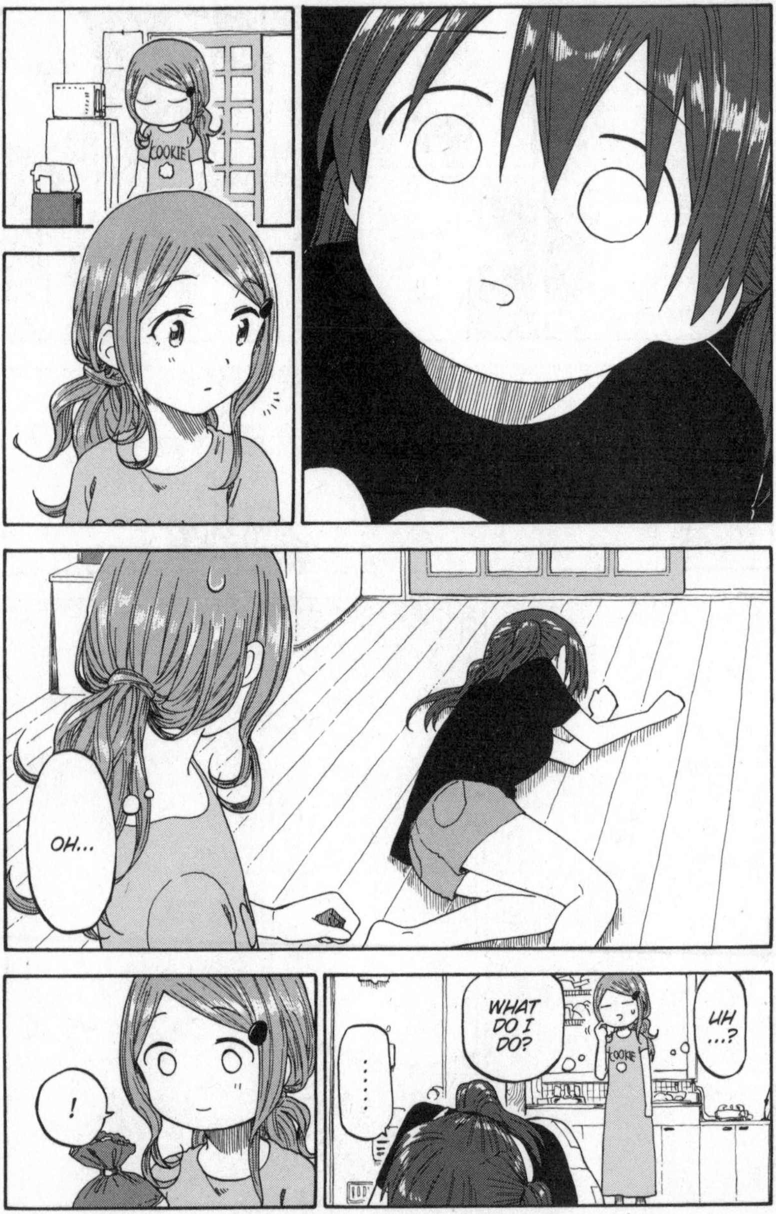
COOKIE
OH...
UH ...?
WHAT DO I DO?
......
!

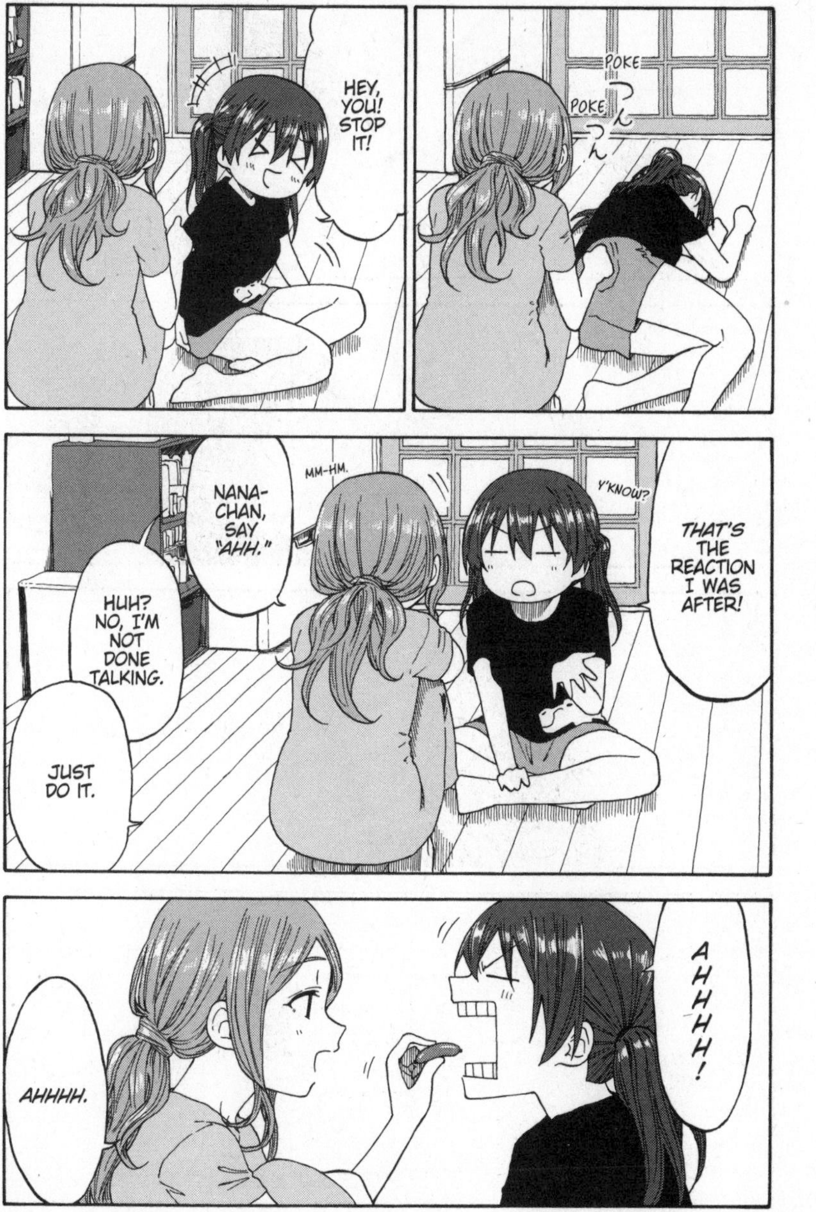

POKE
POKE
HEY, YOU! STOP IT!
THAT'S THE REACTION I WAS AFTER!
Y'KNOW?
MM-HM.
NANA-CHAN, SAY "AHH."
HUH? NO, I'M NOT DONE TALKING.
JUST DO IT.
AHHHHH!
AHHHH.

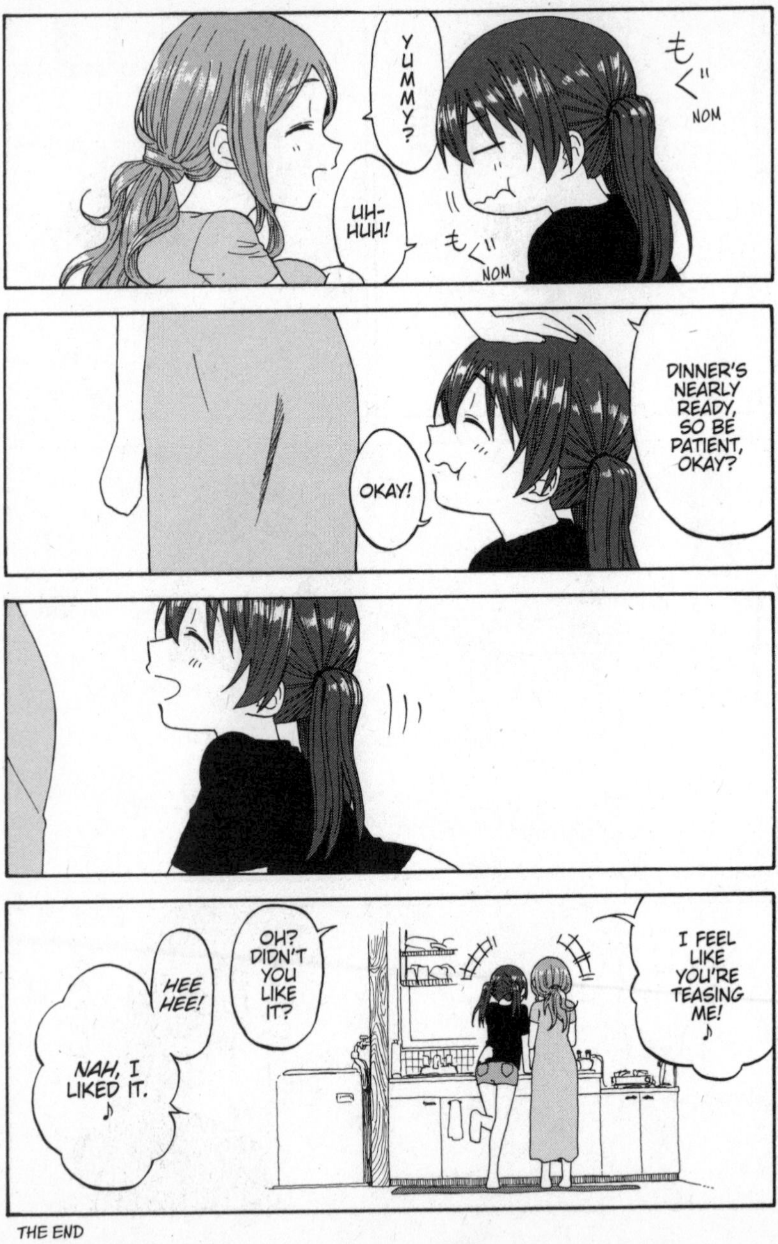
もぐ NOM
YUMMY?
UH-HUH!
もぐ NOM
DINNER'S NEARLY READY, SO BE PATIENT, OKAY?
OKAY!
I FEEL LIKE YOU'RE TEASING ME! ♪
OH? DIDN'T YOU LIKE IT?
HEE HEE!
NAH, I LIKED IT. ♪

THE END

Our **Wonderful Days**
Tsurezure Biyori

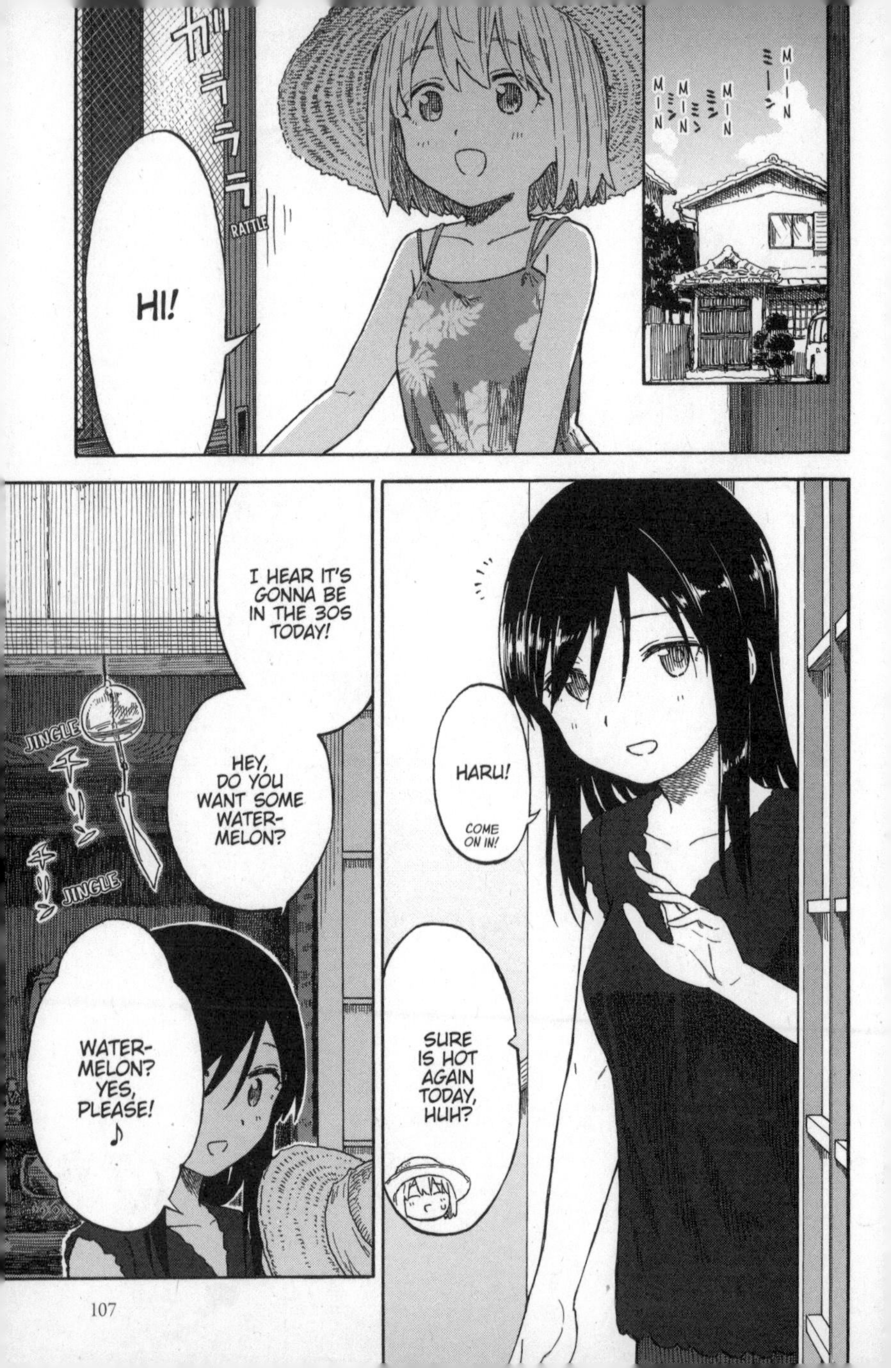
MI-N
MI-N
MI-N
MI-N
RATTLE
HI!
HARU!
COME ON IN!
SURE IS HOT AGAIN TODAY, HUH?
I HEAR IT'S GONNA BE IN THE 30S TODAY!
HEY, DO YOU WANT SOME WATER-MELON?
JINGLE
JINGLE
WATER-MELON? YES, PLEASE! ♪

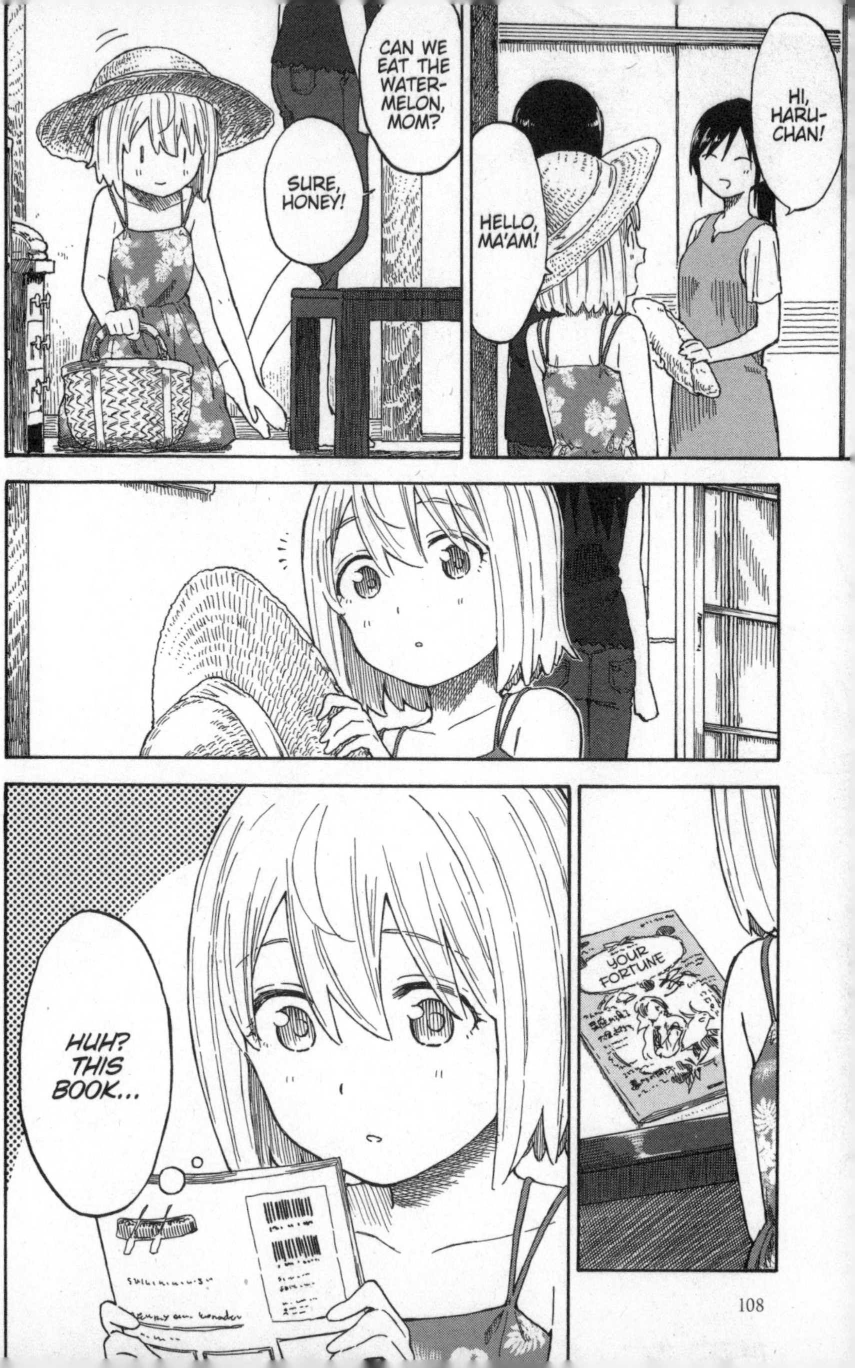
HI, HARU-CHAN!
HELLO, MA'AM!
CAN WE EAT THE WATER-MELON, MOM?
SURE, HONEY!
YOUR FORTUNE
HUH? THIS BOOK...

Chapter 17
A Taste of Watermelon

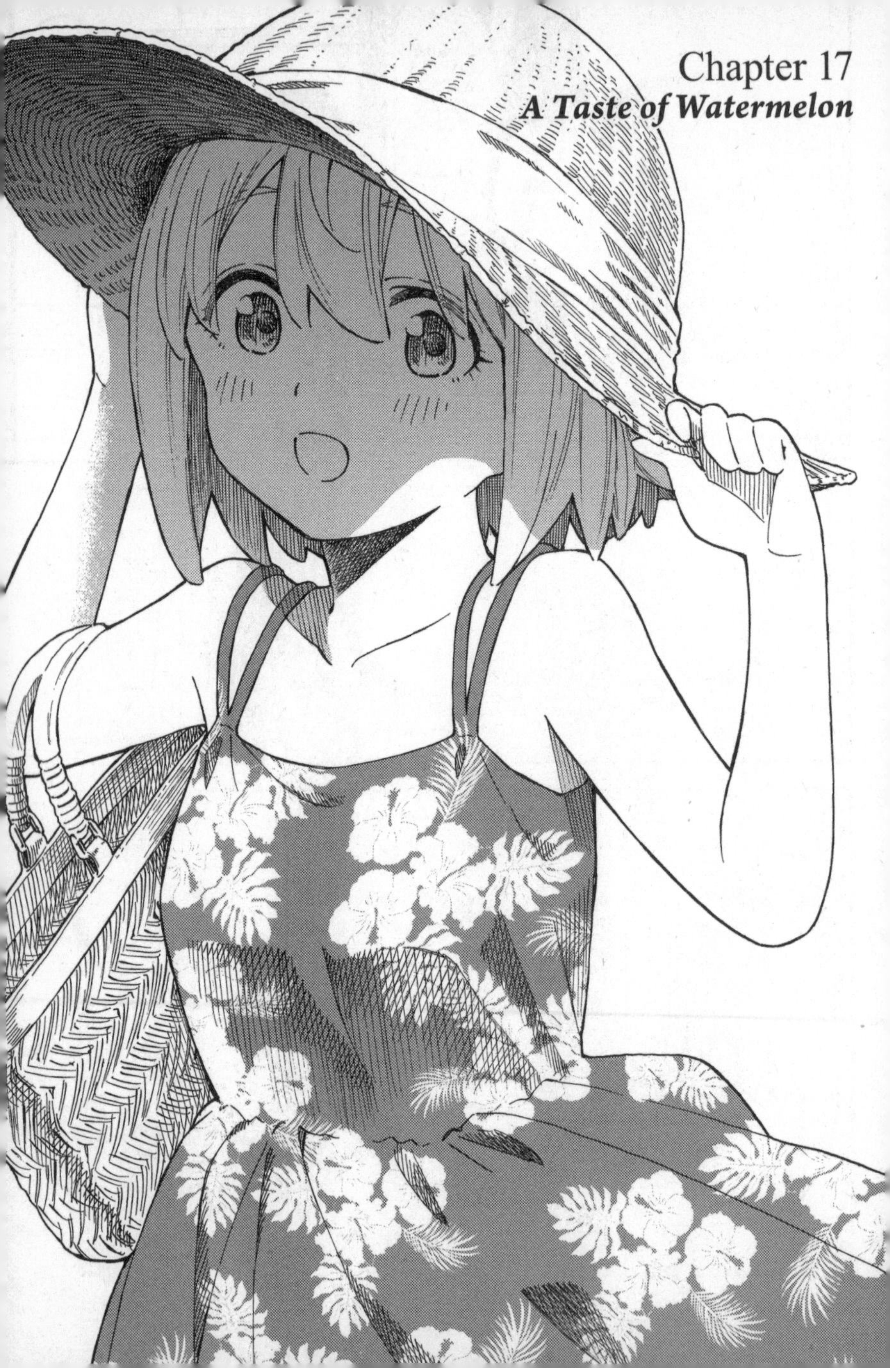

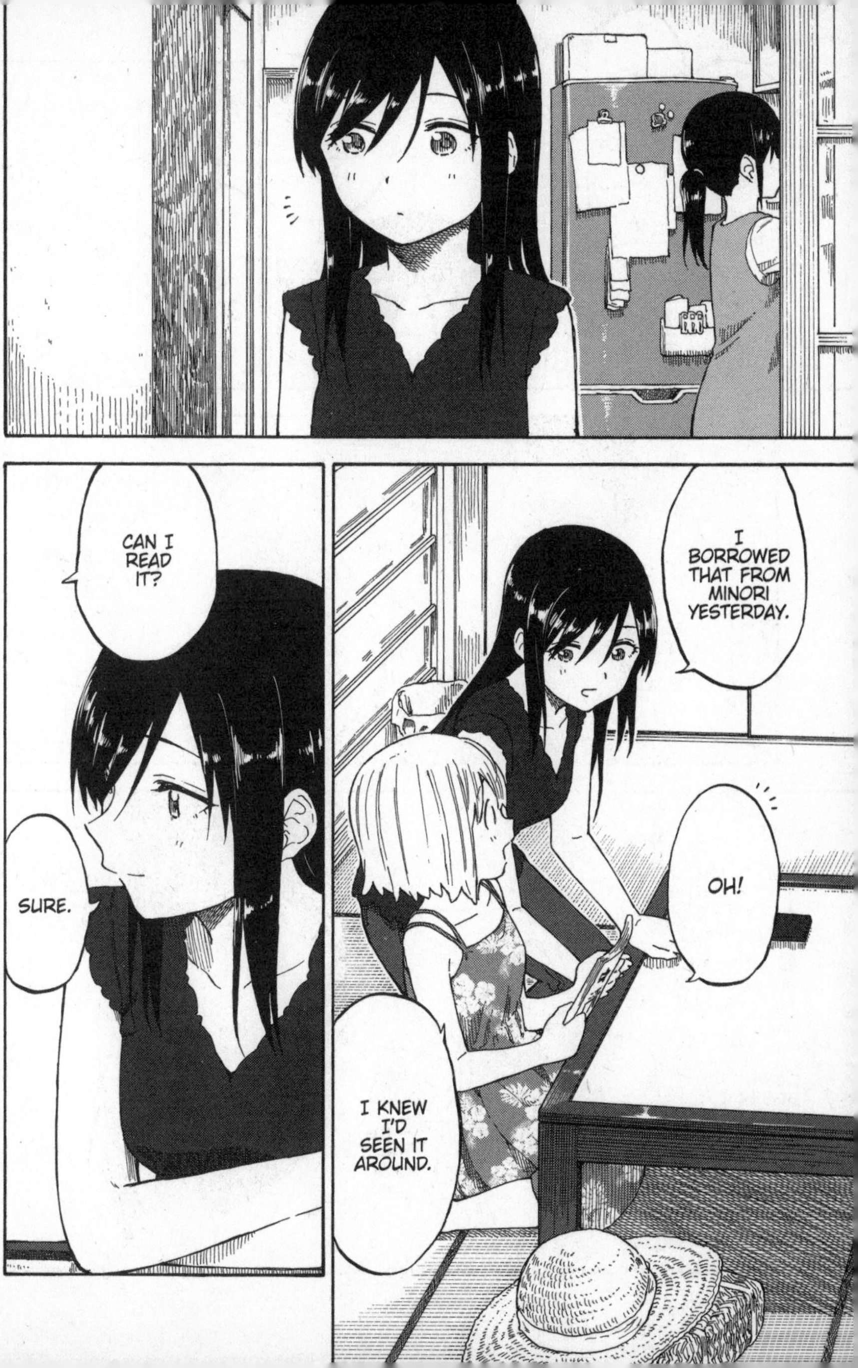
I BORROWED THAT FROM MINORI YESTERDAY.
OH!
I KNEW I'D SEEN IT AROUND.
CAN I READ IT?
SURE.

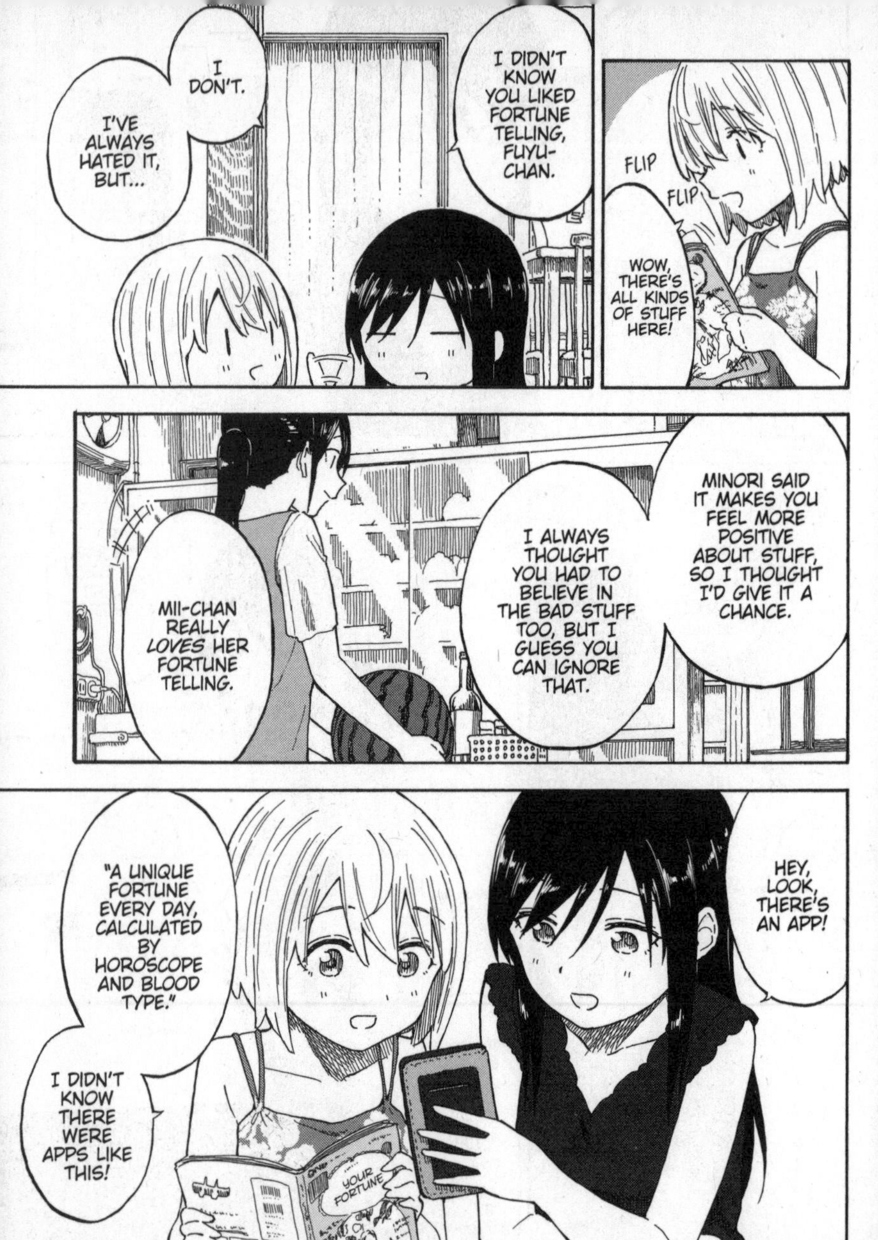
FLIP
FLIP
WOW, THERE'S ALL KINDS OF STUFF HERE!
I DIDN'T KNOW YOU LIKED FORTUNE TELLING, FUYU-CHAN.
I DON'T.
I'VE ALWAYS HATED IT, BUT...
MINORI SAID IT MAKES YOU FEEL MORE POSITIVE ABOUT STUFF, SO I THOUGHT I'D GIVE IT A CHANCE.
I ALWAYS THOUGHT YOU HAD TO BELIEVE IN THE BAD STUFF TOO, BUT I GUESS YOU CAN IGNORE THAT.
MII-CHAN REALLY *LOVES* HER FORTUNE TELLING.
HEY, LOOK, THERE'S AN APP!
YOUR FORTUNE
"A UNIQUE FORTUNE EVERY DAY, CALCULATED BY HOROSCOPE AND BLOOD TYPE."
I DIDN'T KNOW THERE WERE APPS LIKE THIS!

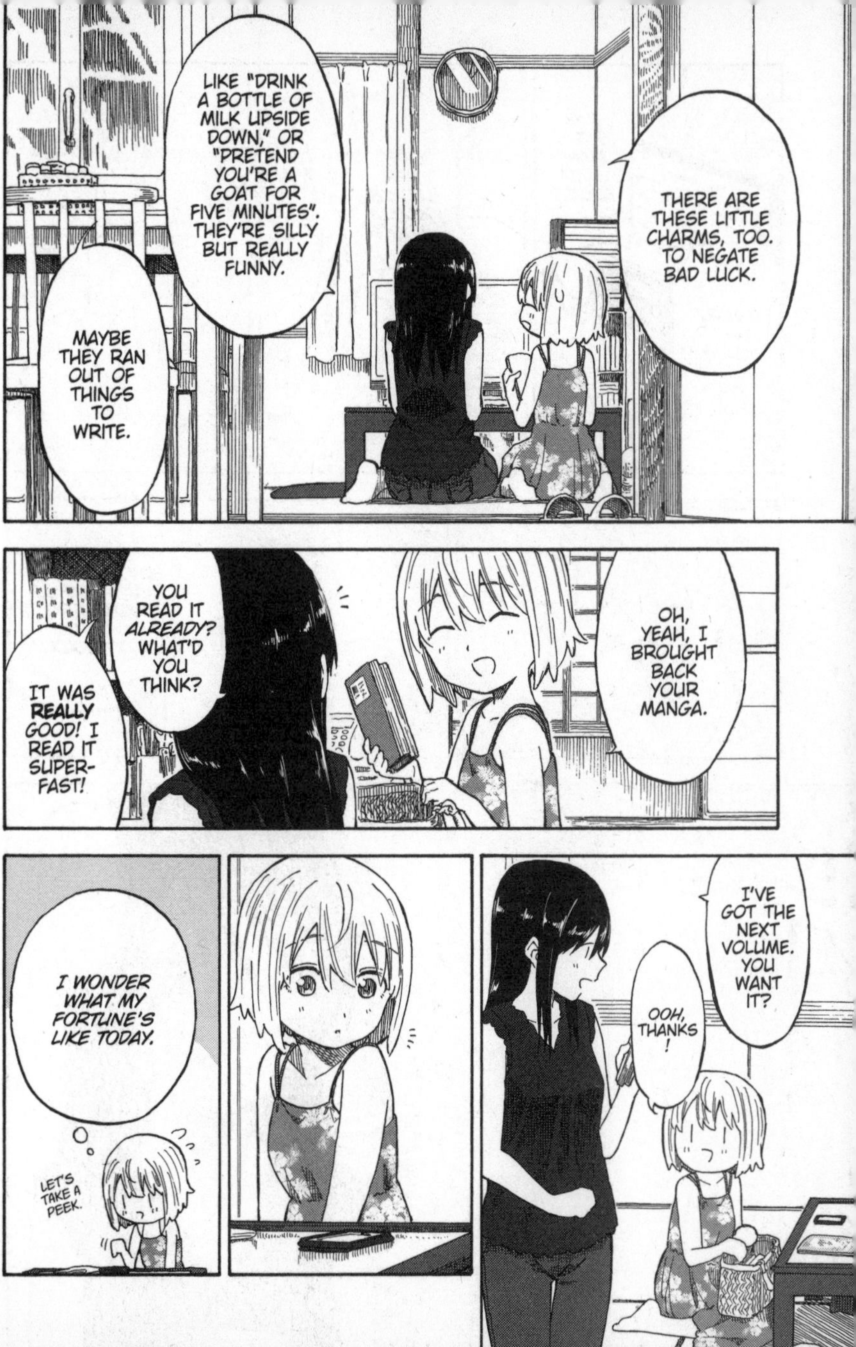
THERE ARE THESE LITTLE CHARMS, TOO. TO NEGATE BAD LUCK.
LIKE "DRINK A BOTTLE OF MILK UPSIDE DOWN," OR "PRETEND YOU'RE A GOAT FOR FIVE MINUTES". THEY'RE SILLY BUT REALLY FUNNY.
MAYBE THEY RAN OUT OF THINGS TO WRITE.
OH, YEAH, I BROUGHT BACK YOUR MANGA.
YOU READ IT *ALREADY*? WHAT'D YOU THINK?
IT WAS **REALLY** GOOD! I READ IT SUPER-FAST!
I'VE GOT THE NEXT VOLUME. YOU WANT IT?
OOH, THANKS!
I WONDER WHAT MY FORTUNE'S LIKE TODAY.
LET'S TAKE A PEEK.

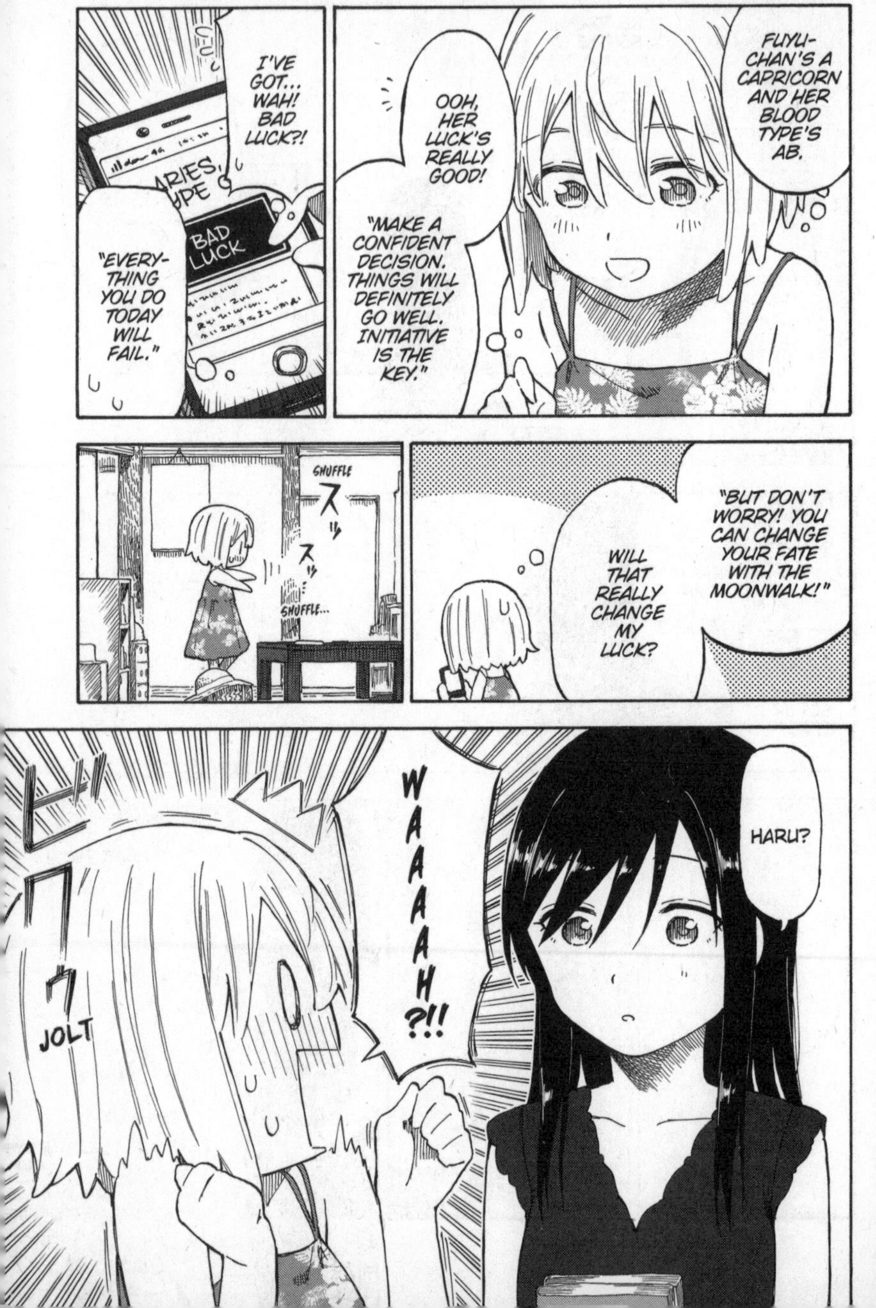

FUYU-CHAN'S A CAPRICORN AND HER BLOOD TYPE'S AB.
OOH, HER LUCK'S REALLY GOOD!
"MAKE A CONFIDENT DECISION. THINGS WILL DEFINITELY GO WELL. INITIATIVE IS THE KEY."
I'VE GOT... WAH! BAD LUCK?!
BAD LUCK
"EVERYTHING YOU DO TODAY WILL FAIL."
"BUT DON'T WORRY! YOU CAN CHANGE YOUR FATE WITH THE MOONWALK!"
WILL THAT REALLY CHANGE MY LUCK?
SHUFFLE
スッ
スッ
SHUFFLE...
HARU?
WAAAAAH?!!
ビクッ
JOLT

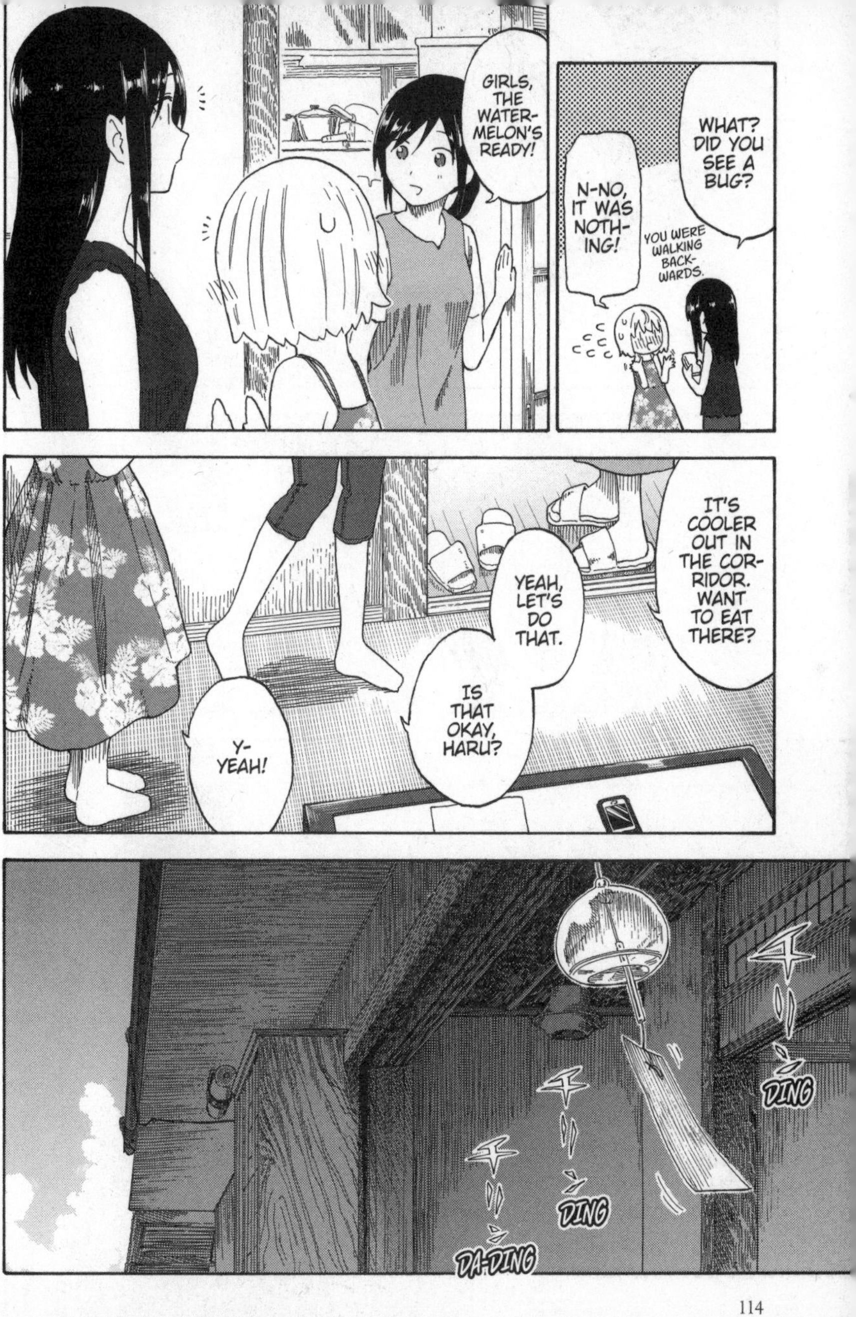
WHAT? DID YOU SEE A BUG?
N-NO, IT WAS NOTH-ING!
YOU WERE WALKING BACK-WARDS.
GIRLS, THE WATER-MELON'S READY!
IT'S COOLER OUT IN THE COR-RIDOR. WANT TO EAT THERE?
YEAH, LET'S DO THAT.
IS THAT OKAY, HARU?
Y-YEAH!
DING
DING
DA-DING

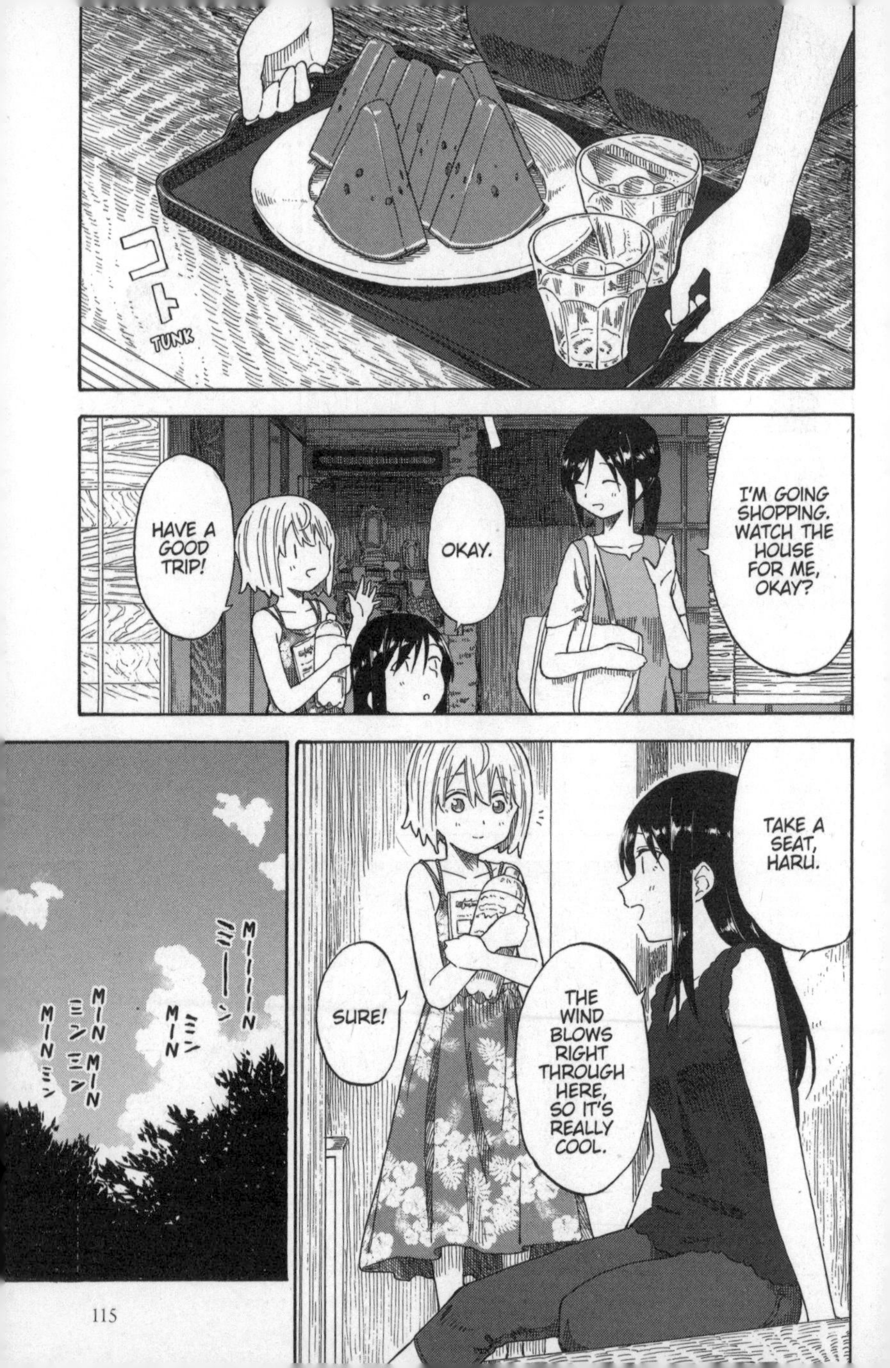
コト
TUNK
I'M GOING SHOPPING. WATCH THE HOUSE FOR ME, OKAY?
OKAY.
HAVE A GOOD TRIP!
TAKE A SEAT, HARU.
THE WIND BLOWS RIGHT THROUGH HERE, SO IT'S REALLY COOL.
SURE!
ミーーン
MIIIIN
ミン
MIN
ミンミンミン
MIN MIN MIN

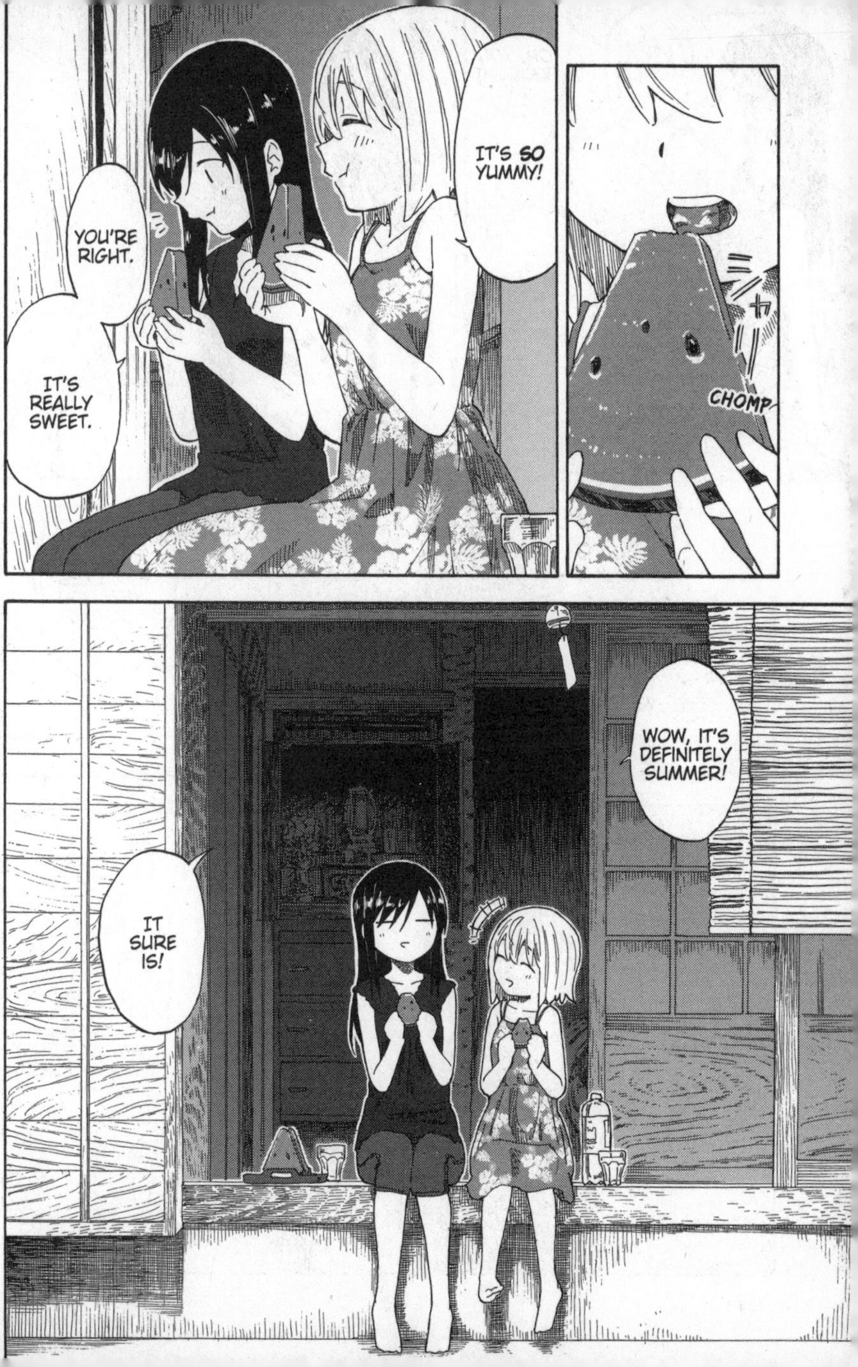
CHOMP
IT'S SO YUMMY!
YOU'RE RIGHT.
IT'S REALLY SWEET.
WOW, IT'S DEFINITELY SUMMER!
IT SURE IS!

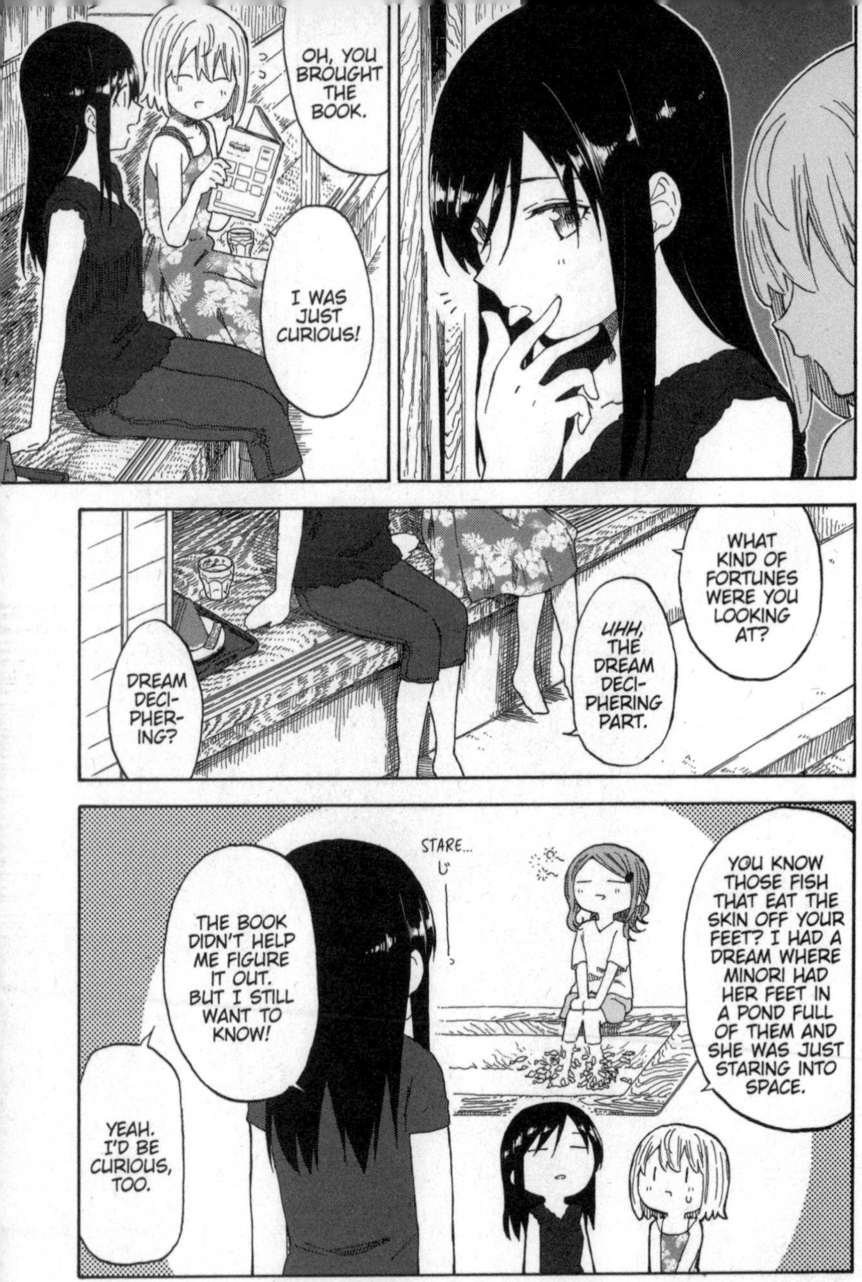
OH, YOU BROUGHT THE BOOK.
I WAS JUST CURIOUS!
WHAT KIND OF FORTUNES WERE YOU LOOKING AT?
UHH, THE DREAM DECI-PHERING PART.
DREAM DECI-PHER-ING?
YOU KNOW THOSE FISH THAT EAT THE SKIN OFF YOUR FEET? I HAD A DREAM WHERE MINORI HAD HER FEET IN A POND FULL OF THEM AND SHE WAS JUST STARING INTO SPACE.
STARE...
じー
THE BOOK DIDN'T HELP ME FIGURE IT OUT. BUT I STILL WANT TO KNOW!
YEAH. I'D BE CURIOUS, TOO.

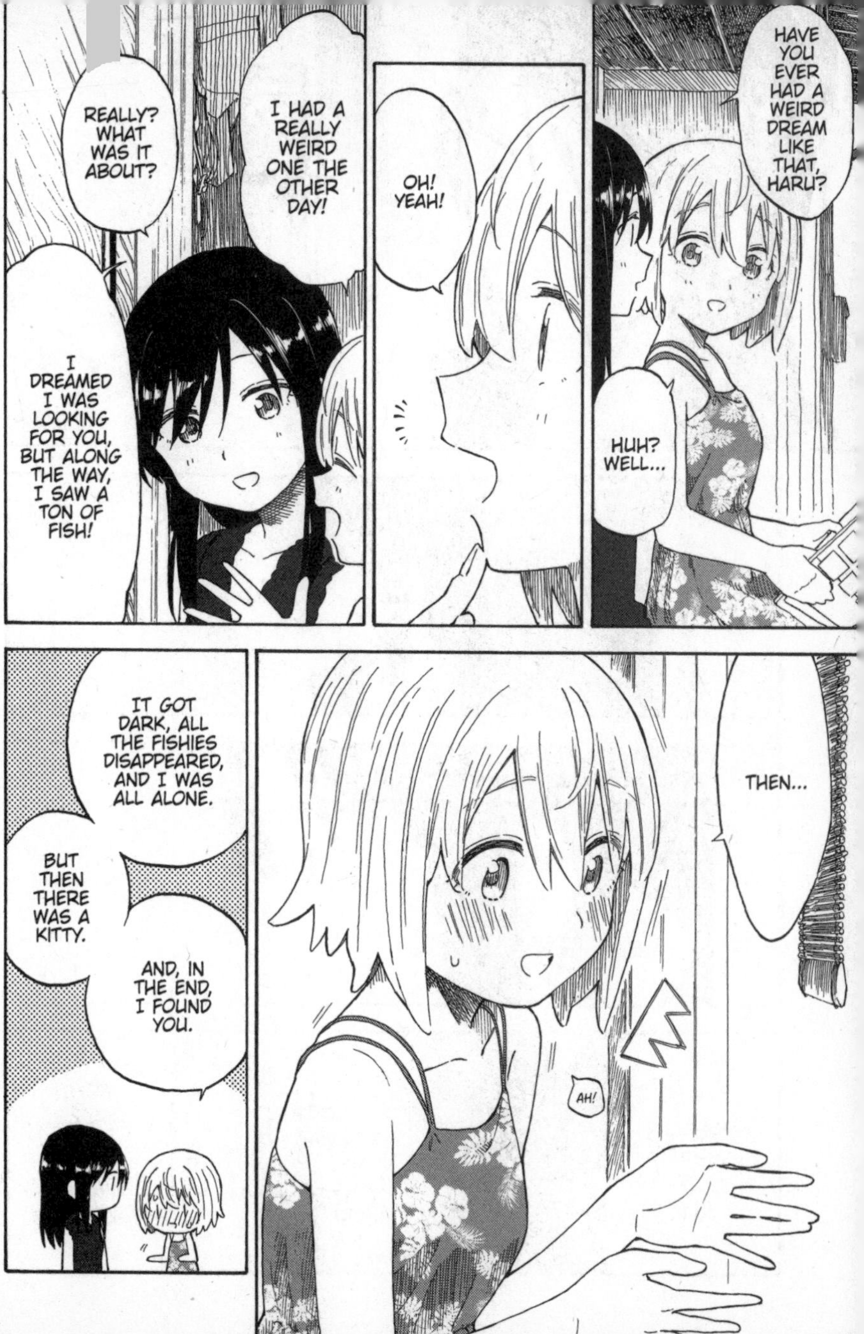
HAVE YOU EVER HAD A WEIRD DREAM LIKE THAT, HARU?
HUH? WELL...
OH! YEAH!
I HAD A REALLY WEIRD ONE THE OTHER DAY!
REALLY? WHAT WAS IT ABOUT?
I DREAMED I WAS LOOKING FOR YOU, BUT ALONG THE WAY, I SAW A TON OF FISH!
THEN...
AH!
IT GOT DARK, ALL THE FISHIES DISAPPEARED, AND I WAS ALL ALONE.
BUT THEN THERE WAS A KITTY.
AND, IN THE END, I FOUND YOU.

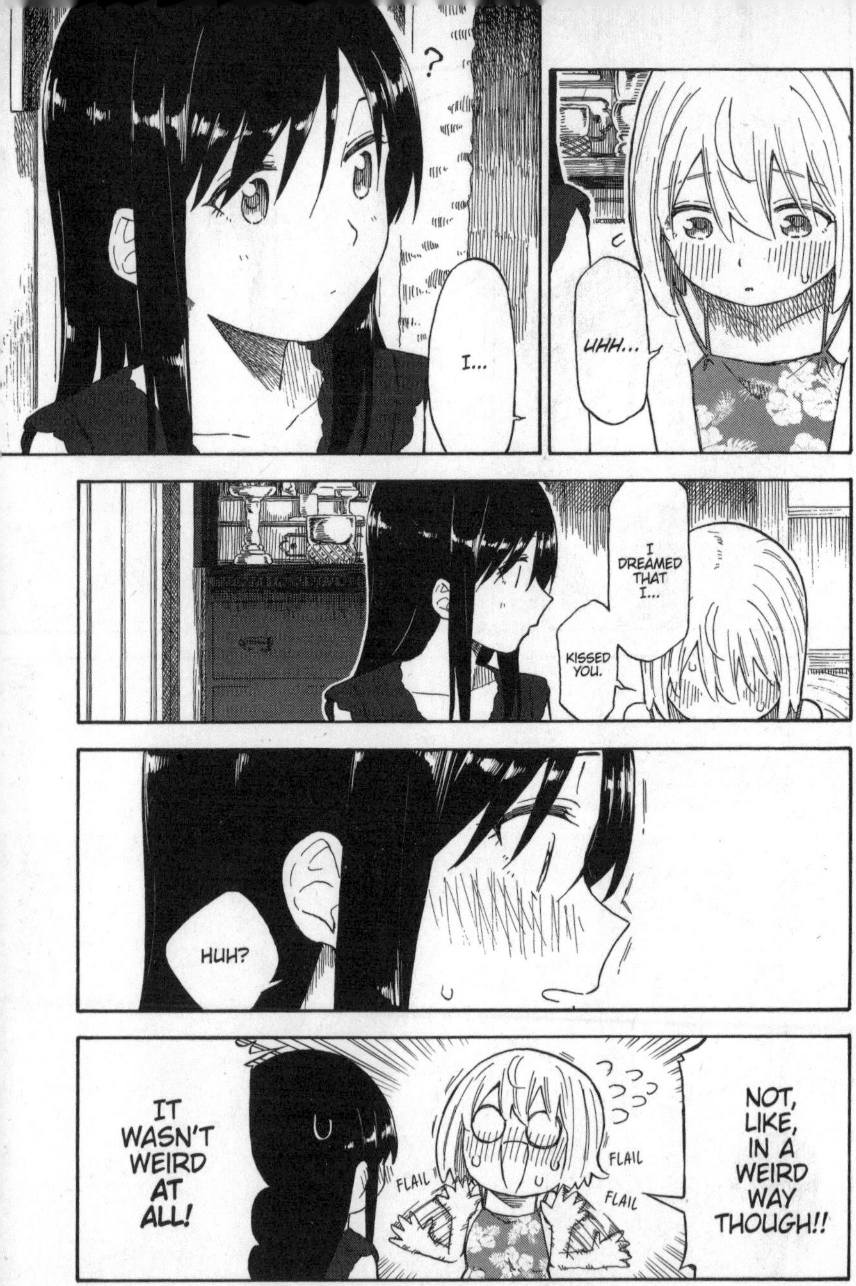
UHH...
?
I...
I DREAMED THAT I...
KISSED YOU.
HUH?
NOT, LIKE, IN A WEIRD WAY THOUGH!!
FLAIL
FLAIL
FLAIL
IT WASN'T WEIRD AT ALL!

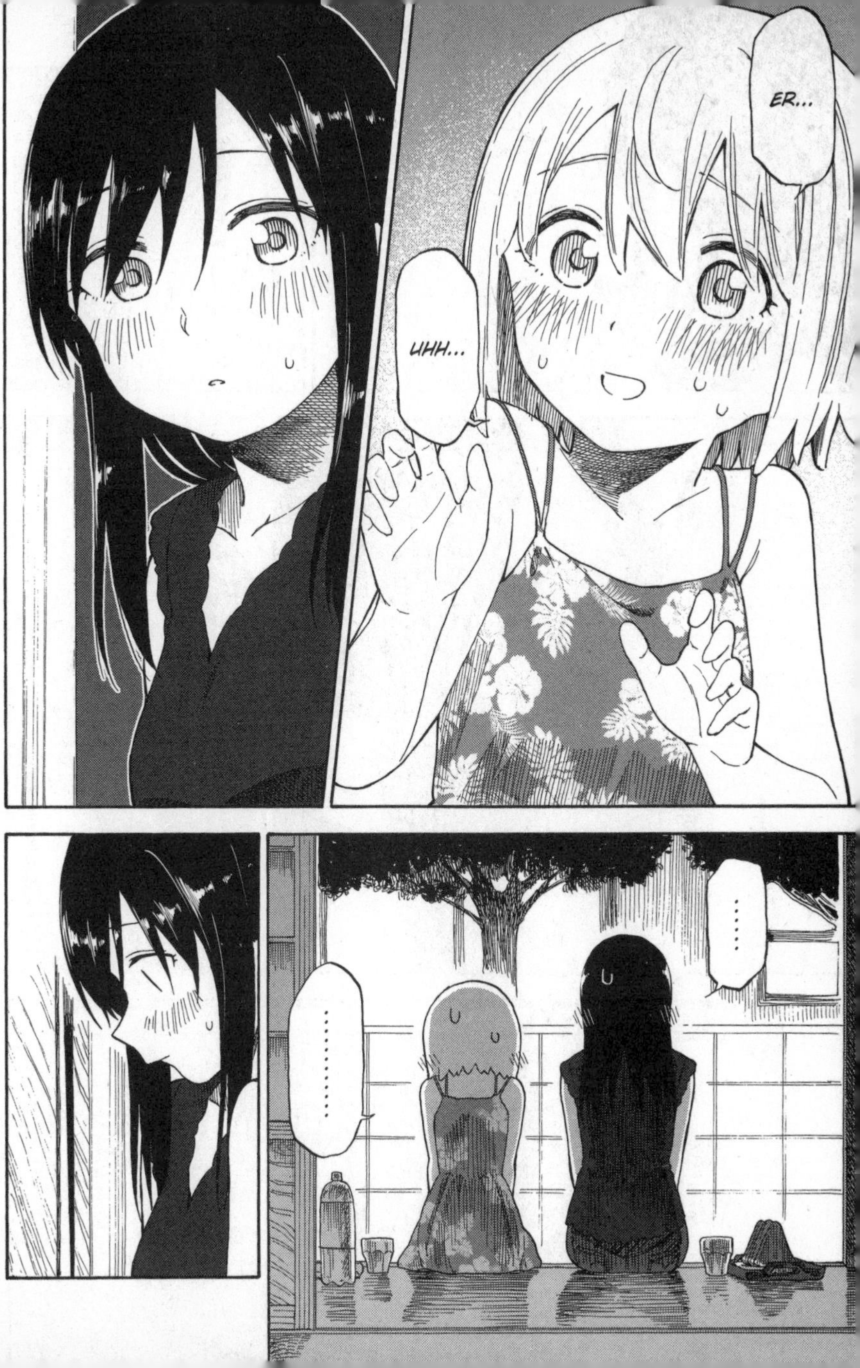
ER...
UHH...
......
....

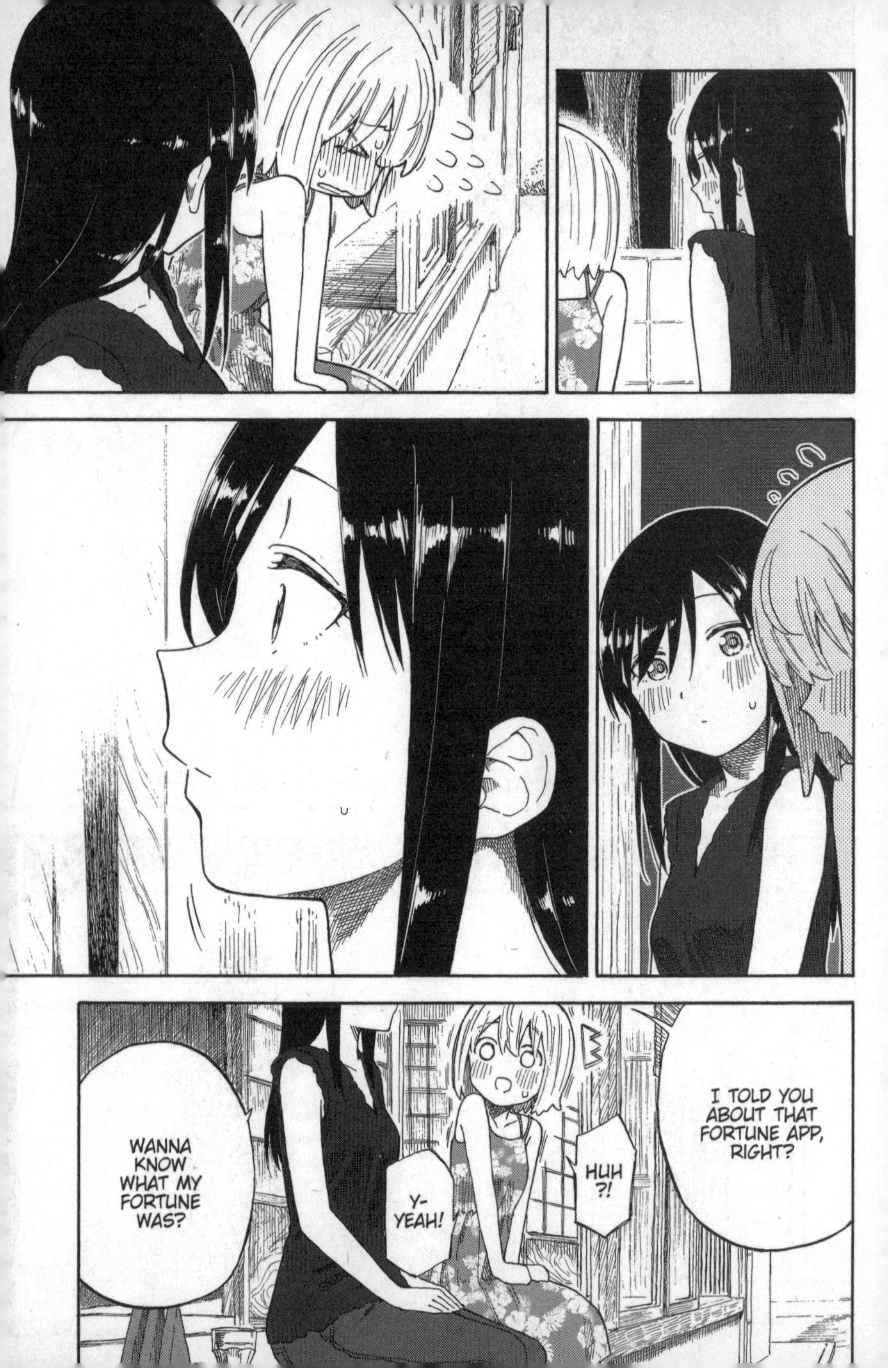
I TOLD YOU ABOUT THAT FORTUNE APP, RIGHT?
HUH ?!
Y- YEAH!
WANNA KNOW WHAT MY FORTUNE WAS?

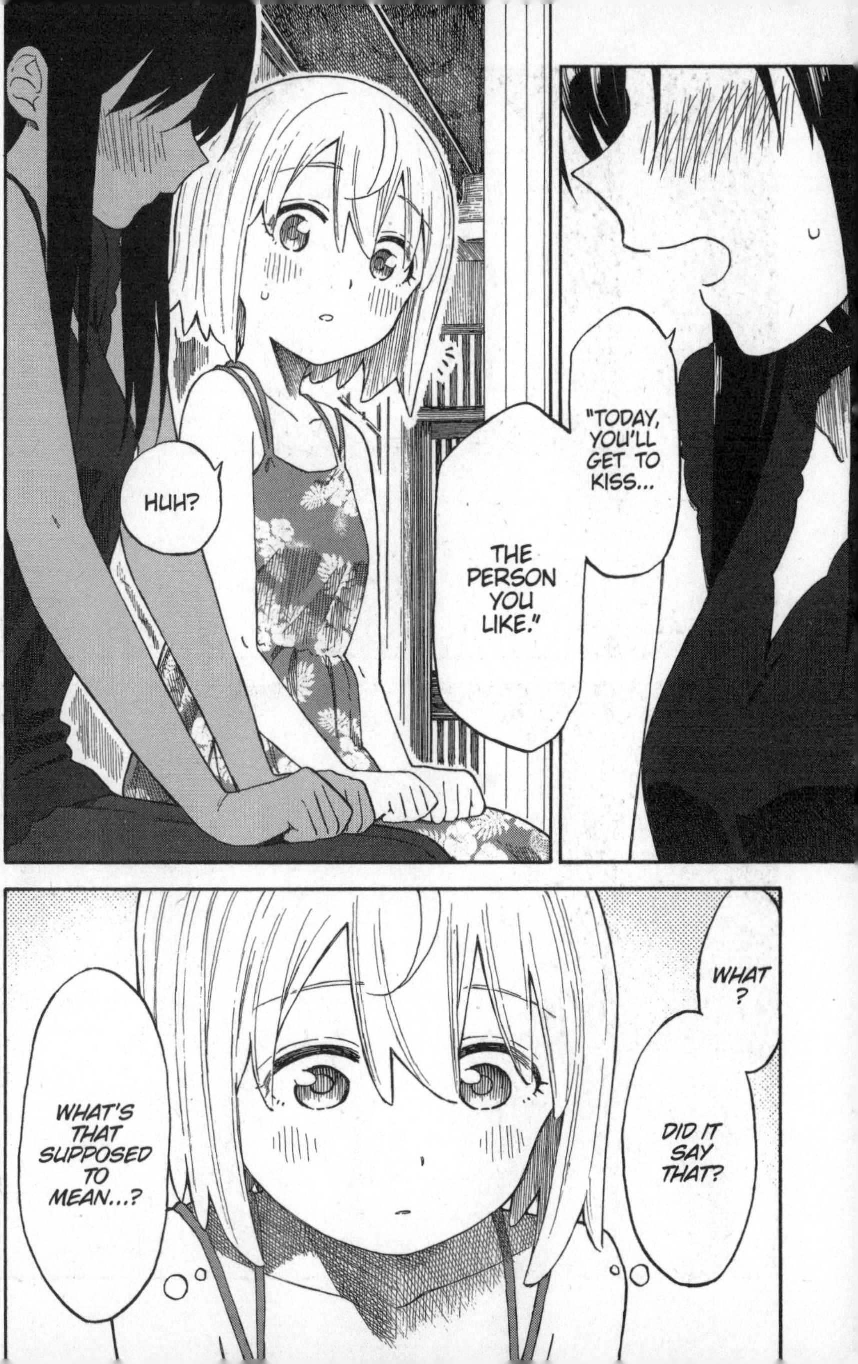
"TODAY, YOU'LL GET TO KISS...
THE PERSON YOU LIKE."
HUH?
WHAT?
DID IT SAY THAT?
WHAT'S THAT SUPPOSED TO MEAN...?

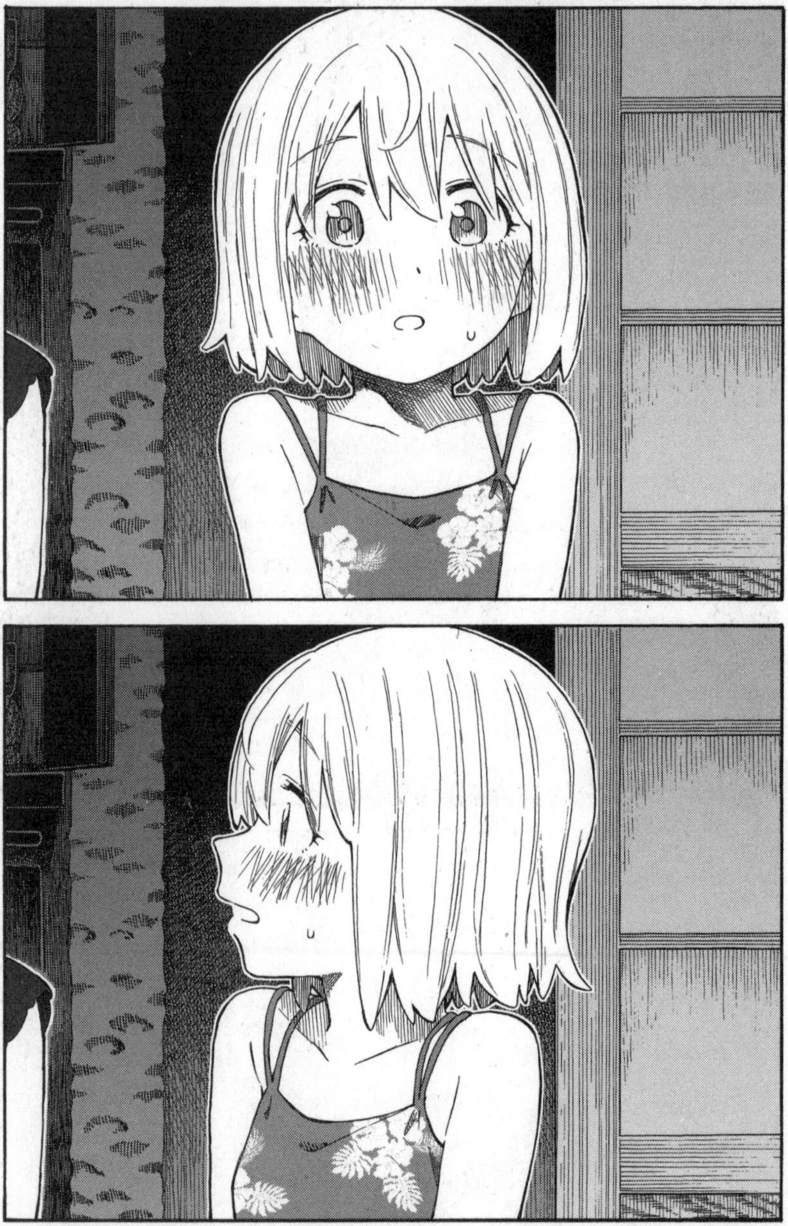

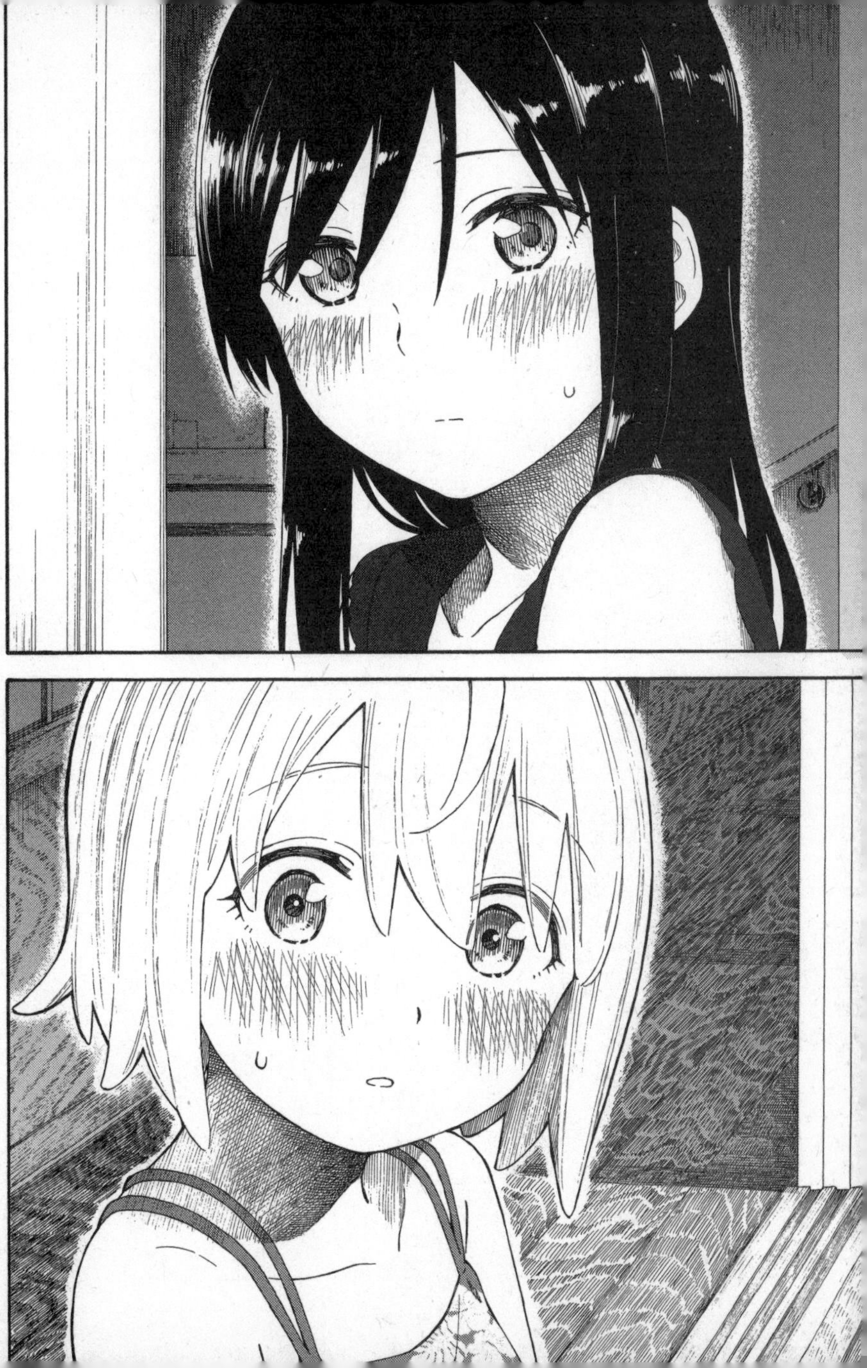

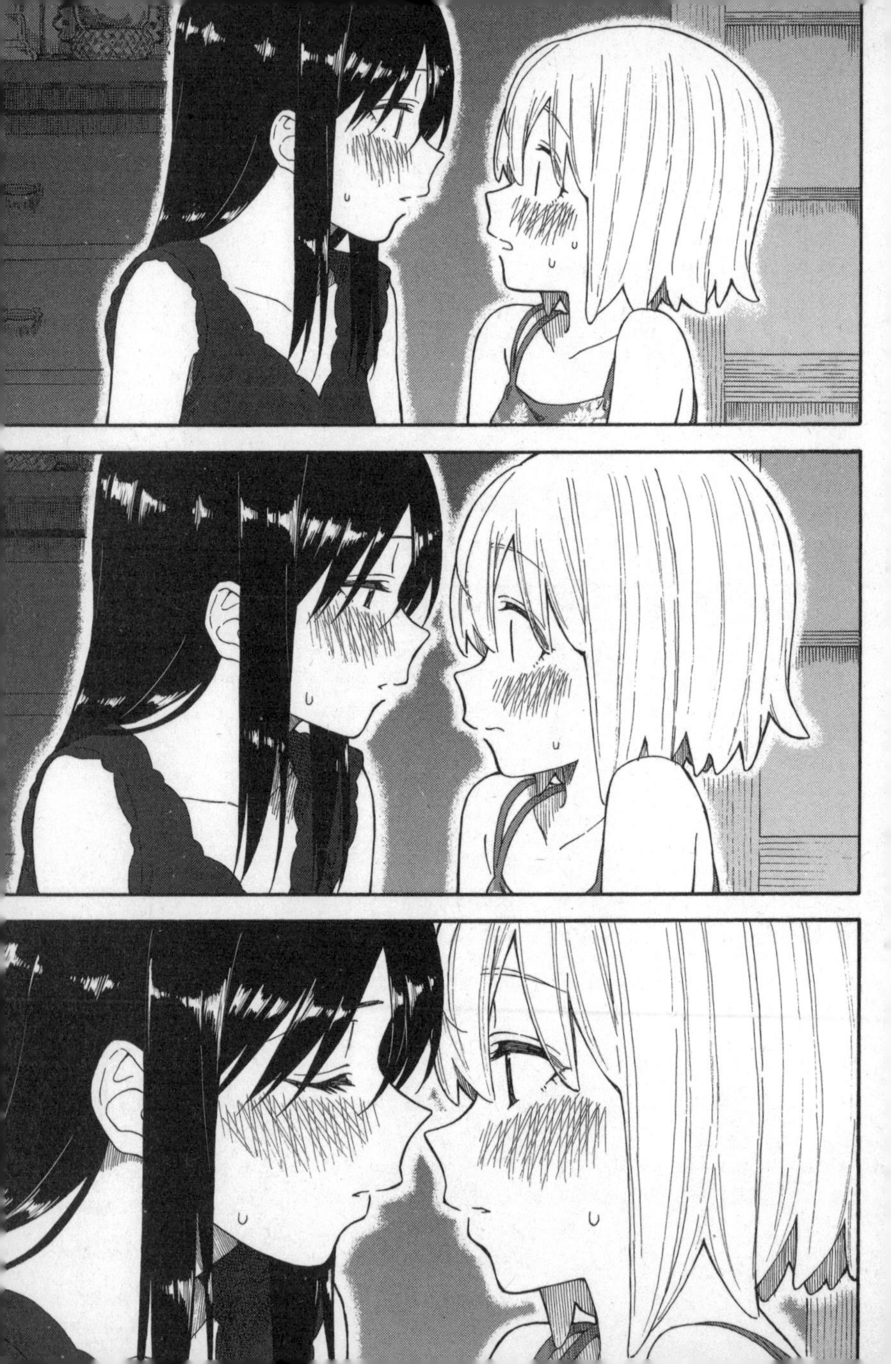

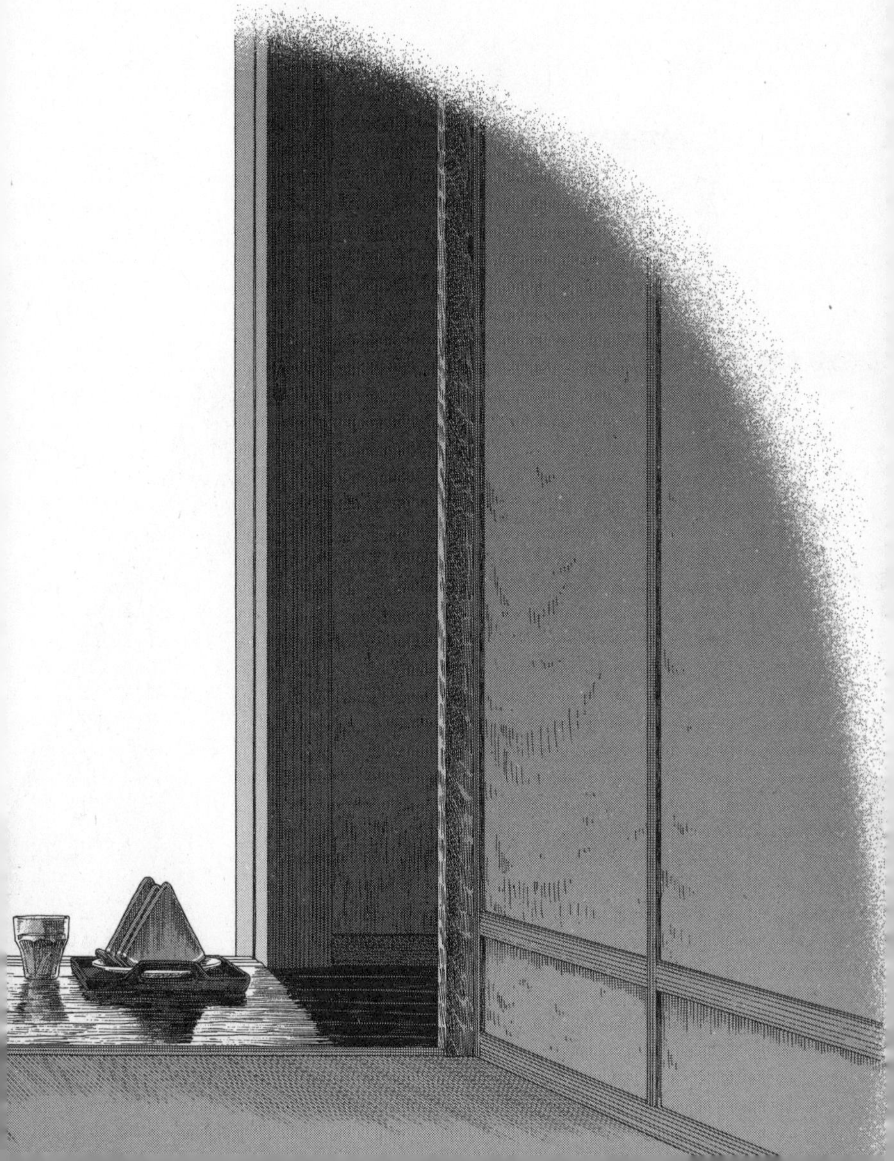

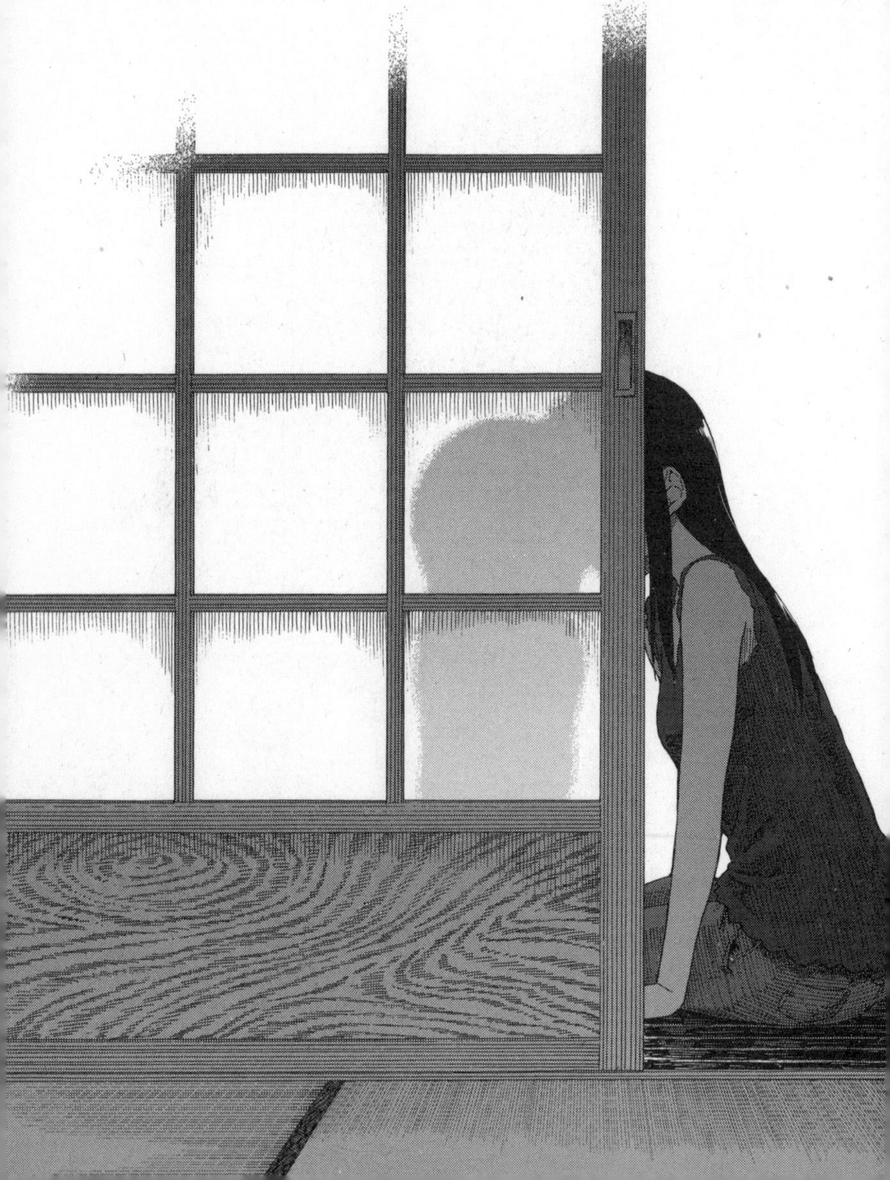

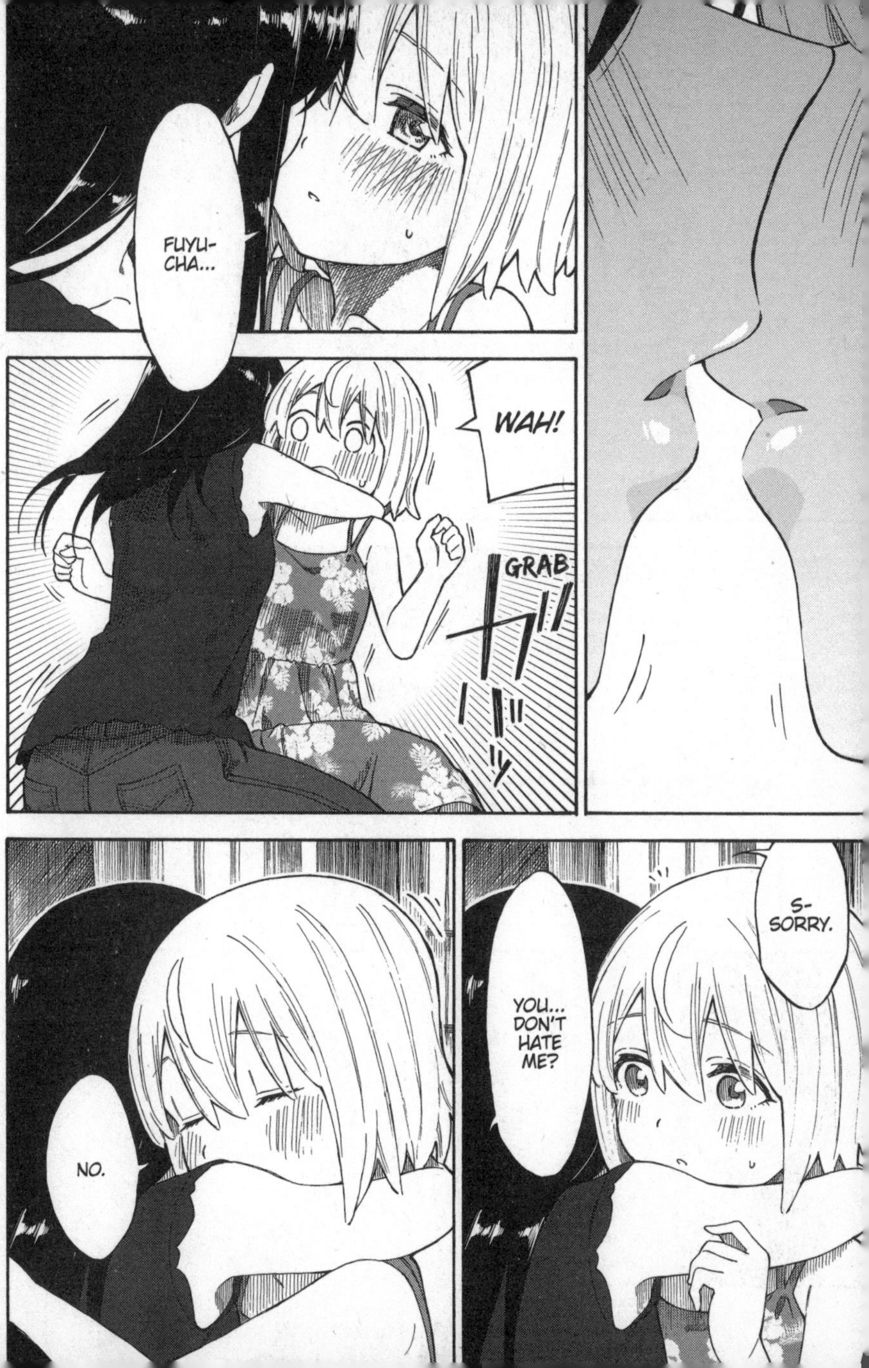

FUYU-CHA...
WAH!
GRAB
S-SORRY.
YOU... DON'T HATE ME?
NO.

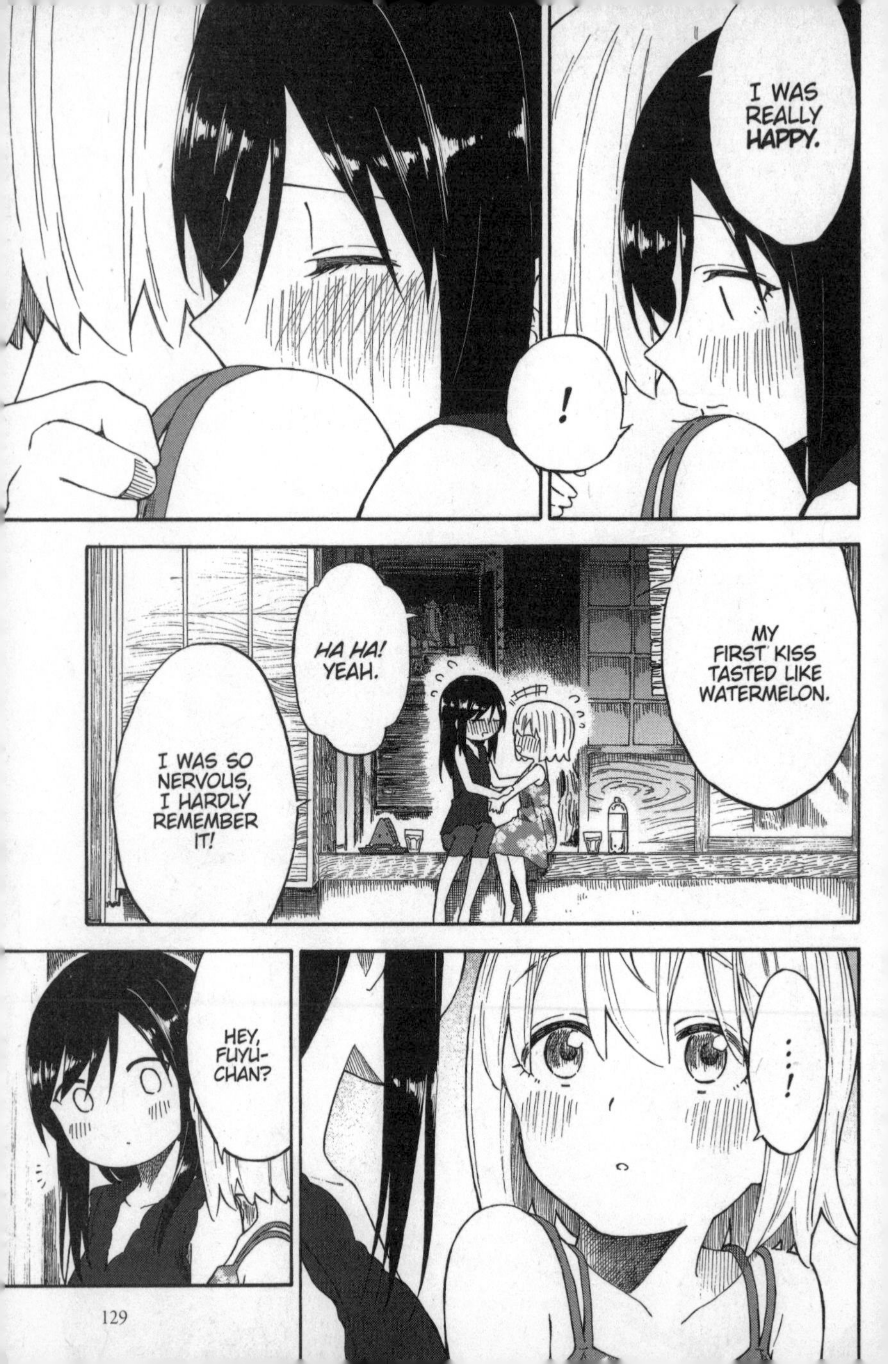

I WAS REALLY HAPPY.
!
MY FIRST KISS TASTED LIKE WATERMELON.
HA HA! YEAH.
I WAS SO NERVOUS, I HARDLY REMEMBER IT!
…!
HEY, FUYU-CHAN?

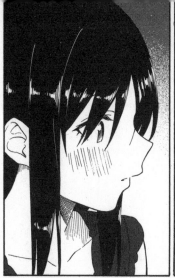

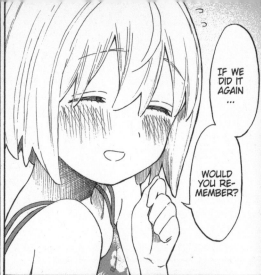

IF WE DID IT AGAIN...

WOULD YOU RE-MEMBER?

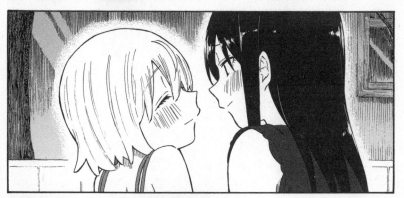

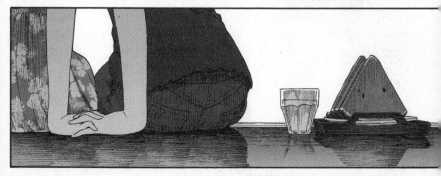

Our Wonderful Days

story & art by Kei Hamuro

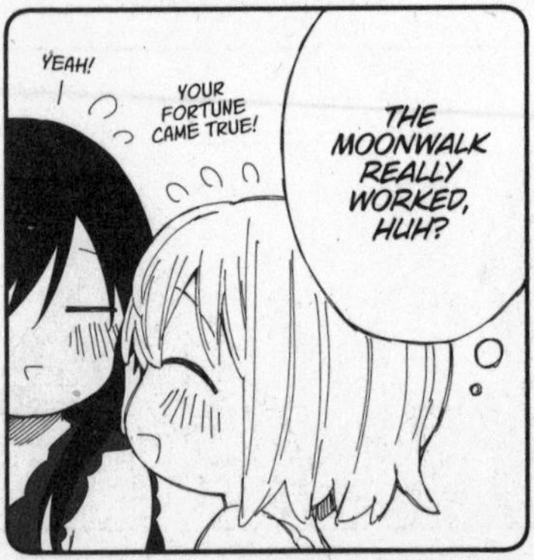

THE MOONWALK REALLY WORKED, HUH?
YOUR FORTUNE CAME TRUE!
YEAH!

Our *Wonderful* Days
Days Tsurezure Biyori

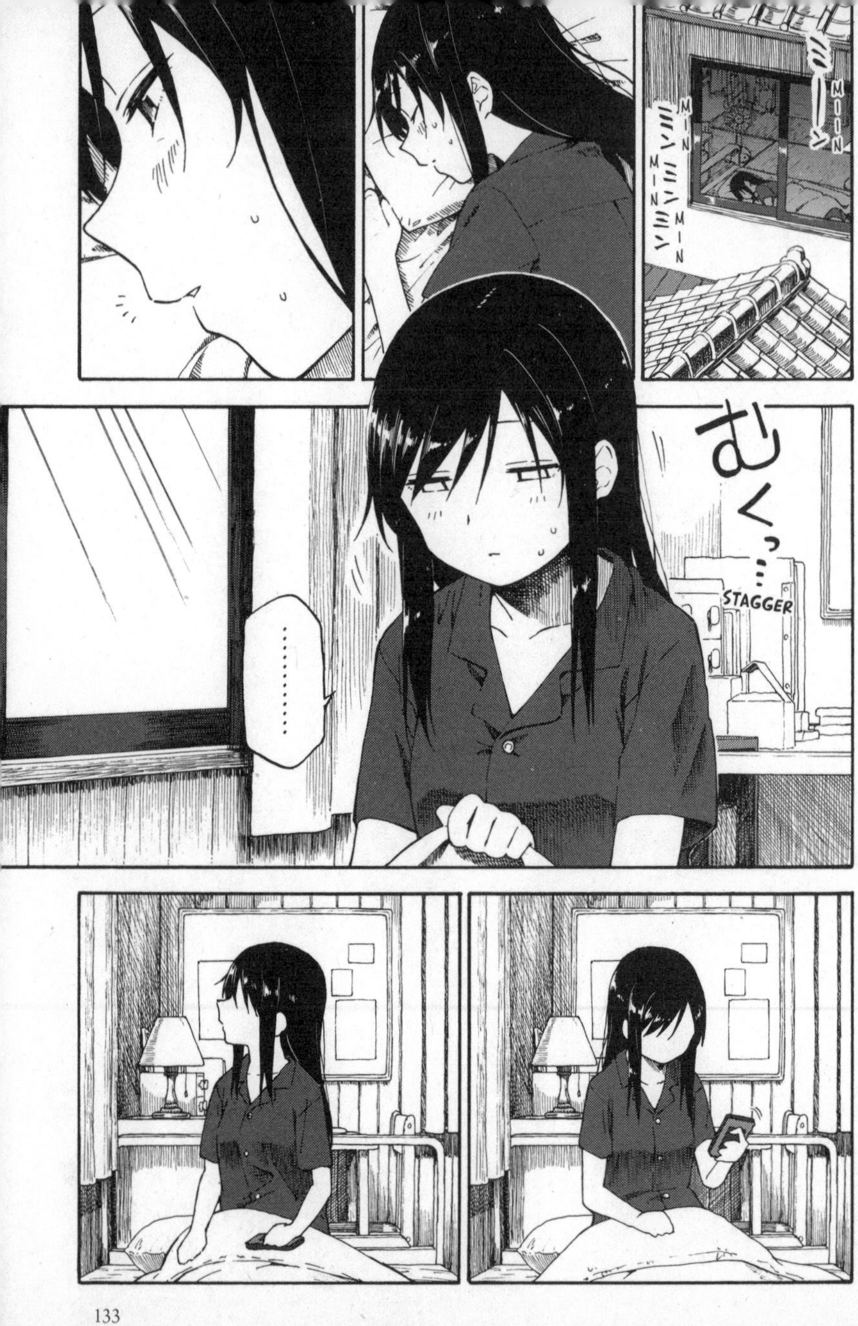
ミーン
M-I-N
ミンミンミン
MIN MIN MIN
むくっ…
STAGGER
……

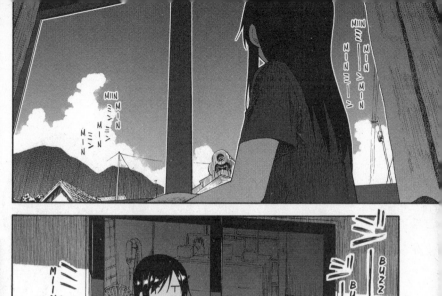

MIIN
VIII VIII MIIN
MIIN
VIII VIII

MIIN
VIII VIIN MIIN-VIIN
MIIN
VIII VIIN

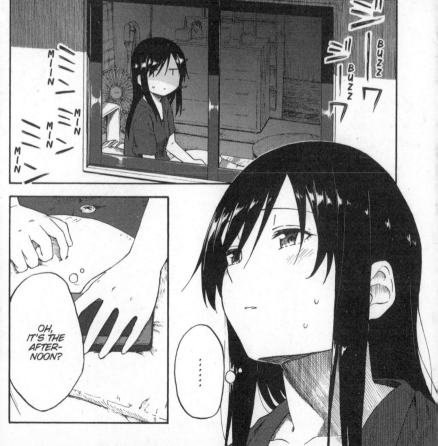

MIIN

MIIN

MIIN
MIN

MIIN
MIN

MIN
MIN

MIN

BUZZ

BUZZ

OH,
IT'S THE
AFTER-
NOON?

. . . . .

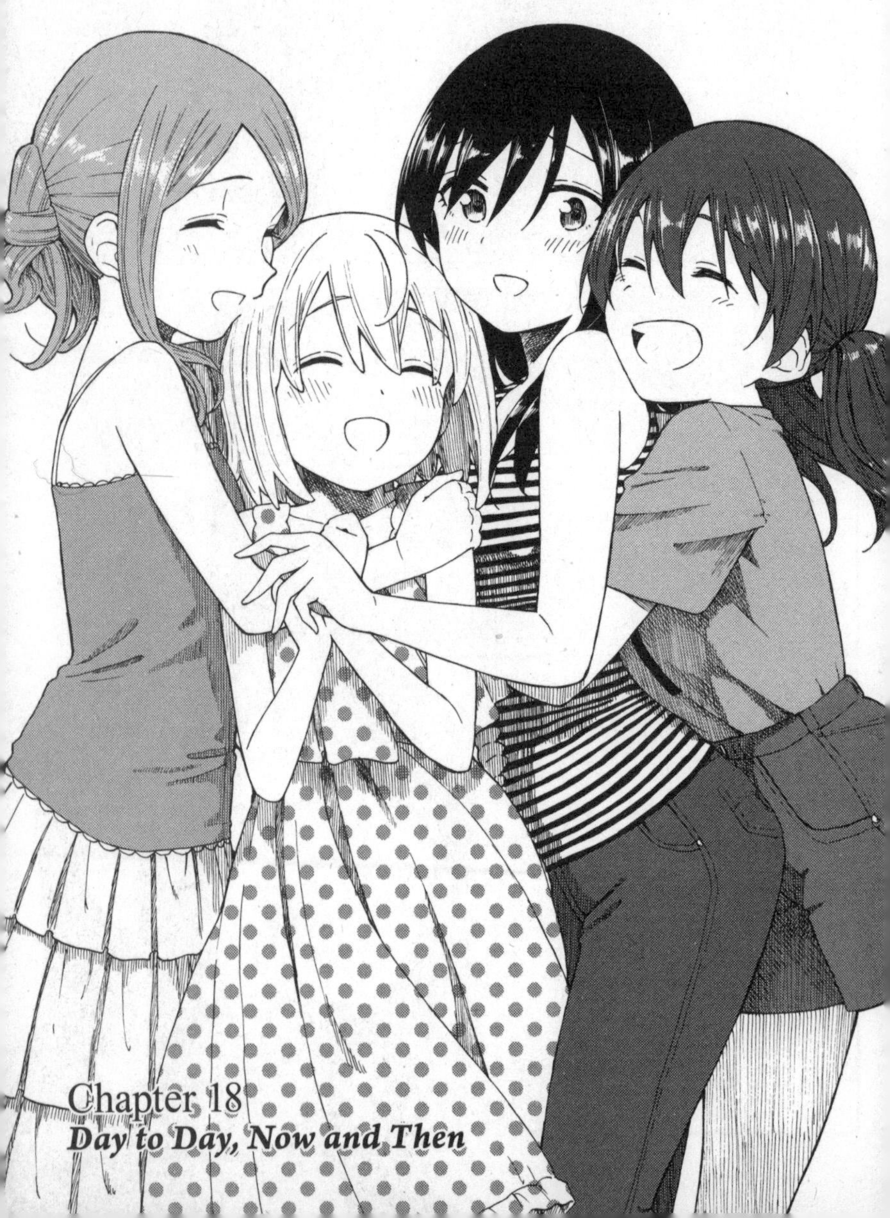

Chapter 18

Day to Day, Now and Then

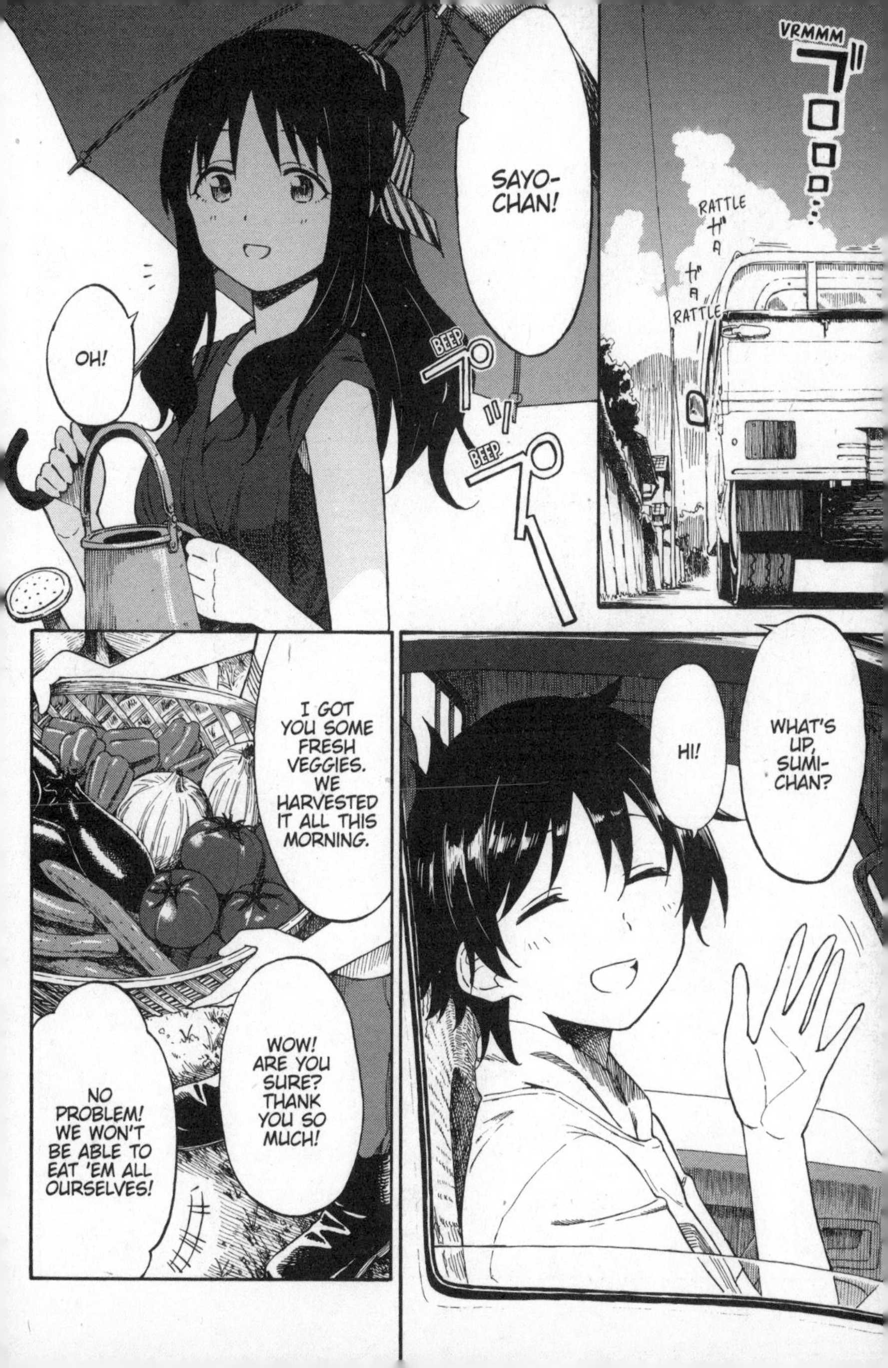
VRMMM
RATTLE
RATTLE
SAYO-CHAN!
BEEP
BEEP
OH!
WHAT'S UP, SUMI-CHAN?
HI!
I GOT YOU SOME FRESH VEGGIES. WE HARVESTED IT ALL THIS MORNING.
WOW! ARE YOU SURE? THANK YOU SO MUCH!
NO PROBLEM! WE WON'T BE ABLE TO EAT 'EM ALL OURSELVES!

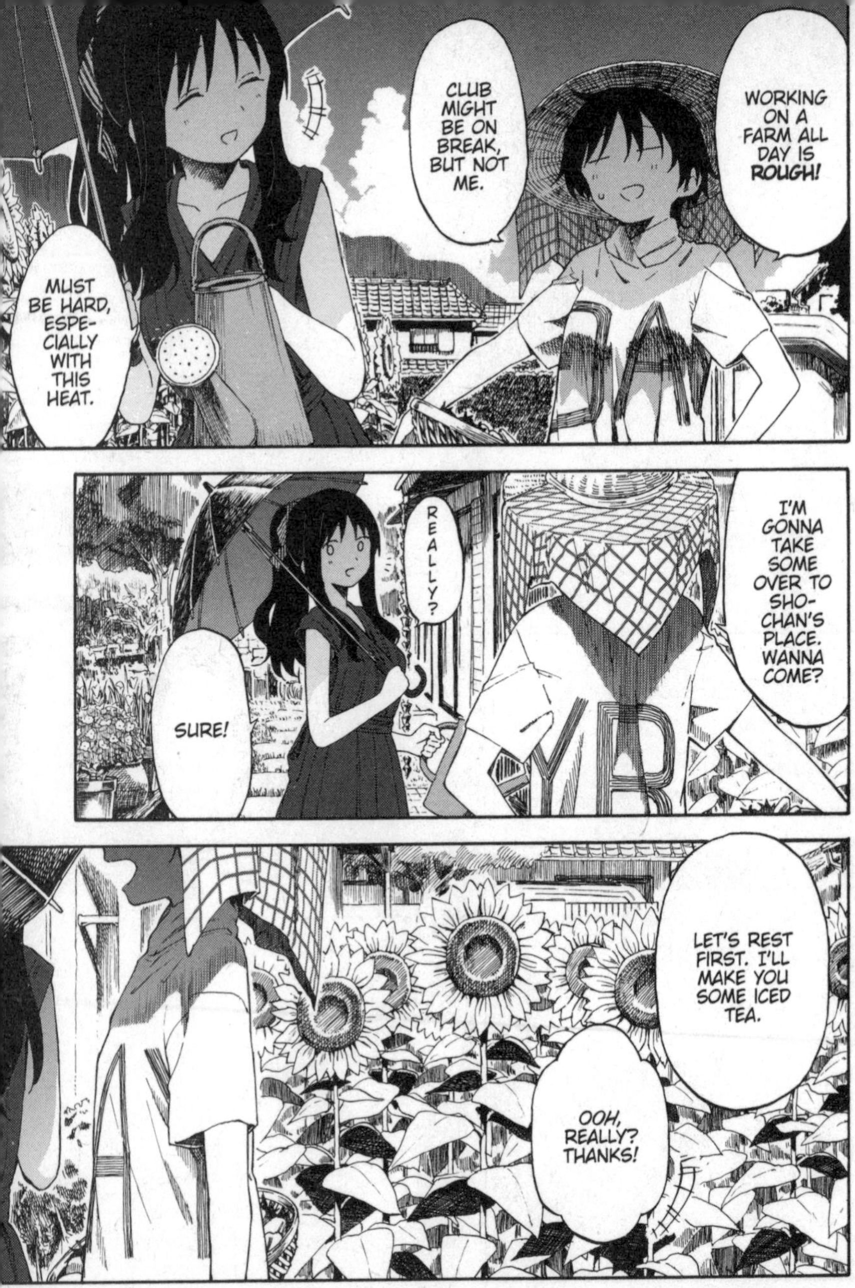
WORKING ON A FARM ALL DAY IS ROUGH!
CLUB MIGHT BE ON BREAK, BUT NOT ME.
MUST BE HARD, ESPECIALLY WITH THIS HEAT.
I'M GONNA TAKE SOME OVER TO SHO-CHAN'S PLACE. WANNA COME?
REALLY?
SURE!
LET'S REST FIRST. I'LL MAKE YOU SOME ICED TEA.
OOH, REALLY? THANKS!

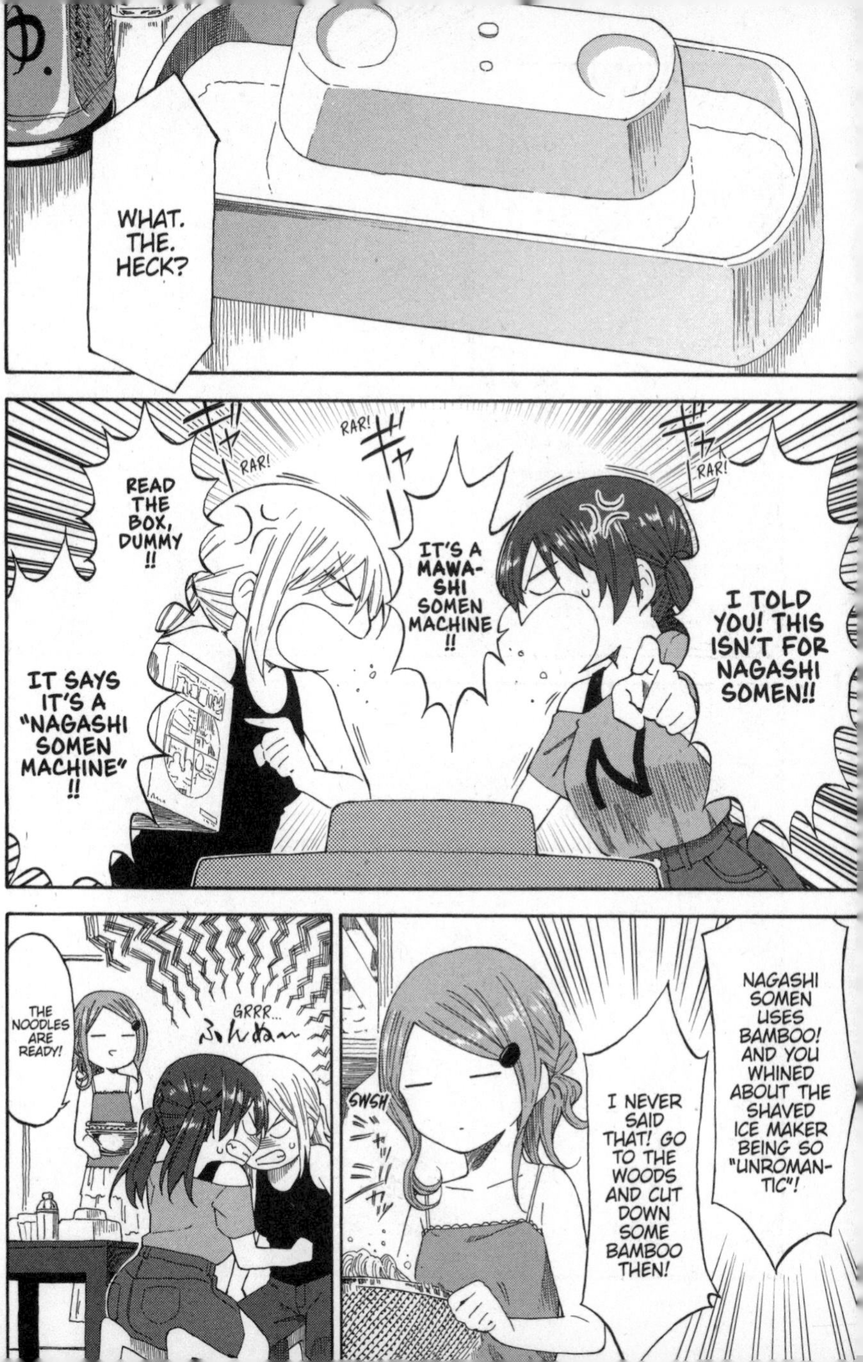

WHAT. THE. HECK?
I TOLD YOU! THIS ISN'T FOR NAGASHI SOMEN!!
RAR!
IT'S A MAWA-SHI SOMEN MACHINE!!
RAR!
RAR!
READ THE BOX, DUMMY!!
IT SAYS IT'S A "NAGASHI SOMEN MACHINE"!!
NAGASHI SOMEN USES BAMBOO! AND YOU WHINED ABOUT THE SHAVED ICE MAKER BEING SO "UNROMAN-TIC"!
I NEVER SAID THAT! GO TO THE WOODS AND CUT DOWN SOME BAMBOO THEN!
SWSH
GRRR...
ふんぬ〜
THE NOODLES ARE READY!

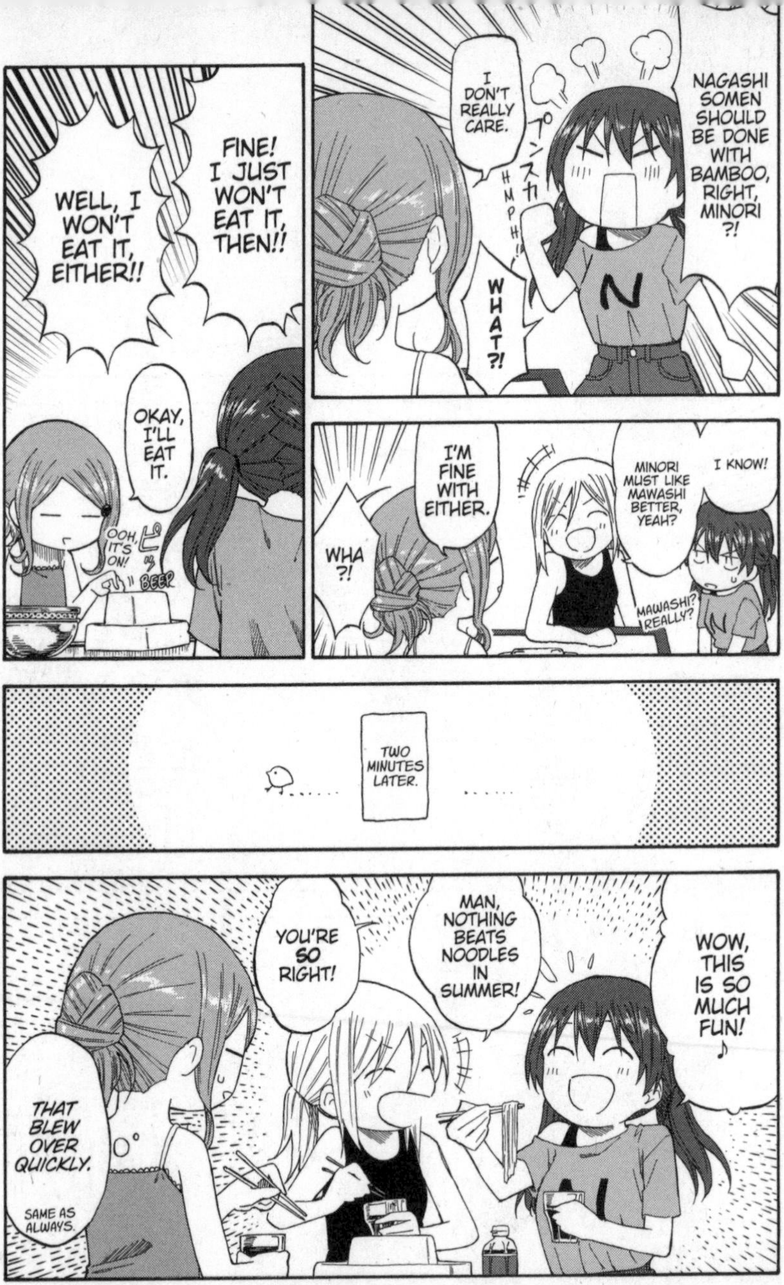
NAGASHI SOMEN SHOULD BE DONE WITH BAMBOO, RIGHT, MINORI?!
プンスカ HMPH!!
I DON'T REALLY CARE.
WHAT?!
I KNOW!
MINORI MUST LIKE MAWASHI BETTER, YEAH?
MAWASHI? REALLY?
I'M FINE WITH EITHER.
WHA?!
FINE! I JUST WON'T EAT IT, THEN!!
WELL, I WON'T EAT IT, EITHER!!
OKAY, I'LL EAT IT.
OOH, IT'S ON!
ピッ BEEP
TWO MINUTES LATER.
WOW, THIS IS SO MUCH FUN! ♪
MAN, NOTHING BEATS NOODLES IN SUMMER!
YOU'RE SO RIGHT!
THAT BLEW OVER QUICKLY.
SAME AS ALWAYS.

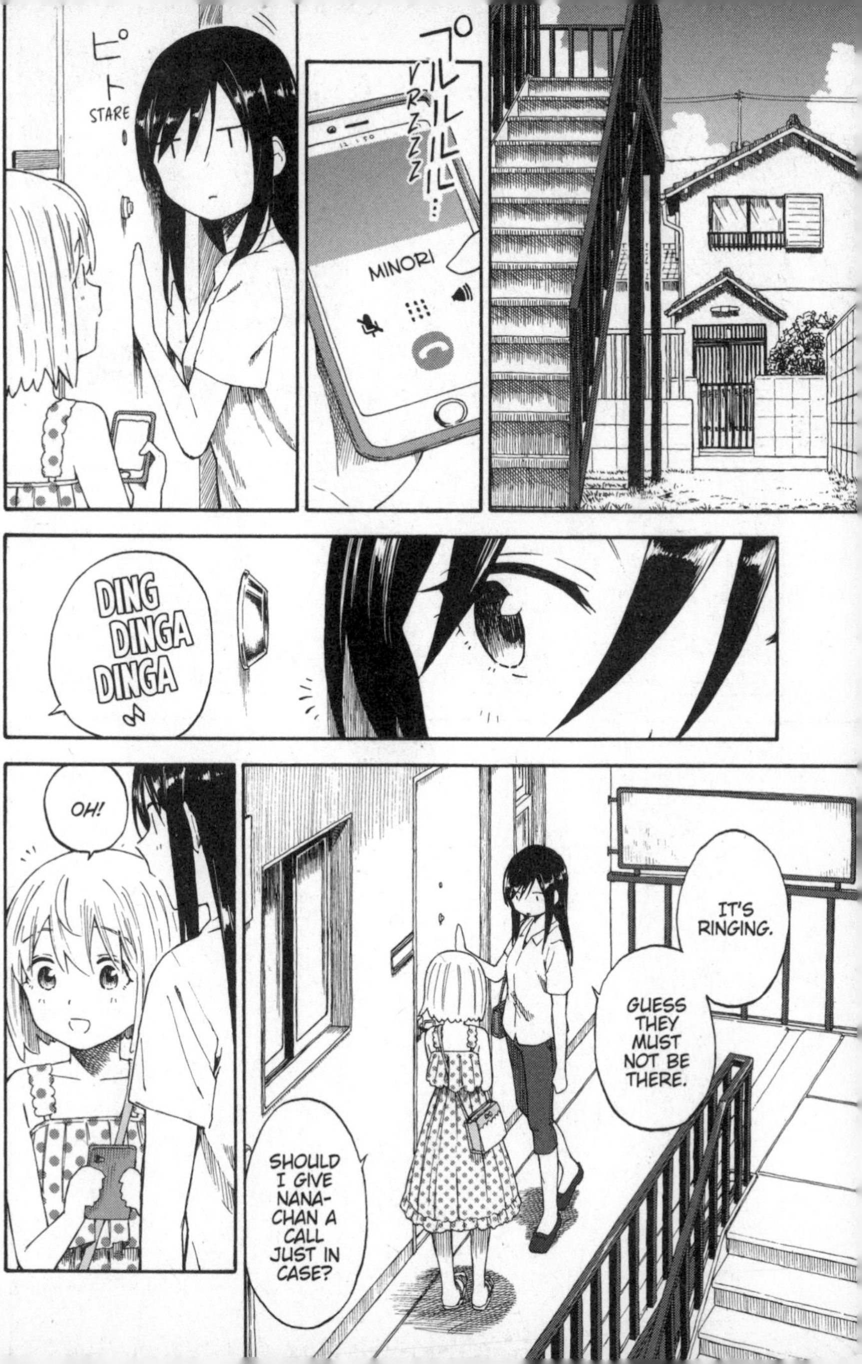
プルルルル…
VRZZZ
MINORI
ピト
STARE
DING DINGA DINGA
IT'S RINGING.
GUESS THEY MUST NOT BE THERE.
SHOULD I GIVE NANA-CHAN A CALL JUST IN CASE?
OH!

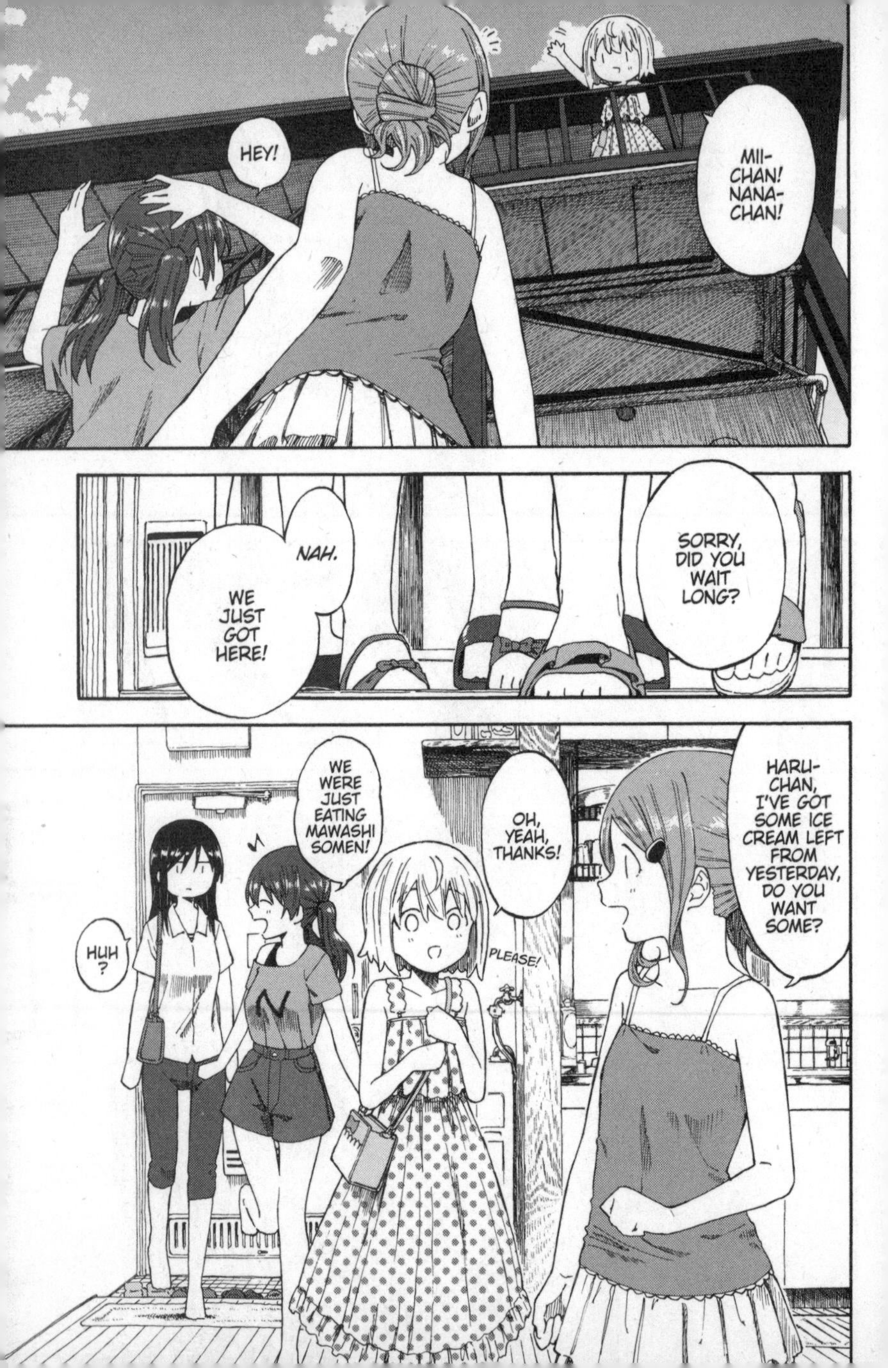
MII-CHAN! NANA-CHAN!
HEY!
SORRY, DID YOU WAIT LONG?
NAH. WE JUST GOT HERE!
HARU-CHAN, I'VE GOT SOME ICE CREAM LEFT FROM YESTERDAY, DO YOU WANT SOME?
OH, YEAH, THANKS!
PLEASE!
WE WERE JUST EATING MAWASHI SOMEN!
HUH?

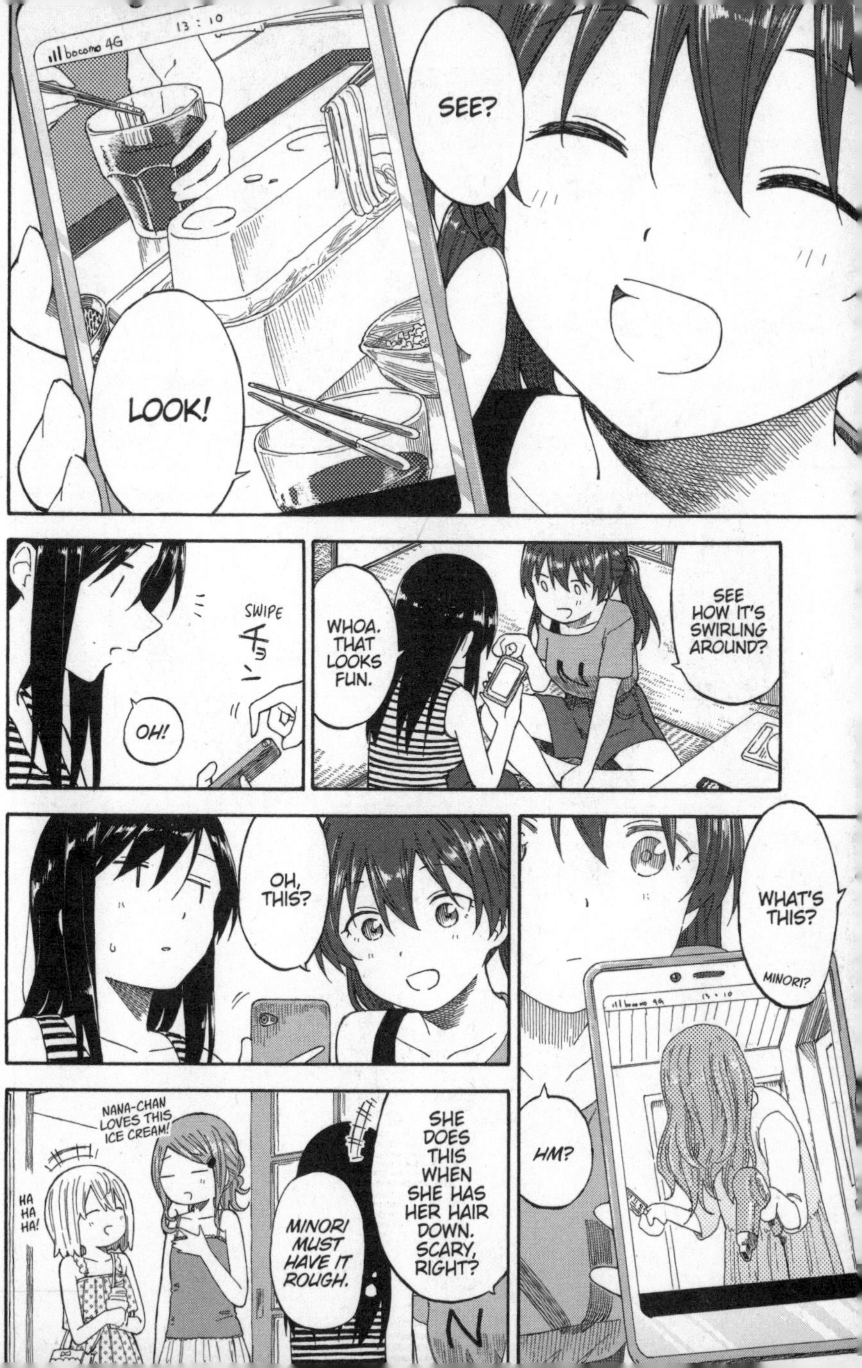
13 : 10
bocomo 4G
SEE?
LOOK!
SEE HOW IT'S SWIRLING AROUND?
WHOA. THAT LOOKS FUN.
SWIPE
OH!
WHAT'S THIS?
MINORI?
HM?
OH, THIS?
SHE DOES THIS WHEN SHE HAS HER HAIR DOWN. SCARY, RIGHT?
MINORI MUST HAVE IT ROUGH.
NANA-CHAN LOVES THIS ICE CREAM!
HA HA HA!

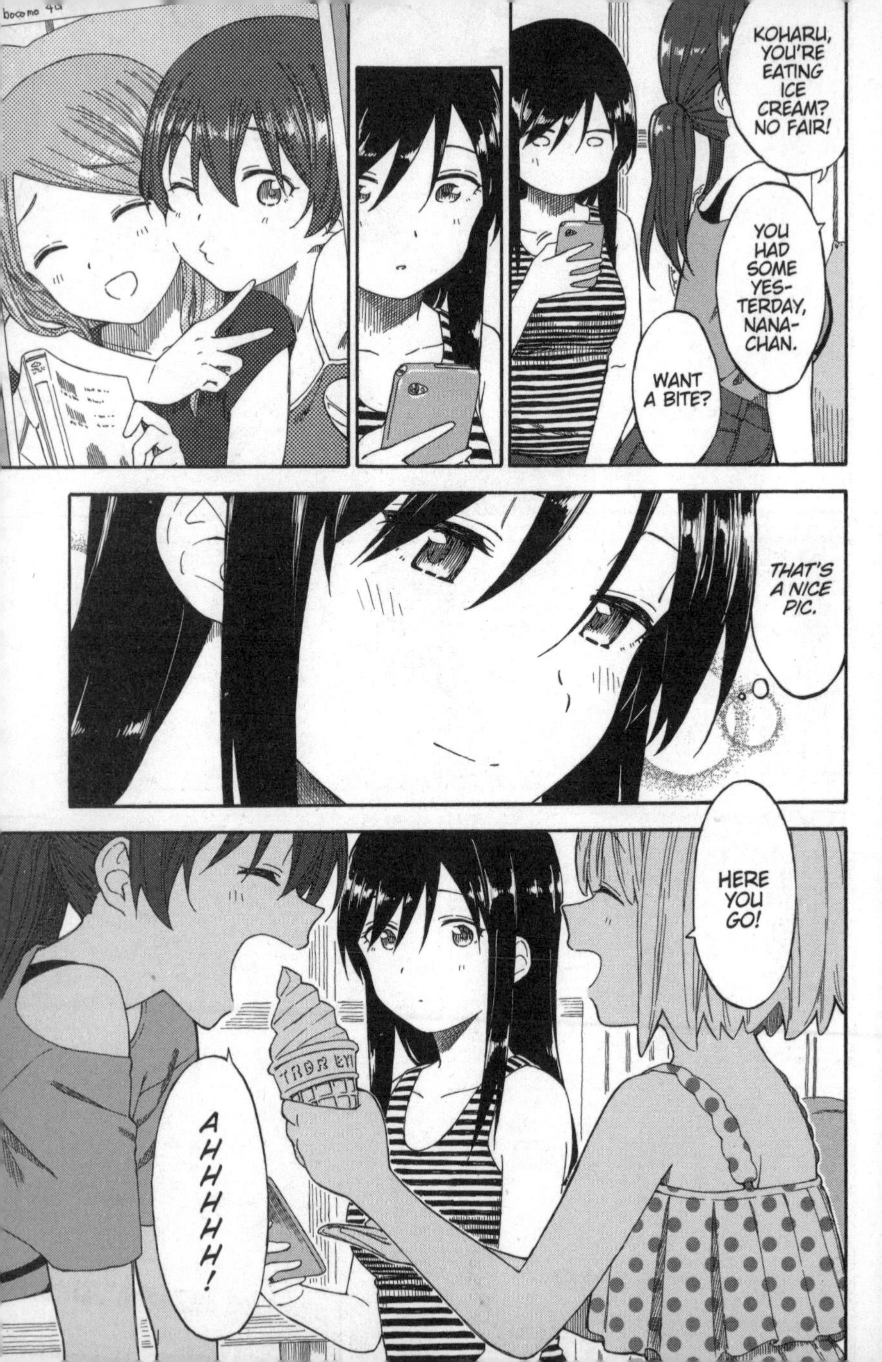
KOHARU, YOU'RE EATING ICE CREAM? NO FAIR!
YOU HAD SOME YES-TERDAY, NANA-CHAN.
WANT A BITE?
THAT'S A NICE PIC.
HERE YOU GO!
AHHHHH!

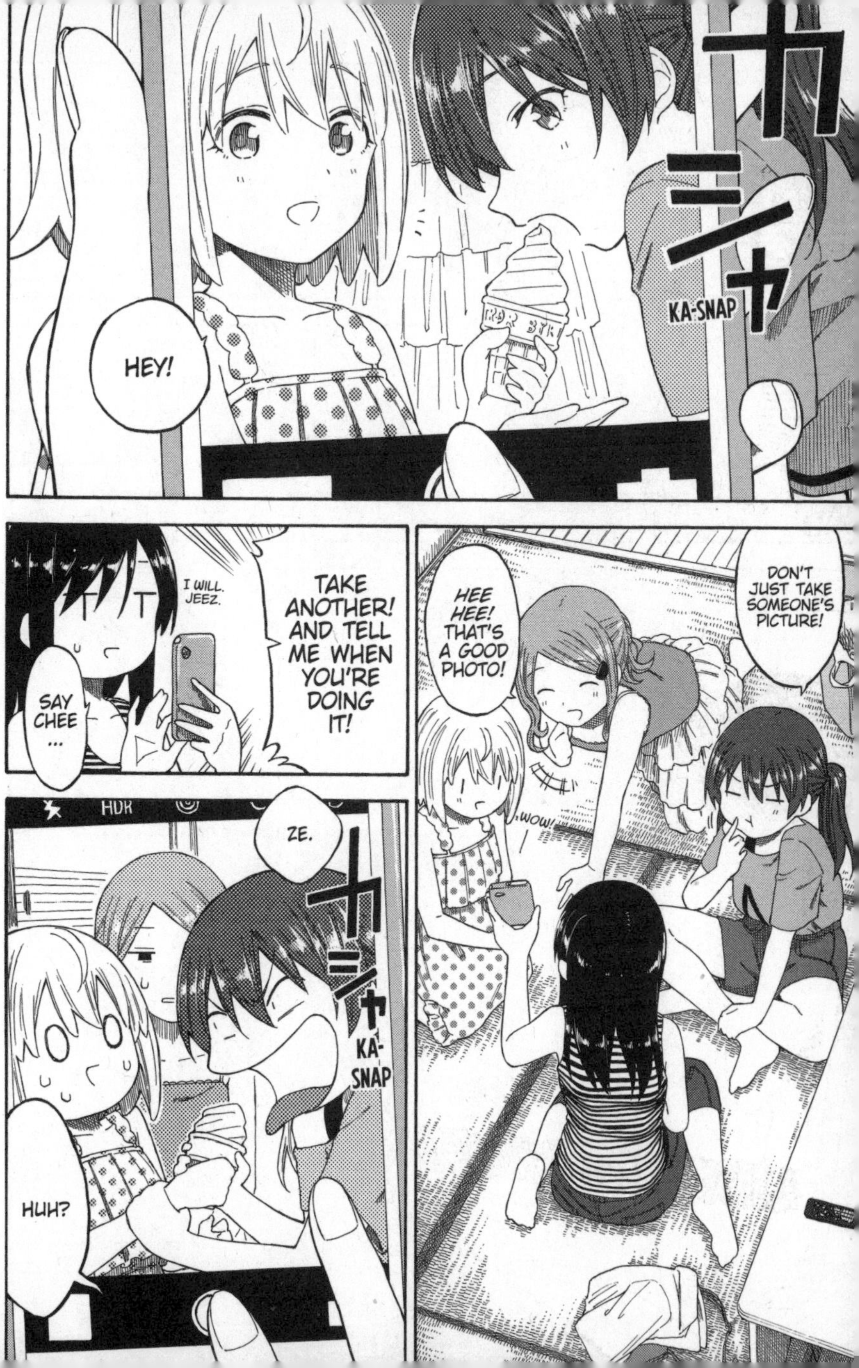
カシャ
KA-SNAP
HEY!
DON'T JUST TAKE SOMEONE'S PICTURE!
HEE HEE! THAT'S A GOOD PHOTO!
WOW!
TAKE ANOTHER! AND TELL ME WHEN YOU'RE DOING IT!
I WILL. JEEZ.
SAY CHEE ...
HDR
ZE.
カシャ
KA-SNAP
HUH?

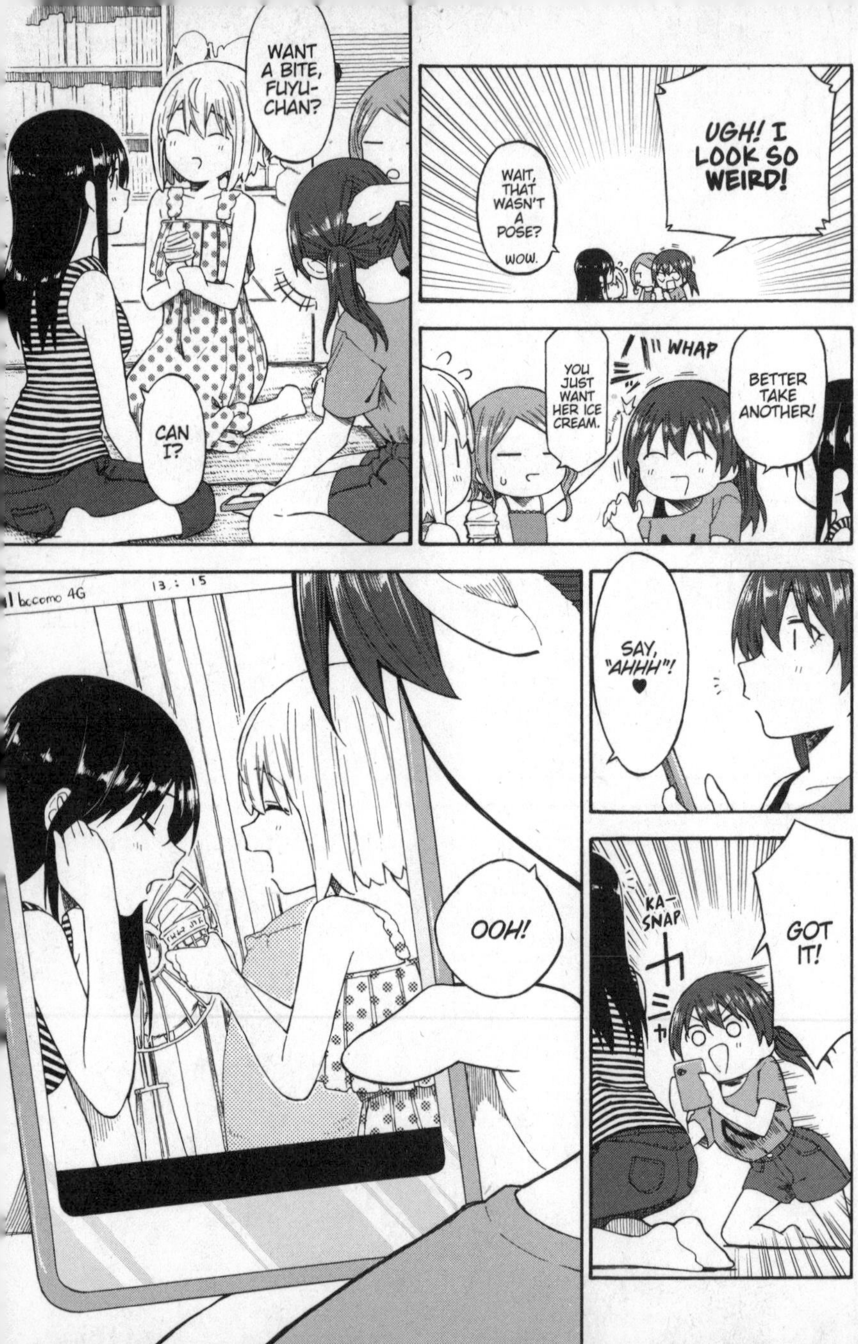
UGH! I LOOK SO WEIRD!
WAIT, THAT WASN'T A POSE? WOW.
BETTER TAKE ANOTHER!
WHAP
YOU JUST WANT HER ICE CREAM.
WANT A BITE, FUYU-CHAN?
CAN I?
SAY, "AHHH"! ♥
GOT IT!
KA-SNAP
13:15
OOH!

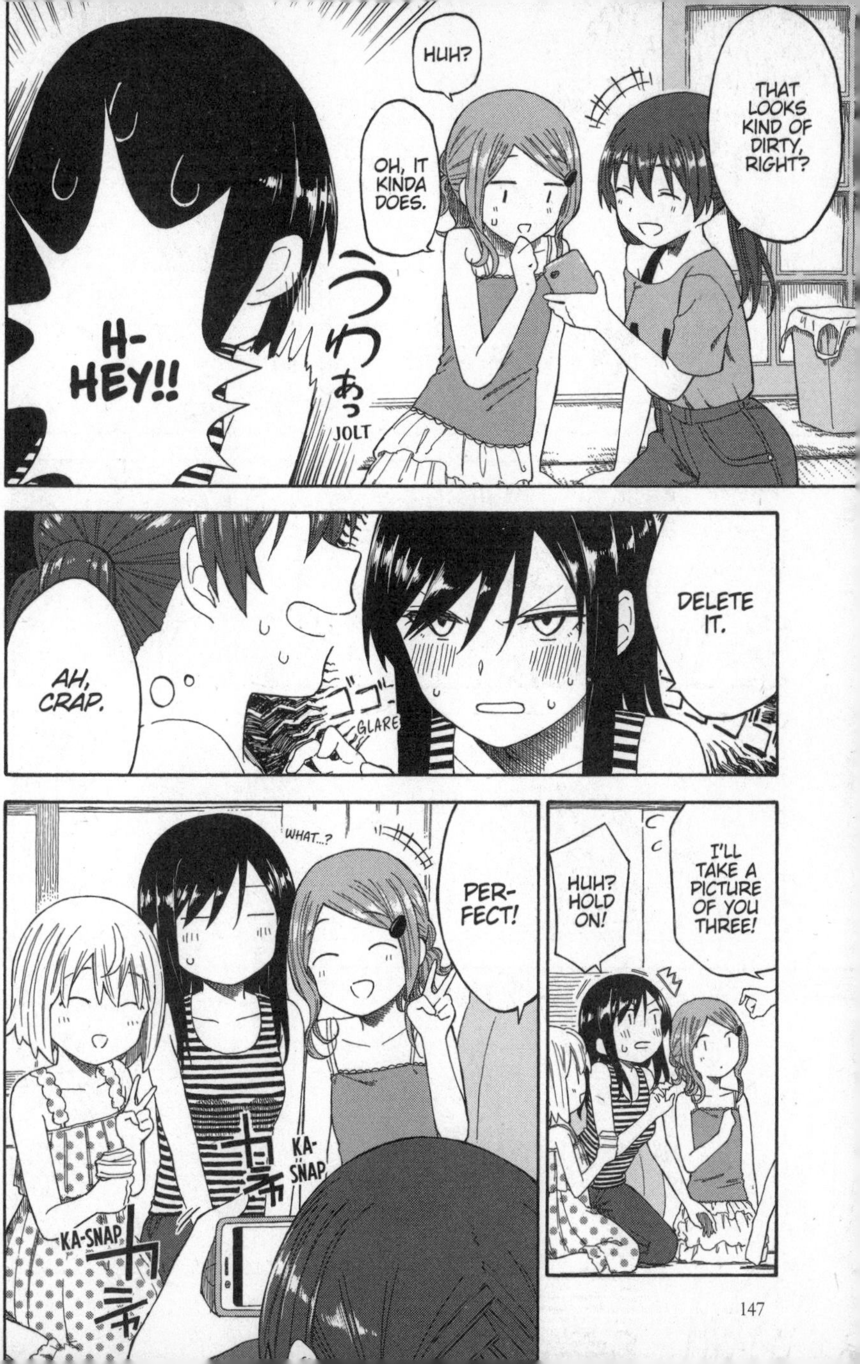
THAT LOOKS KIND OF DIRTY, RIGHT?
HUH?
OH, IT KINDA DOES.
うわあっ
JOLT
H-HEY!!
DELETE IT.
ゴゴ
GLARE
AH, CRAP.
I'LL TAKE A PICTURE OF YOU THREE!
HUH? HOLD ON!
PER-FECT!
WHAT...?
KA-SNAP
KA-SNAP

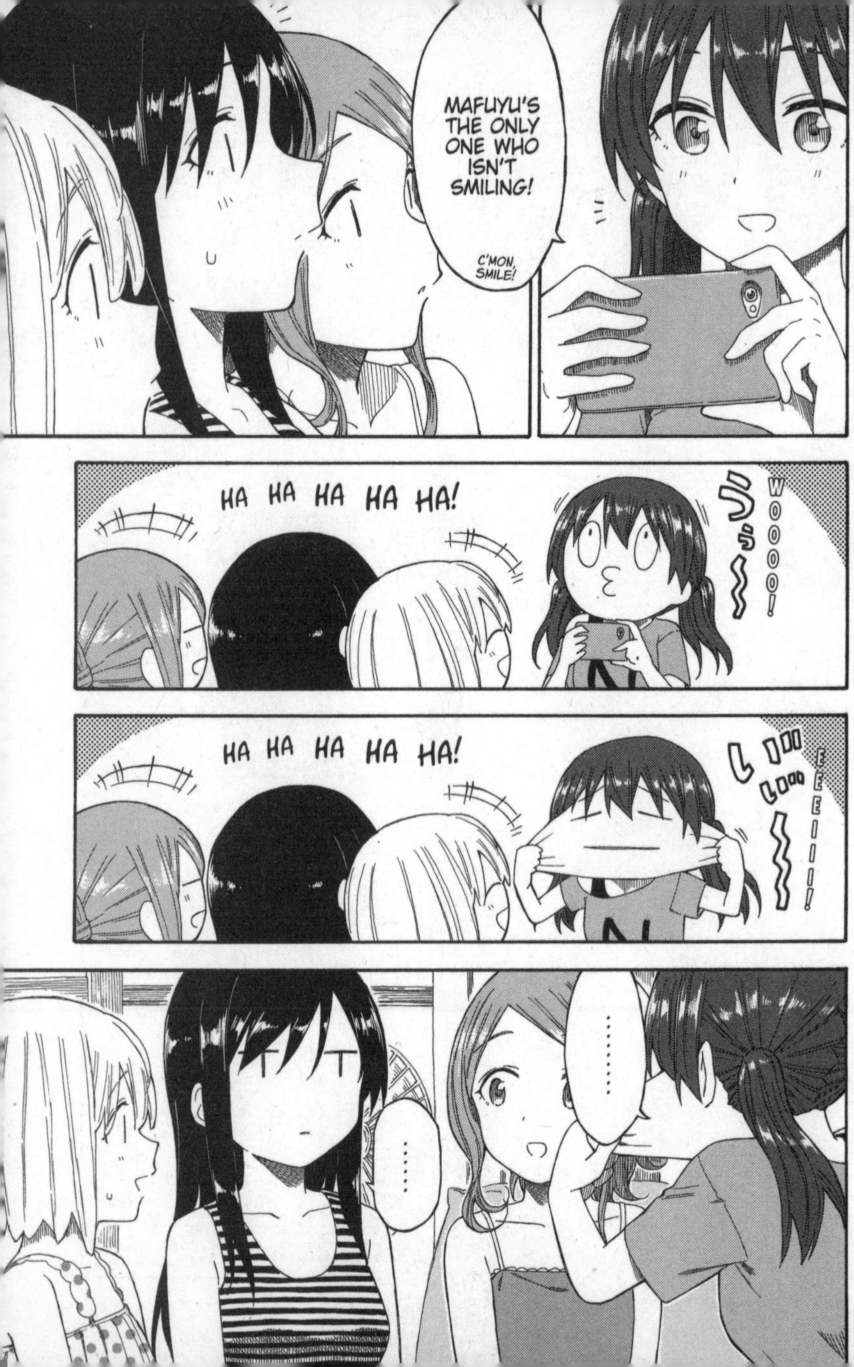

MAFUYU'S THE ONLY ONE WHO ISN'T SMILING!
C'MON, SMILE!
WOOOOO!
HA HA HA HA HA!
EEEIIII!
HA HA HA HA HA!
......
......

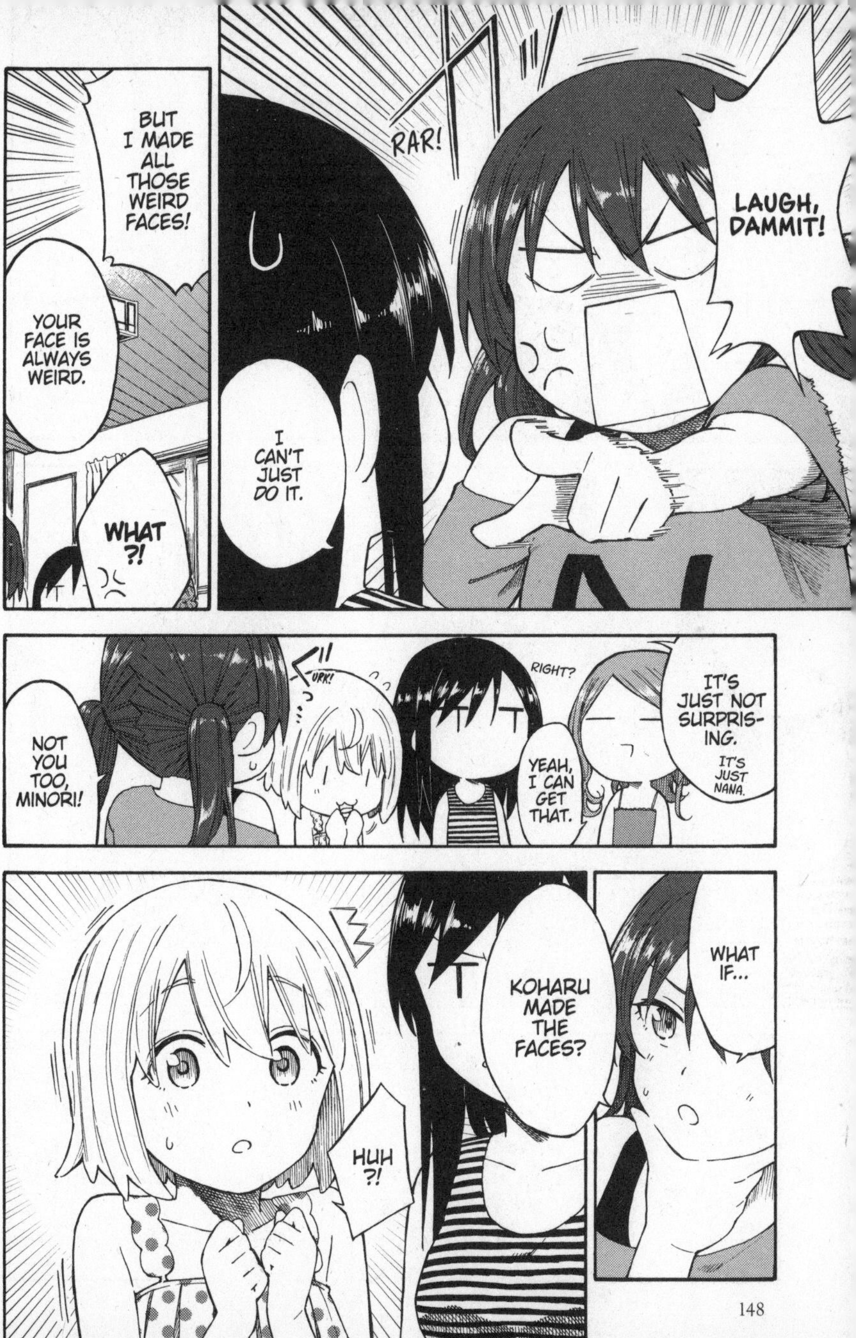
LAUGH, DAMMIT!
RAR!
I CAN'T JUST DO IT.
BUT I MADE ALL THOSE WEIRD FACES!
YOUR FACE IS ALWAYS WEIRD.
WHAT?!
IT'S JUST NOT SURPRISING.
IT'S JUST NANA.
RIGHT?
YEAH, I CAN GET THAT.
URK!
NOT YOU TOO, MINORI!
WHAT IF...
KOHARU MADE THE FACES?
HUH?!

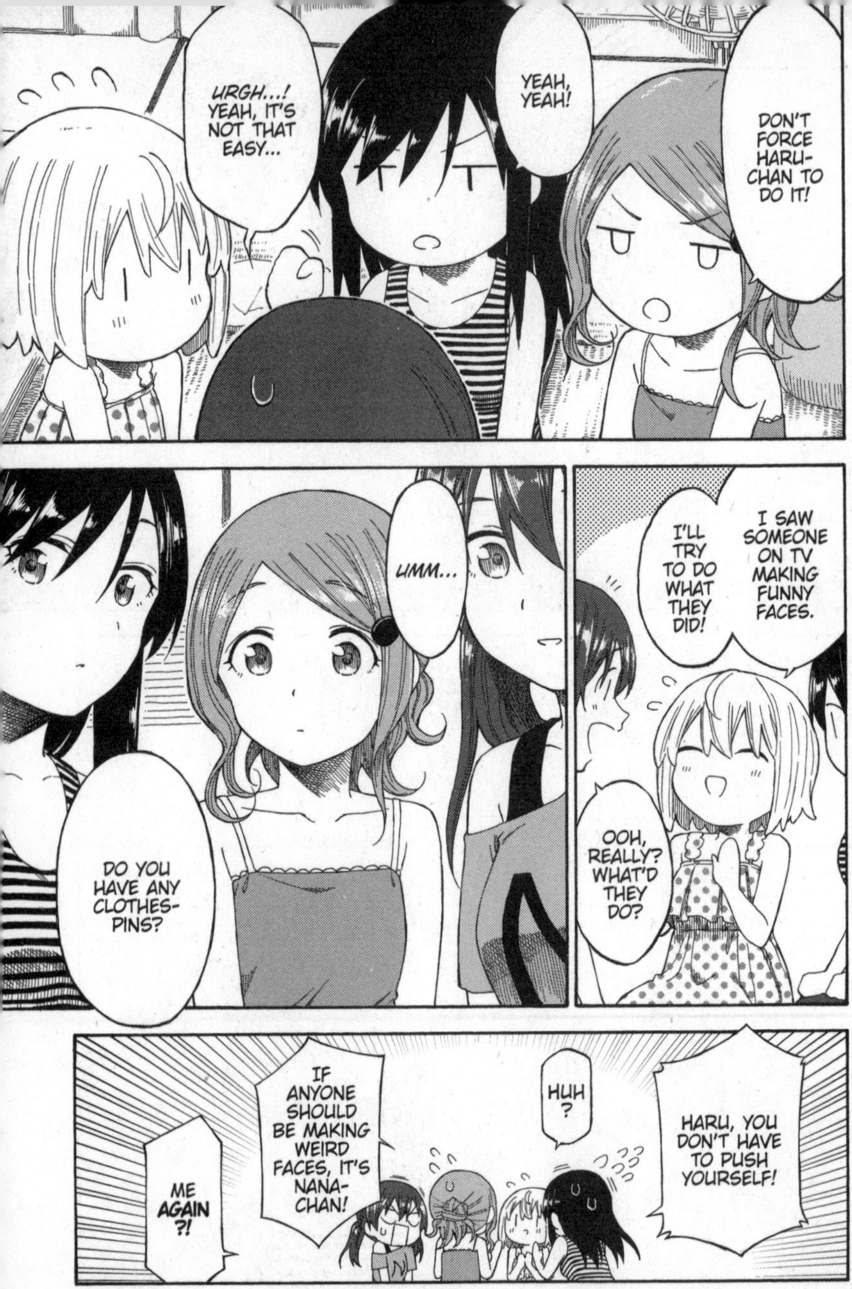
DON'T FORCE HARU-CHAN TO DO IT!
YEAH, YEAH!
URGH...! YEAH, IT'S NOT THAT EASY...
I SAW SOMEONE ON TV MAKING FUNNY FACES.
I'LL TRY TO DO WHAT THEY DID!
OOH, REALLY? WHAT'D THEY DO?
UMM...
DO YOU HAVE ANY CLOTHES-PINS?
HARU, YOU DON'T HAVE TO PUSH YOURSELF!
HUH?
IF ANYONE SHOULD BE MAKING WEIRD FACES, IT'S NANA-CHAN!
ME AGAIN?!

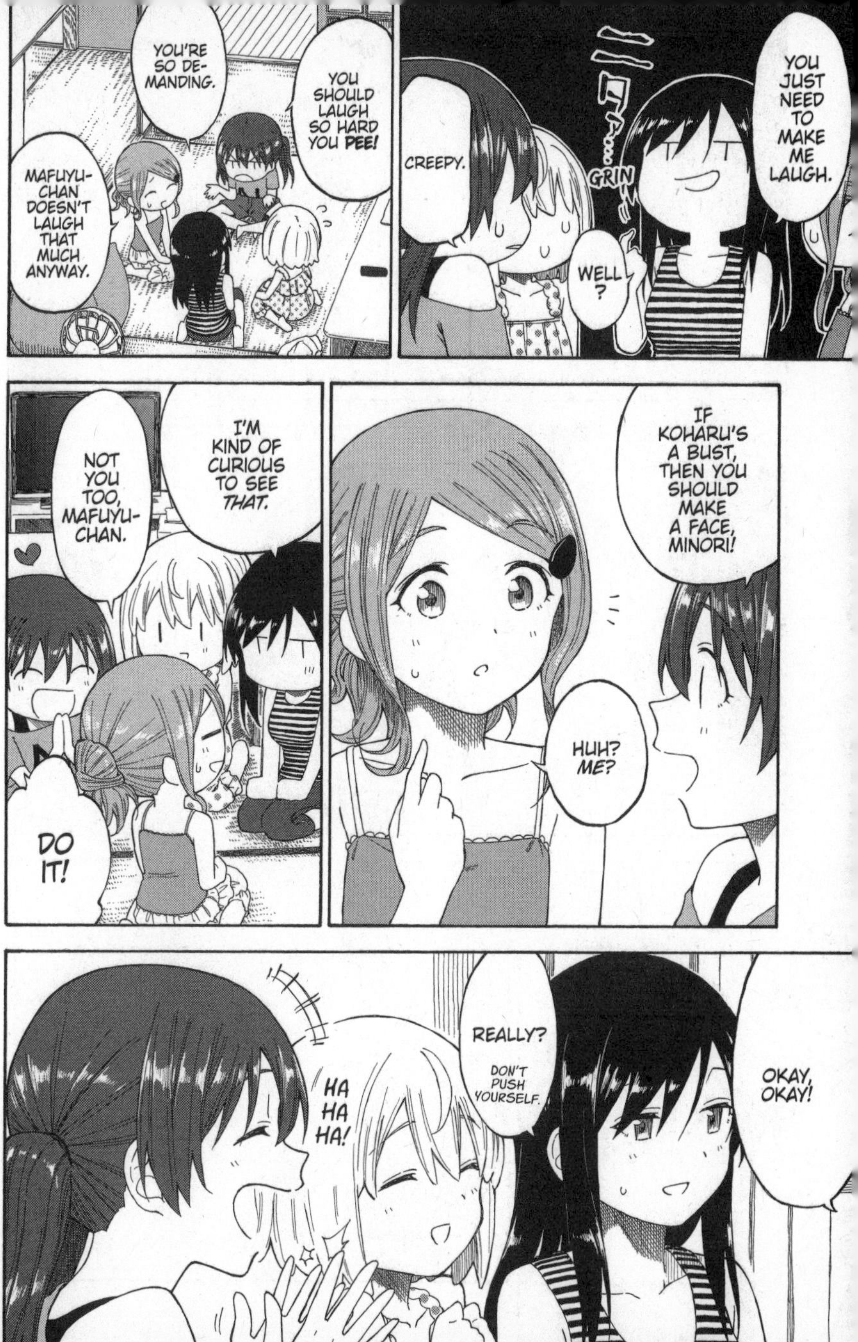
YOU JUST NEED TO MAKE ME LAUGH.
GRIN
WELL?
CREEPY.
YOU SHOULD LAUGH SO HARD YOU PEE!
YOU'RE SO DE-MANDING.
MAFUYU-CHAN DOESN'T LAUGH THAT MUCH ANYWAY.
IF KOHARU'S A BUST, THEN YOU SHOULD MAKE A FACE, MINORI!
HUH? ME?
I'M KIND OF CURIOUS TO SEE THAT.
NOT YOU TOO, MAFUYU-CHAN.
DO IT!
OKAY, OKAY!
REALLY?
DON'T PUSH YOURSELF.
HA HA HA!

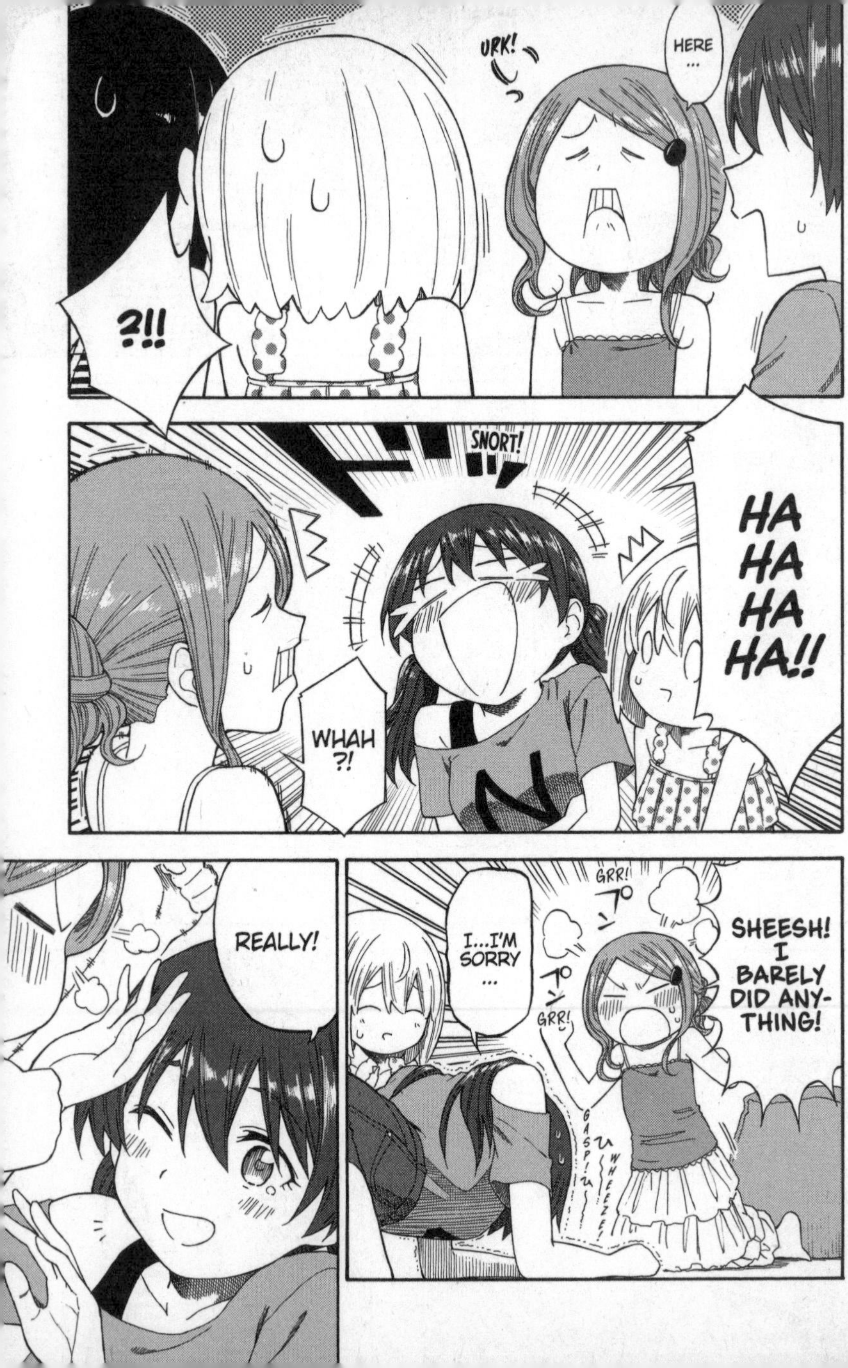
HERE ...
URK!
?!!
HA HA HA HA HA!!
SNORT!
WHAH ?!
GRR!
SHEESH! I BARELY DID ANY-THING!
I...I'M SORRY ...
GRR!
GASP!
WHEEZE!
REALLY!

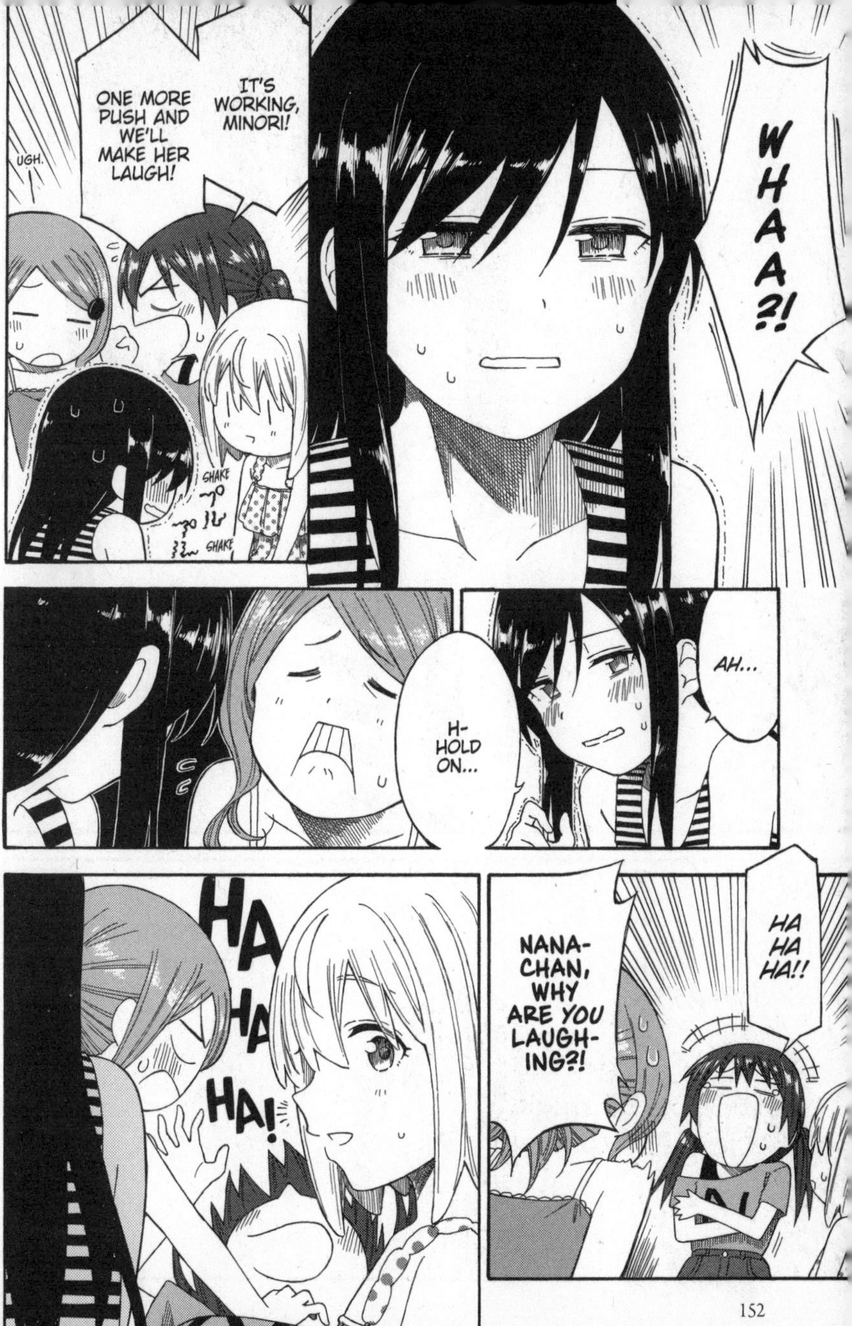
WHAAA?!
IT'S WORKING, MINORI!
ONE MORE PUSH AND WE'LL MAKE HER LAUGH!
UGH.
SHAKE
SHAKE
AH...
H-HOLD ON...
HA HA HA!!
NANA-CHAN, WHY ARE YOU LAUGH-ING?!
HA HA HA!

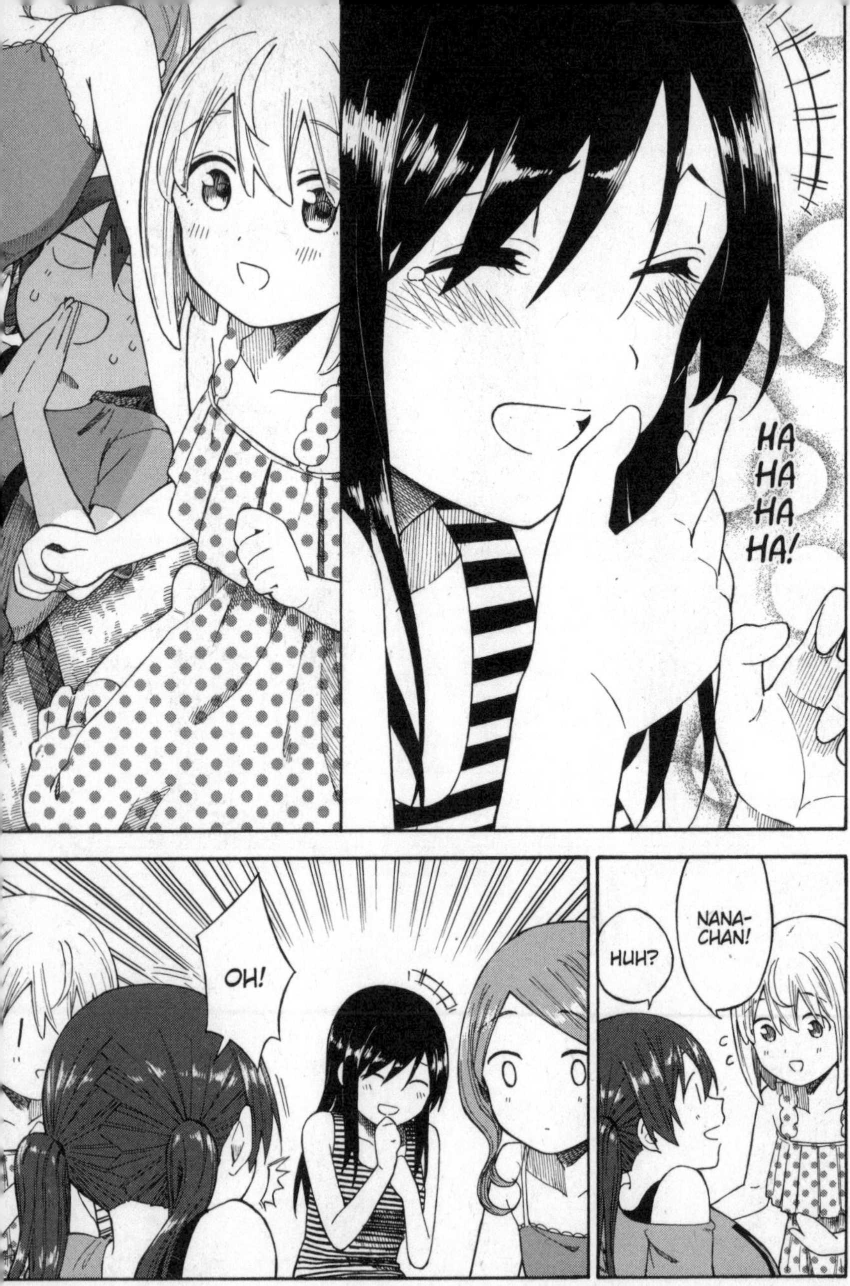
HA HA HA HA!
NANA-CHAN!
HUH?
OH!

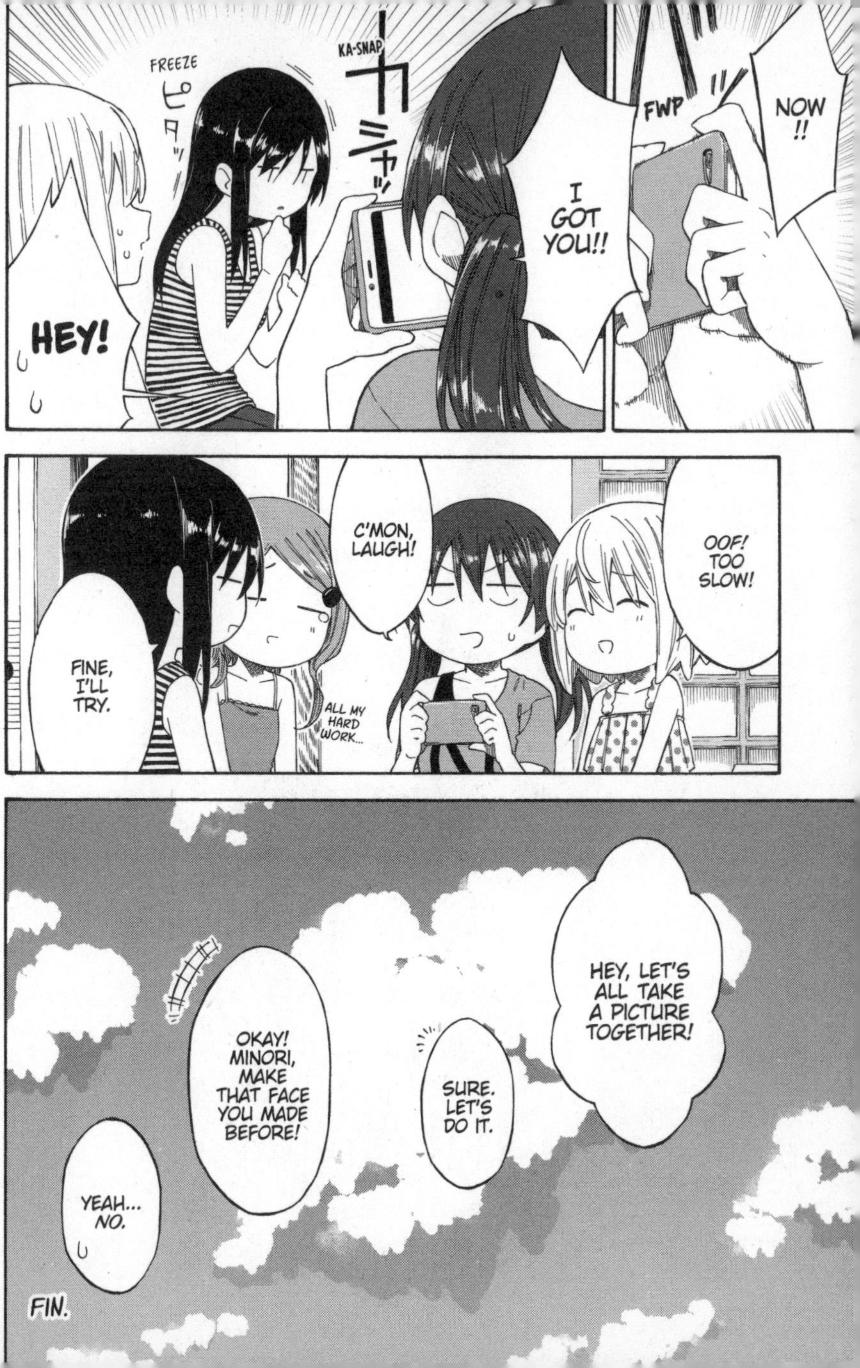
NOW!!
FWP
I GOT YOU!!
KA-SNAP
カシャッ
FREEZE
ピタッ
HEY!
OOF! TOO SLOW!
C'MON, LAUGH!
ALL MY HARD WORK...
FINE, I'LL TRY.
HEY, LET'S ALL TAKE A PICTURE TOGETHER!
SURE. LET'S DO IT.
OKAY! MINORI, MAKE THAT FACE YOU MADE BEFORE!
YEAH... NO.
FIN.

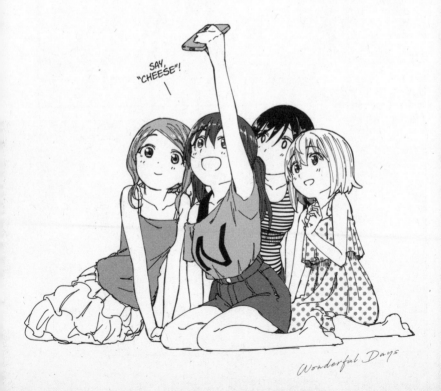

SAY,
"CHEESE"!

Wonderful Days

THE DIFFERENCE BETWEEN THEM

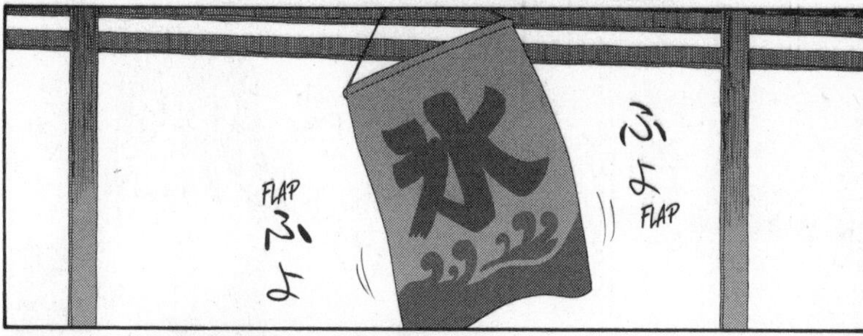
ふよ
FLAP
FLAP
ふよ

Banner: Ice.

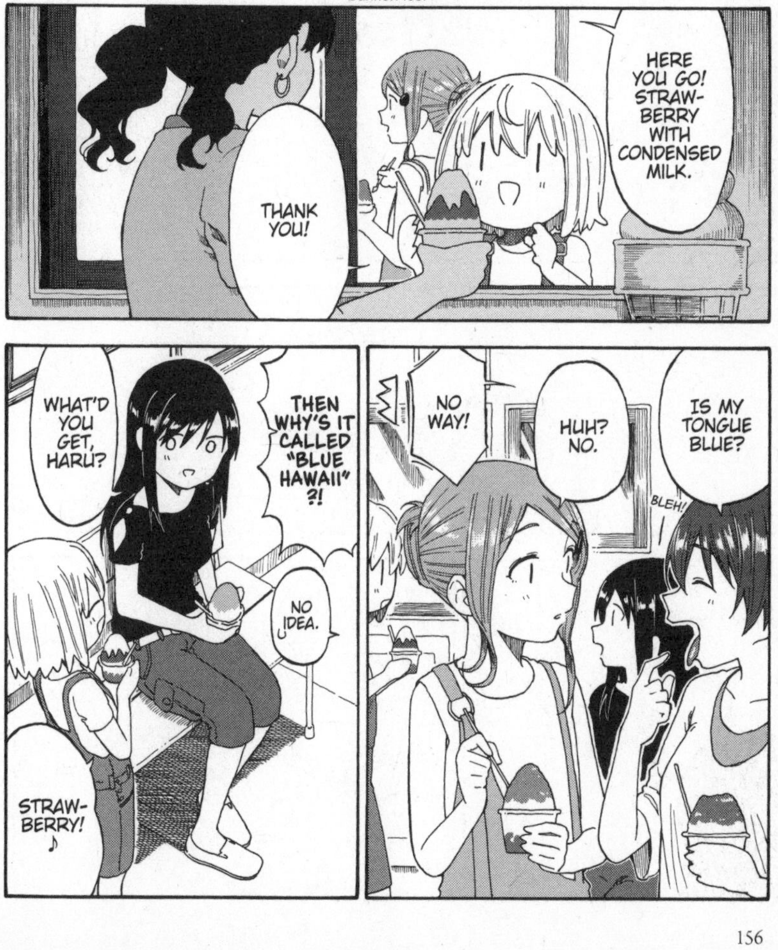
HERE YOU GO! STRAW-BERRY WITH CONDENSED MILK.
THANK YOU!
IS MY TONGUE BLUE?
BLEH!
HUH? NO.
NO WAY!
THEN WHY'S IT CALLED "BLUE HAWAII"?!
WHAT'D YOU GET, HARU?
NO IDEA.
STRAW-BERRY! ♪

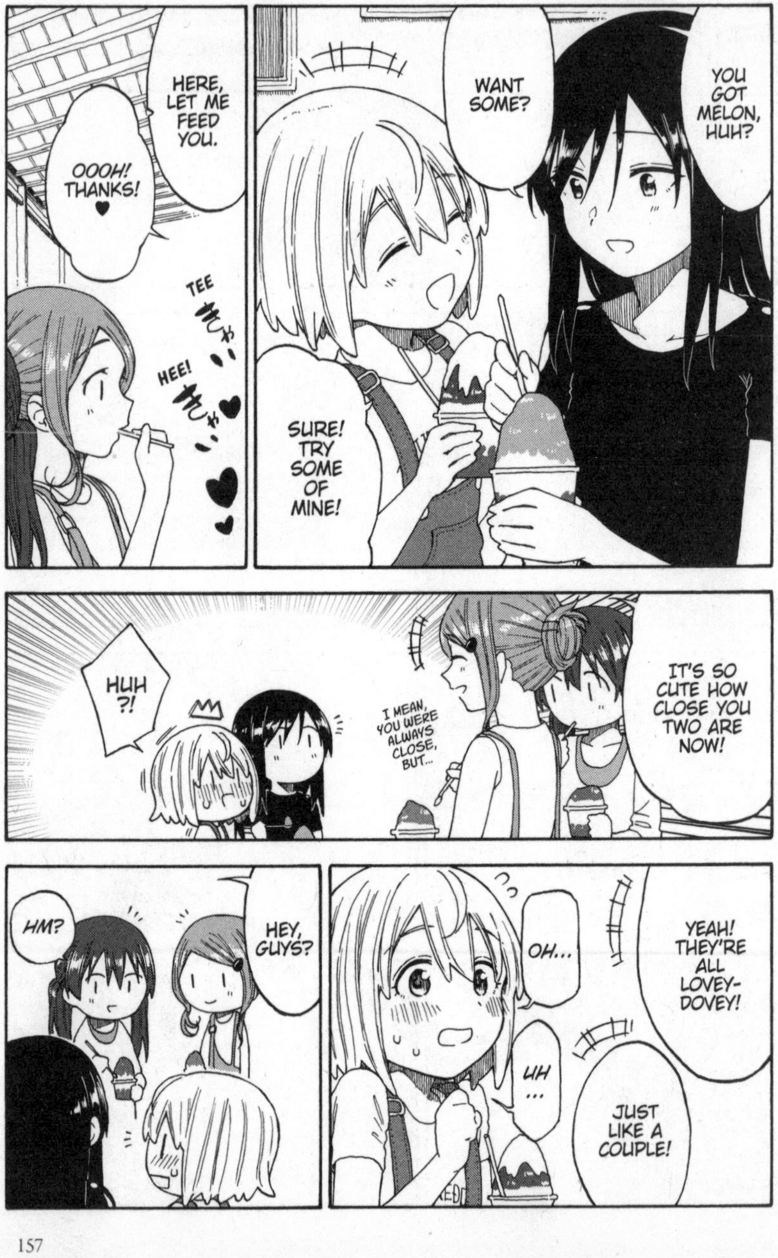
YOU GOT MELON, HUH?
WANT SOME?
SURE! TRY SOME OF MINE!
HERE, LET ME FEED YOU.
OOOH! THANKS! ♥
TEE HEE!
きゃい きゃい
IT'S SO CUTE HOW CLOSE YOU TWO ARE NOW!
I MEAN, YOU WERE ALWAYS CLOSE, BUT...
HUH ?!
YEAH! THEY'RE ALL LOVEY-DOVEY!
JUST LIKE A COUPLE!
OH...
UH ...
HEY, GUYS?
HM?

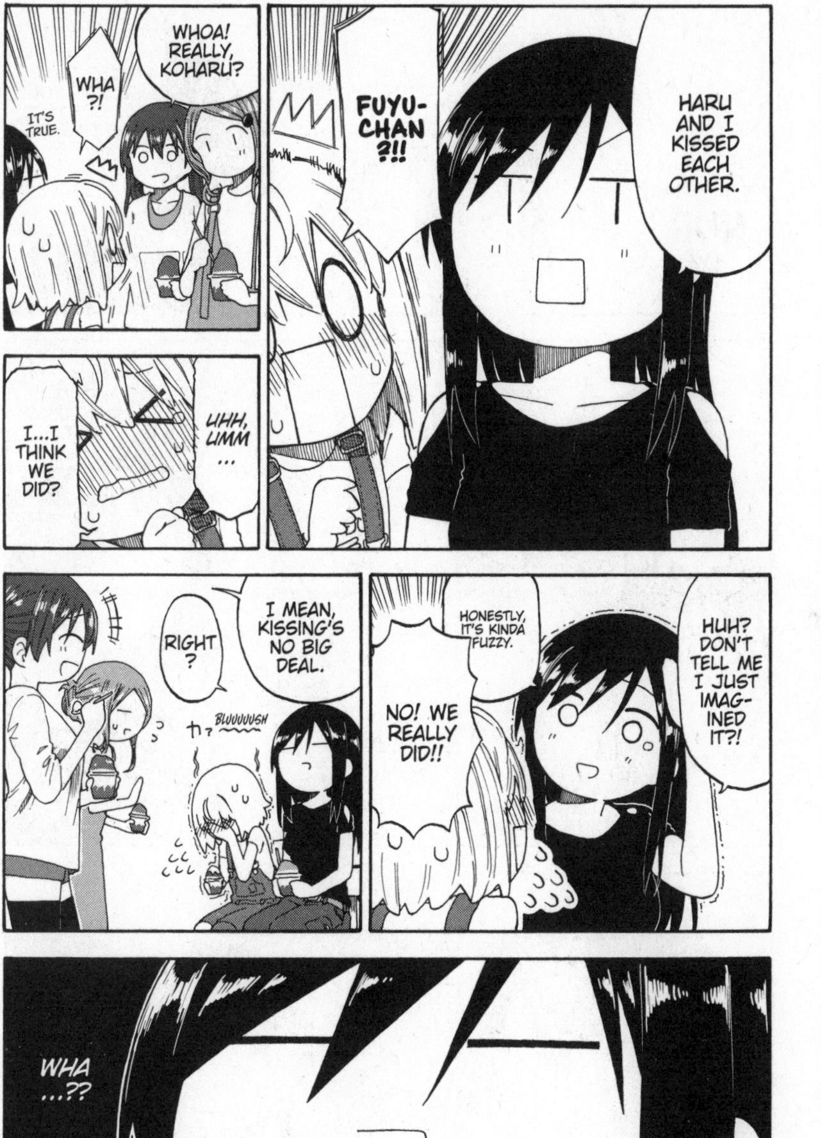
HARU AND I KISSED EACH OTHER.
FUYU-CHAN ?!!
WHOA! REALLY, KOHARU?
WHA ?!
IT'S TRUE.
UHH, UMM ...
I...I THINK WE DID?
HUH? DON'T TELL ME I JUST IMAG-INED IT?!
HONESTLY, IT'S KINDA FUZZY.
NO! WE REALLY DID!!
I MEAN, KISSING'S NO BIG DEAL.
RIGHT ?
BLUUUUUSH
WHA ...??

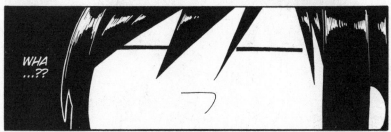

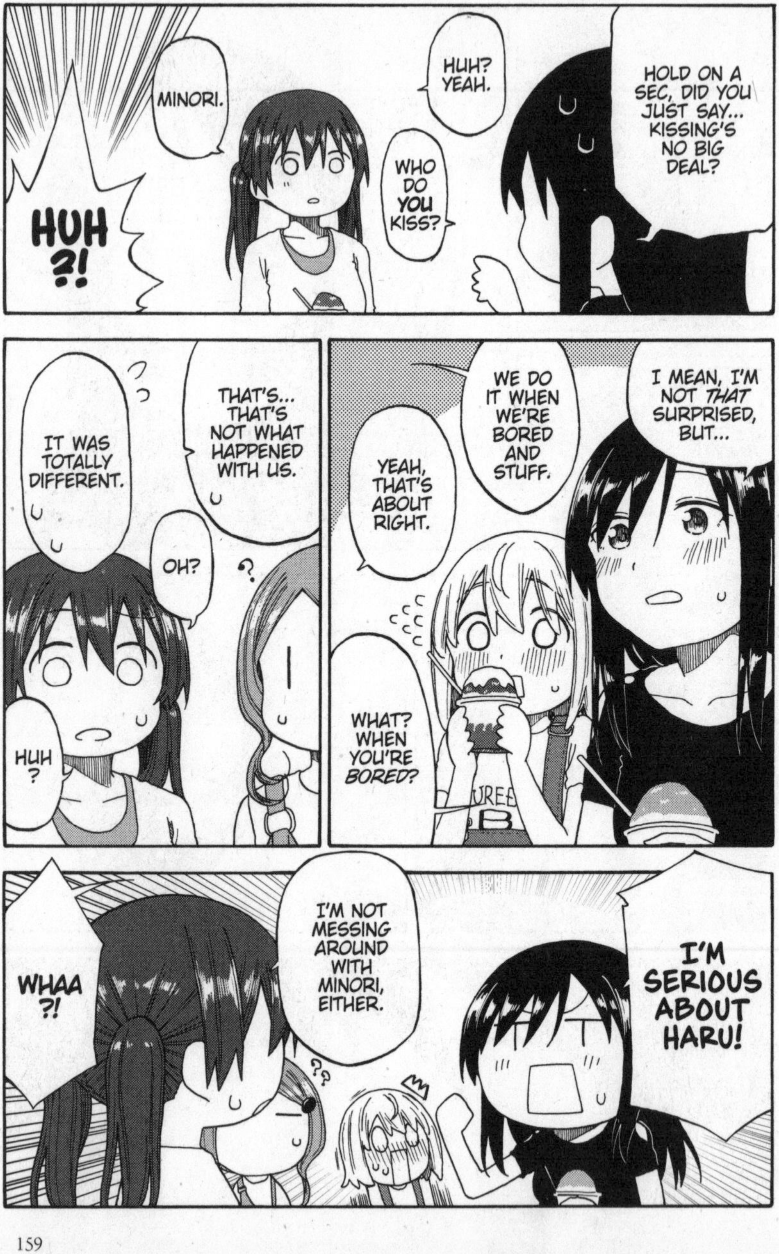
HOLD ON A SEC, DID YOU JUST SAY... KISSING'S NO BIG DEAL?
HUH? YEAH.
WHO DO YOU KISS?
MINORI.
HUH ?!
I MEAN, I'M NOT *THAT* SURPRISED, BUT...
WE DO IT WHEN WE'RE BORED AND STUFF.
YEAH, THAT'S ABOUT RIGHT.
WHAT? WHEN YOU'RE *BORED*?
THAT'S... THAT'S NOT WHAT HAPPENED WITH US.
IT WAS TOTALLY DIFFERENT.
OH?
HUH ?
I'M SERIOUS ABOUT HARU!
I'M NOT MESSING AROUND WITH MINORI, EITHER.
WHAA ?!

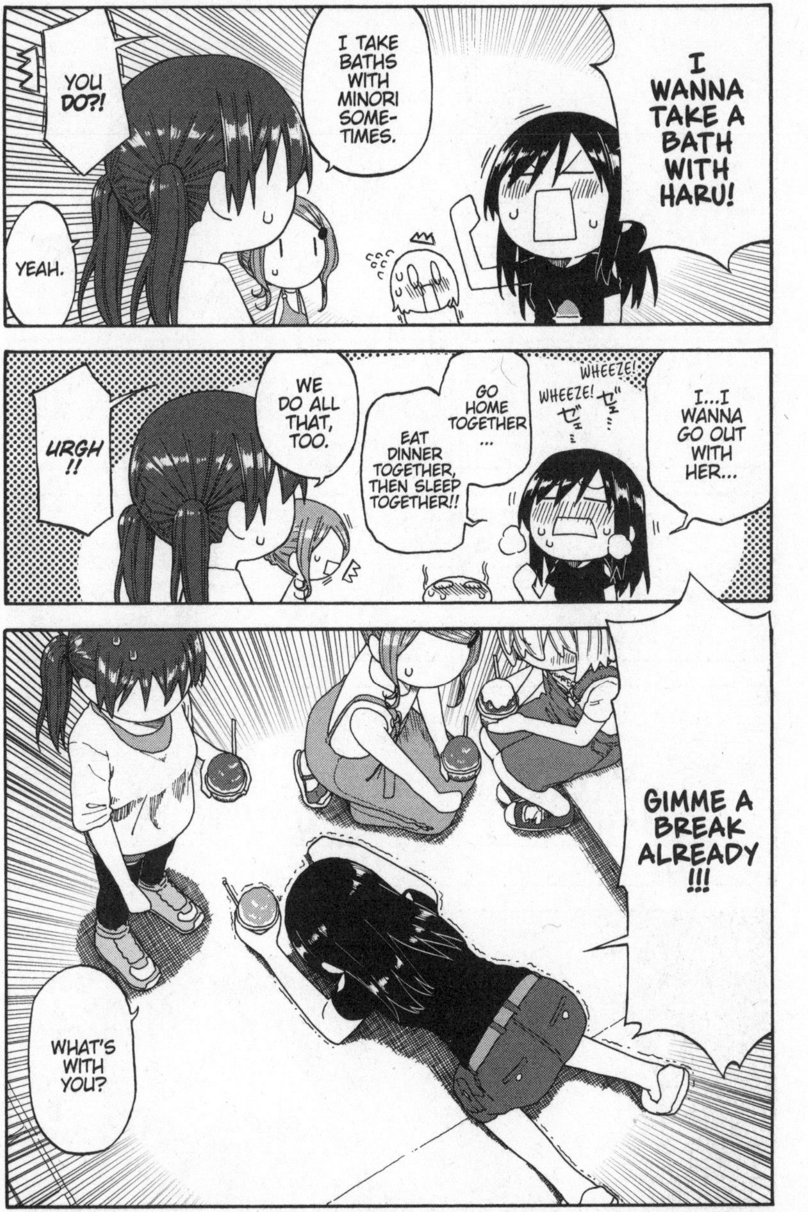
I WANNA TAKE A BATH WITH HARU!
I TAKE BATHS WITH MINORI SOMETIMES.
YOU DO?!
YEAH.
I...I WANNA GO OUT WITH HER...
WHEEZE! ゼェ
WHEEZE! ゼェ
GO HOME TOGETHER ...
EAT DINNER TOGETHER, THEN SLEEP TOGETHER!!
WE DO ALL THAT, TOO.
URGH !!
GIMME A BREAK ALREADY !!!
WHAT'S WITH YOU?

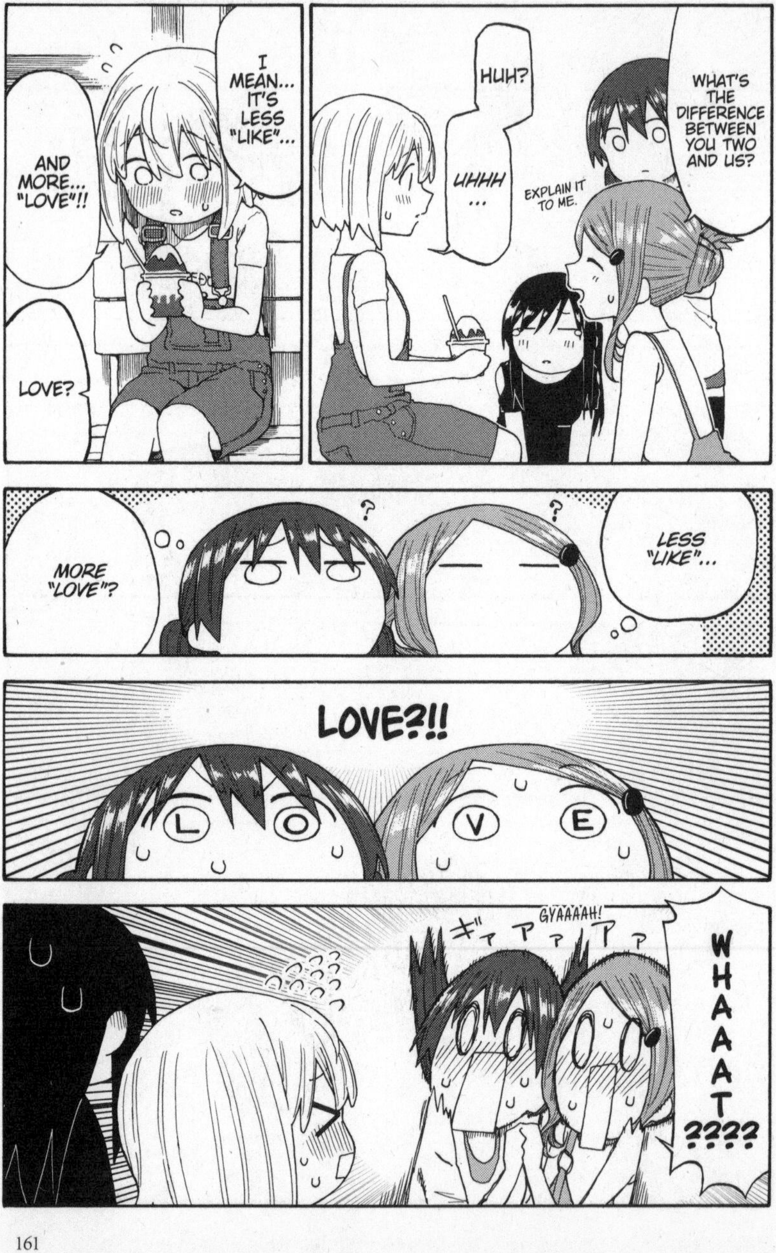
WHAT'S THE DIFFERENCE BETWEEN YOU TWO AND US?
HUH?
EXPLAIN IT TO ME.
UHHH...
I MEAN... IT'S LESS "LIKE"...
AND MORE... "LOVE"!!
LOVE?
LESS "LIKE"...
MORE "LOVE"?
LOVE?!!
L O V E
WHAAAT????
GYAAAAH!
ギャァァァァ

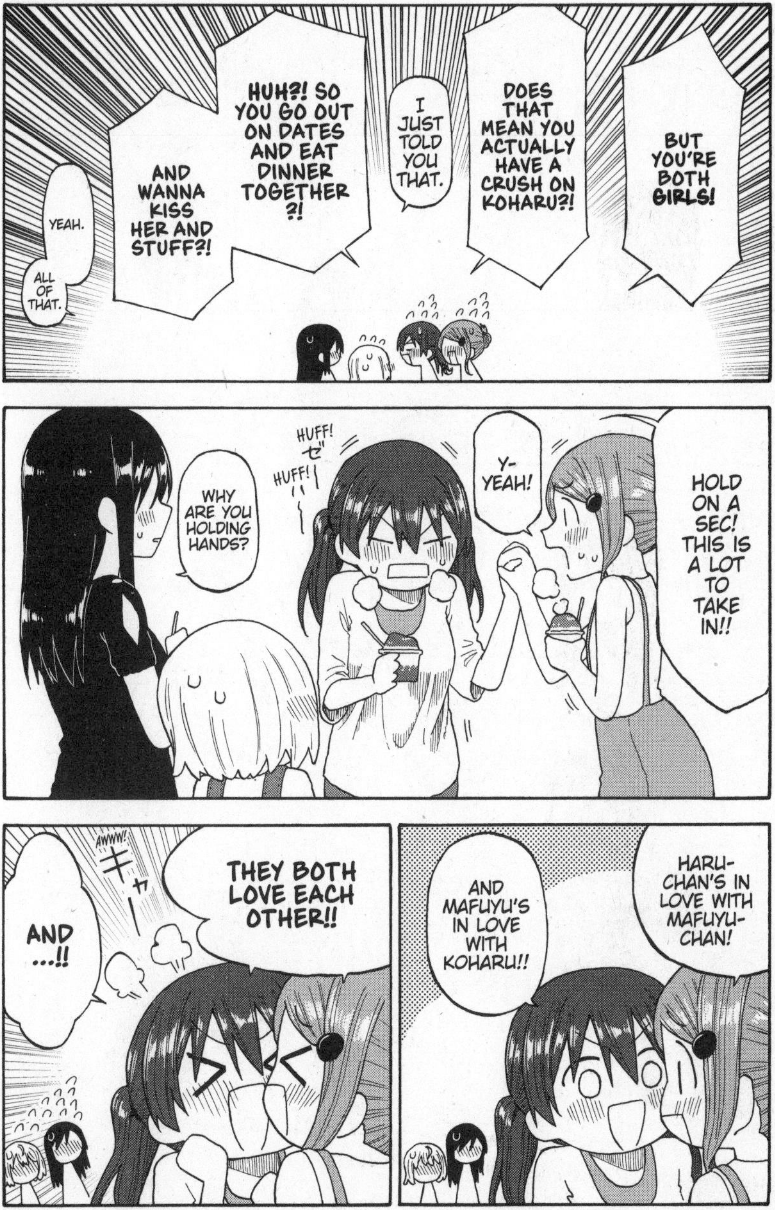
BUT YOU'RE BOTH GIRLS!
DOES THAT MEAN YOU ACTUALLY HAVE A CRUSH ON KOHARU?!
I JUST TOLD YOU THAT.
HUH?! SO YOU GO OUT ON DATES AND EAT DINNER TOGETHER?!
AND WANNA KISS HER AND STUFF?!
YEAH.
ALL OF THAT.
HOLD ON A SEC! THIS IS A LOT TO TAKE IN!!
Y-YEAH!
HUFF! ゼ
HUFF!
WHY ARE YOU HOLDING HANDS?
HARU-CHAN'S IN LOVE WITH MAFUYU-CHAN!
AND MAFUYU'S IN LOVE WITH KOHARU!!
THEY BOTH LOVE EACH OTHER!!
AWWW! キャー
AND ...!!

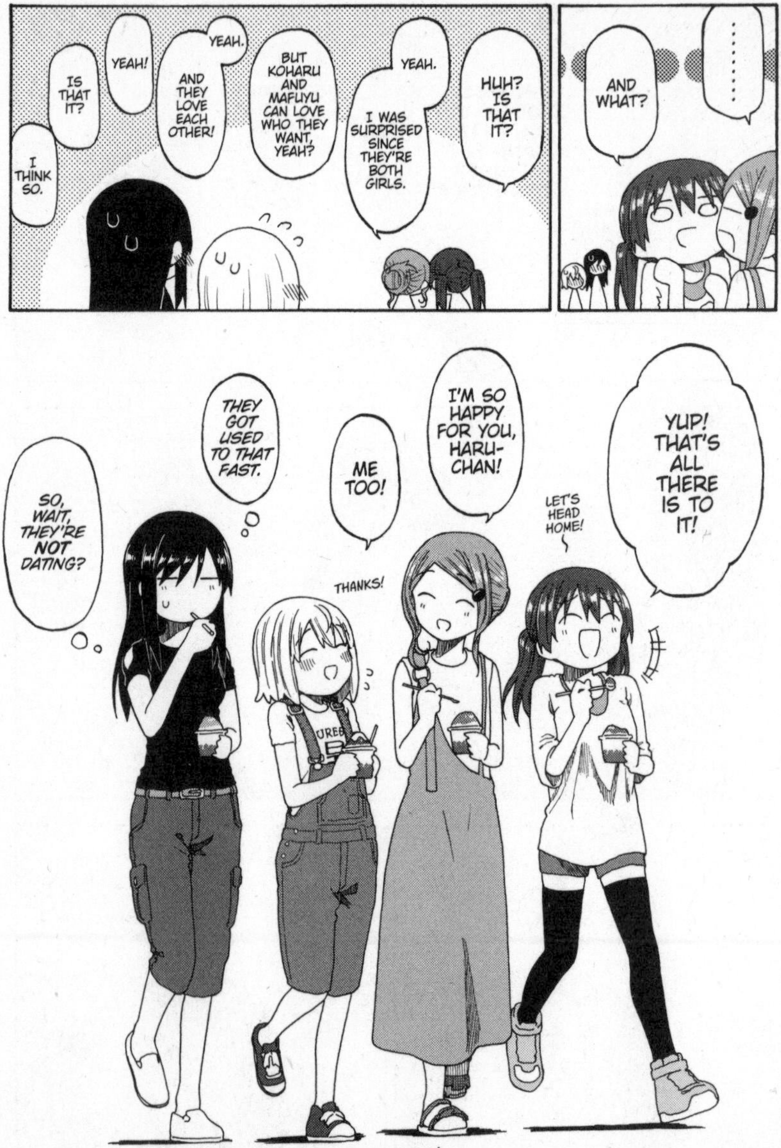
......
AND WHAT?
HUH? IS THAT IT?
YEAH.
I WAS SURPRISED SINCE THEY'RE BOTH GIRLS.
BUT KOHARU AND MAFUYU CAN LOVE WHO THEY WANT, YEAH?
YEAH.
AND THEY LOVE EACH OTHER!
YEAH!
IS THAT IT?
I THINK SO.
YUP! THAT'S ALL THERE IS TO IT!
LET'S HEAD HOME!
I'M SO HAPPY FOR YOU, HARU-CHAN!
ME TOO!
THANKS!
THEY GOT USED TO THAT FAST.
SO, WAIT, THEY'RE NOT DATING?

THANK YOU FOR READING UNTIL THE END!
KEI HAMURO
Kei Hamuro

Our
Wonderful
Days Tsurezure
Biyori

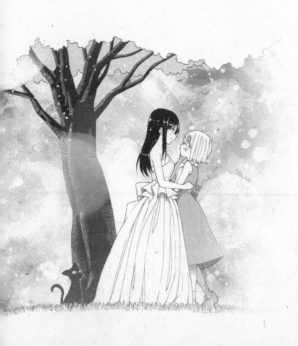

THE ADULTS' LAST SUPPER

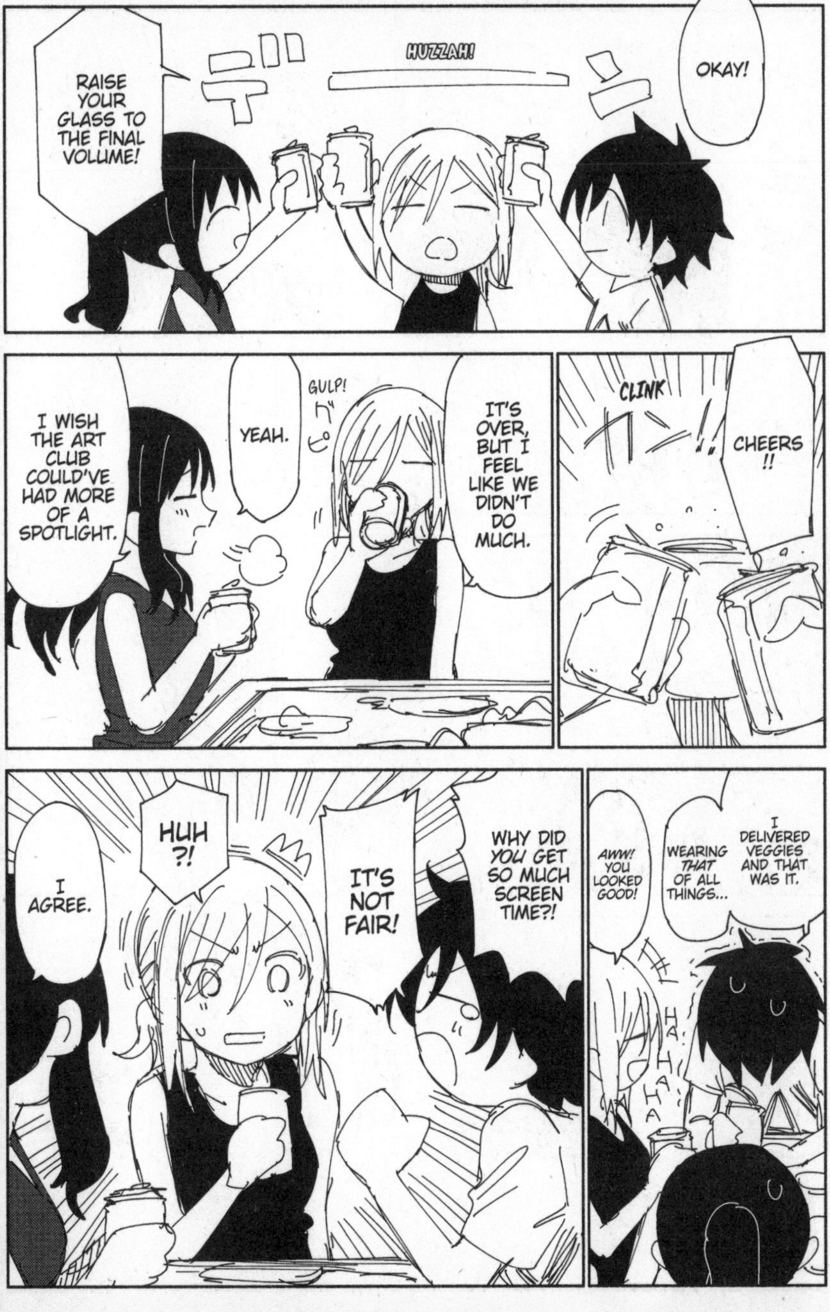

OKAY!
HUZZAH!
RAISE YOUR GLASS TO THE FINAL VOLUME!
CLINK
CHEERS!!
IT'S OVER, BUT I FEEL LIKE WE DIDN'T DO MUCH.
GULP!
YEAH.
I WISH THE ART CLUB COULD'VE HAD MORE OF A SPOTLIGHT.
I DELIVERED VEGGIES AND THAT WAS IT.
WEARING *THAT* OF ALL THINGS...
AWW! YOU LOOKED GOOD!
HA HA HA HA
WHY DID *YOU* GET SO MUCH SCREEN TIME?!
IT'S NOT FAIR!
HUH?!
I AGREE.

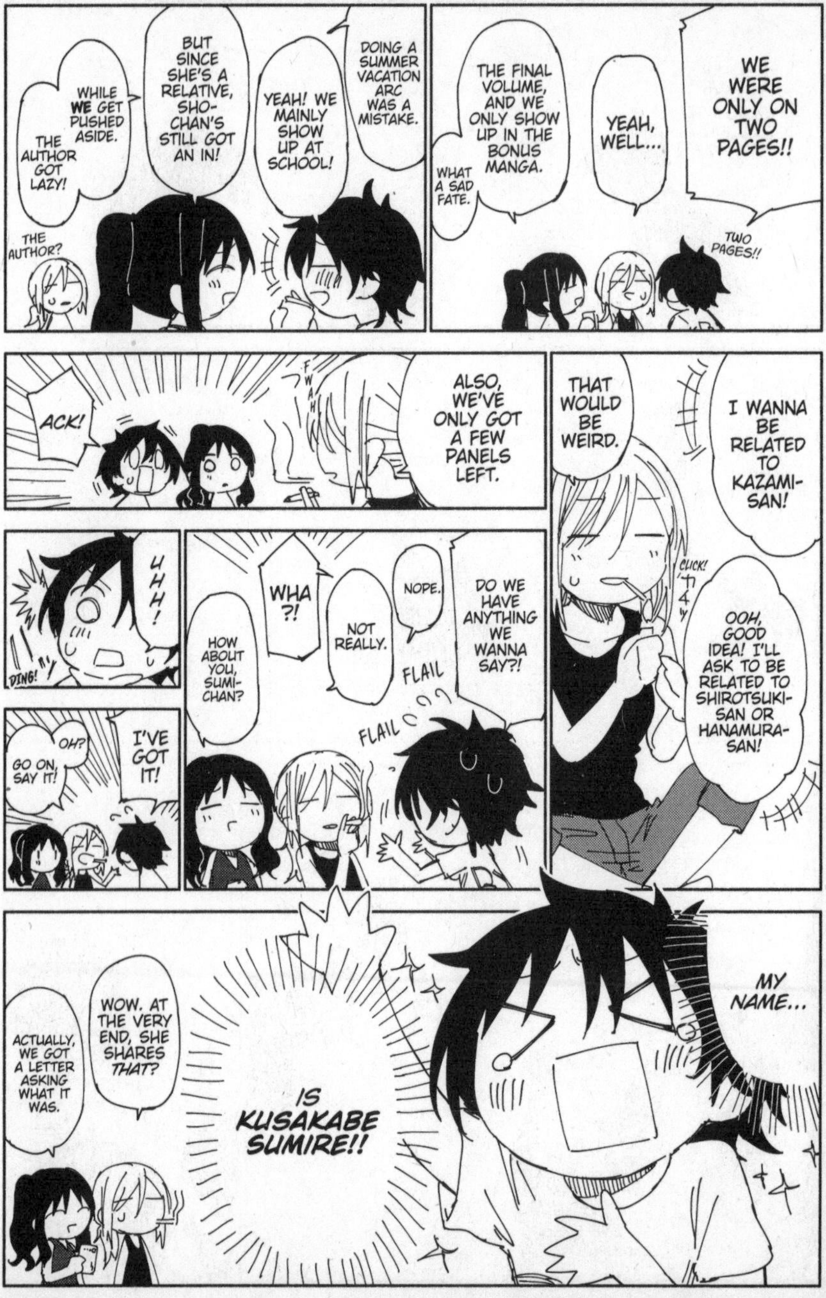

WE WERE ONLY ON TWO PAGES!!
YEAH, WELL...
THE FINAL VOLUME, AND WE ONLY SHOW UP IN THE BONUS MANGA.
WHAT A SAD FATE.
TWO PAGES!!
DOING A SUMMER VACATION ARC WAS A MISTAKE.
YEAH! WE MAINLY SHOW UP AT SCHOOL!
BUT SINCE SHE'S A RELATIVE, SHO-CHAN'S STILL GOT AN IN!
WHILE **WE** GET PUSHED ASIDE.
THE AUTHOR GOT LAZY!
THE AUTHOR?
I WANNA BE RELATED TO KAZAMI-SAN!
THAT WOULD BE WEIRD.
CLICK!
OOH, GOOD IDEA! I'LL ASK TO BE RELATED TO SHIROTSUKI-SAN OR HANAMURA-SAN!
ALSO, WE'VE ONLY GOT A FEW PANELS LEFT.
FWAH
ACK!
DO WE HAVE ANYTHING WE WANNA SAY?!
NOPE.
NOT REALLY.
WHA?!
HOW ABOUT YOU, SUMI-CHAN?
FLAIL
FLAIL
UHH!
DING!
I'VE GOT IT!
OH?
GO ON, SAY IT!
MY NAME...
IS KUSAKABE SUMIRE!!
WOW. AT THE VERY END, SHE SHARES *THAT*?
ACTUALLY, WE GOT A LETTER ASKING WHAT IT WAS.

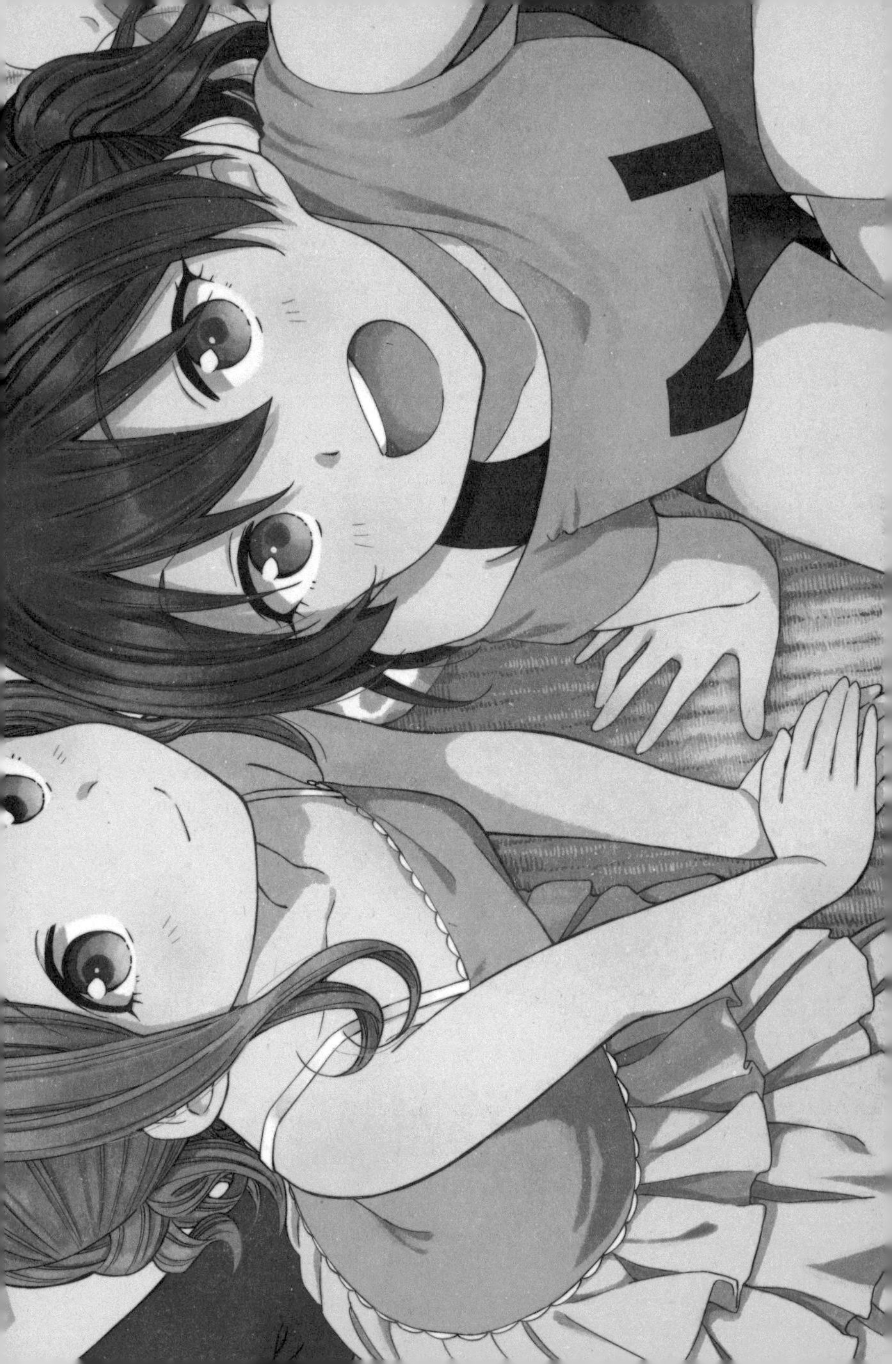

Fall in Love with these *Yuri titles* from Seven Seas Entertainment

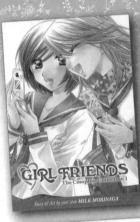
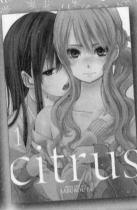
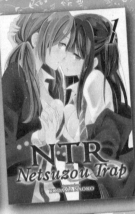
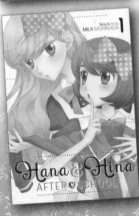
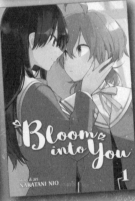
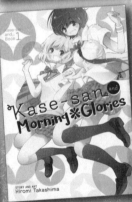

SEVEN SEAS ENTERTAINMENT PRESENTS

Our Wonderful Days
Tsurezure Biyori

story and art by **KEI HAMURO**

VOLUME 3

TRANSLATION
Katrina Leonoudakis

ADAPTATION
Asha Bardon

LETTERING AND RETOUCH
Erika Terriquez

COVER DESIGN
Nicky Lim

PROOFREADER
Stephanie Cohen

EDITOR
Shannon Fay

PREPRESS TECHNICIAN
Rhiannon Rasmussen-Silverstein

PRODUCTION MANAGER
Lissa Pattillo

MANAGING EDITOR
Julie Davis

ASSOCIATE PUBLISHER
Adam Arnold

PUBLISHER
Jason DeAngelis

OUR WONDERFUL DAYS: TSUREZURE BIYORI VOL. 3
© KEI HAMURO 2019
First published in Japan in 2019 by ICHIJINSHA Inc., Tokyo.
English translation rights arranged with KODANSHA.

Seven Seas press and purchase enquiries can be sent to Marketing Manager
Lianne Sentar at press@gomanga.com. Information regarding the distribution
and purchase of digital editions is available from Digital Manager CK Russell
at digital@gomanga.com.

Seven Seas and the Seven Seas logo are trademarks of
Seven Seas Entertainment, LLC. All rights reserved.

ISBN: 978-1-64505-511-2

Printed in Canada

First Printing: July 2020

10 9 8 7 6 5 4 3 2 1

FOLLOW US ONLINE: *www.sevenseasentertainment.com*

READING DIRECTIONS

This book reads from ***right to left***, Japanese style.
If this is your first time reading manga, you start
reading from the top right panel on each page and
take it from there. If you get lost, just follow the
numbered diagram here. It may seem backwards at
first, but you'll get the hang of it! Have fun!!

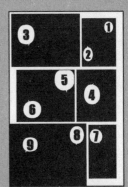

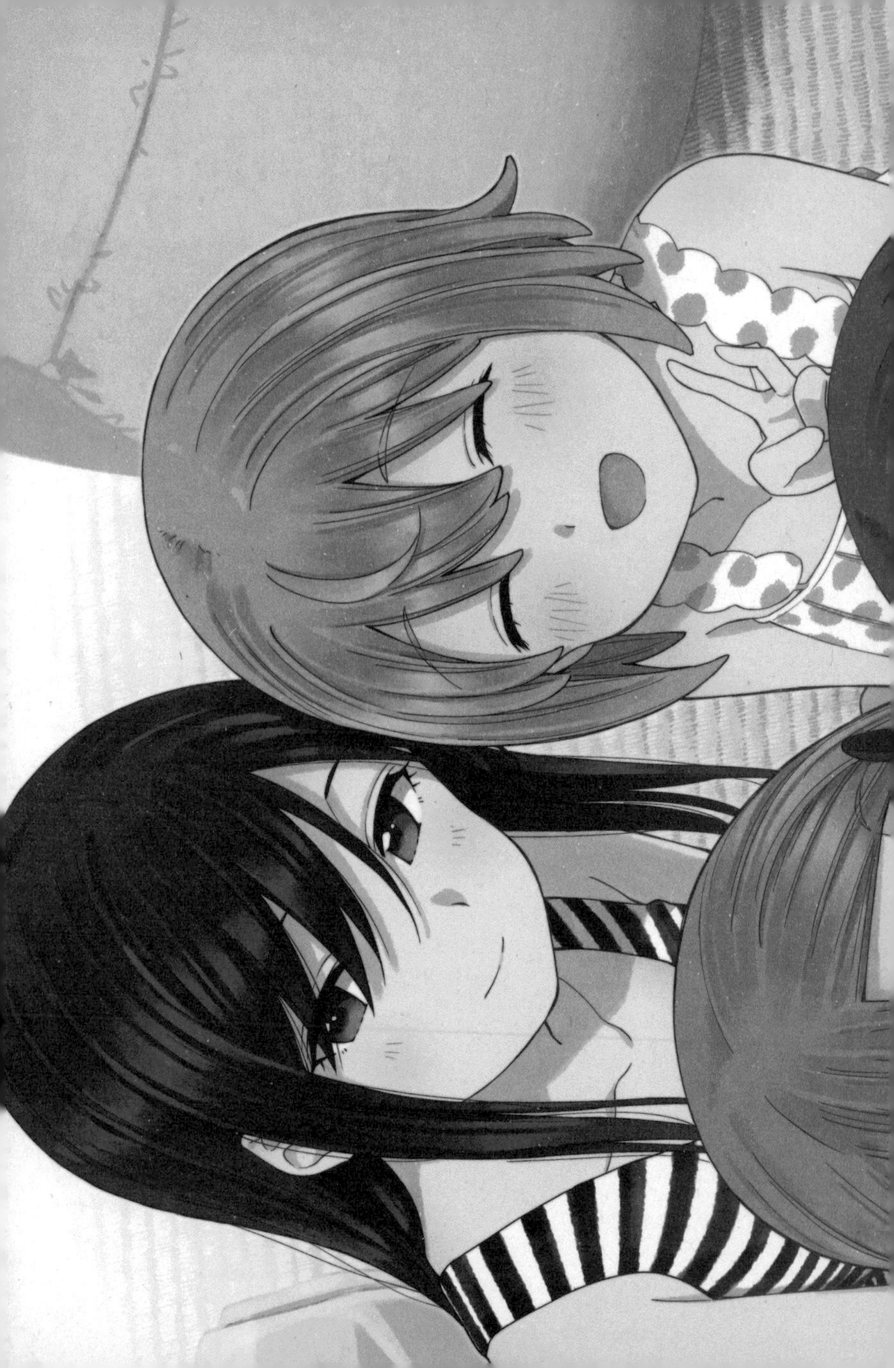

Our Wonderful Days

Tsurezure Biyori